Leading Wisdom

Leading Wisdom

Asian and Asian North American Women Leaders

Su Yon Pak
and
Jung Ha Kim,
EDITORS

WESTMINSTER
JOHN KNOX PRESS
LOUISVILLE · KENTUCKY

Unless otherwise indicated, Scripture quotations are from the New Revised Standard Version of the Bible and are copyright © 1989 by the Division of Christian Education of the National Council of the Churches of Christ in the U.S.A. and are used by permission.

Excerpts from Hal Taussig, "The Thunder: Perfect Mind," in *A New New Testament: A Bible for the 21st Century Combining Traditional and Newly Discovered Texts* (Boston: Houghton Mifflin, 2013) are used by permission. Excerpts from Yoke Lye Kowng, "The Tao of Great Integrity" *Journeys: The Magazine of the American Association of Pastoral Counselors* 11, no. 2 (2009) are used by permission. Excerpts from Carolyn McDade, *Sorrow and Healing* (Wellfleet, MA: Surtsey Publishing, 1993) are used by permission. Excerpts from Hannah Ka, "A New Paradigm of Leadership," in *Leadership Is Discipleship* [in Korean] (Nashville: The Leadership Ministries of General Board of Discipleship, 2015) are used by permission.

Book design by Sharon Adams
Cover design by Lisa Buckley Design

Library of Congress Cataloging-in-Publication Data

Names: Pak, Su Yon, editor. | Kim, Jung Ha, editor.
Title: Leading wisdom : Asian and Asian North American women leaders / Su Yon Pak and Jung Ha Kim, editors.
Description: First edition. | Louisville, KY : Westminster John Knox Press, 2017. | Includes bibliographical references. |
Identifiers: LCCN 2017042865 (print) | LCCN 2017043076 (ebook) | ISBN 9781611648416 (ebk.) | ISBN 9780664263324 (pbk. : alk. paper)
Subjects: LCSH: Women in church work—Asia. | Women in church work—North America. | Leadership in women—Asia. | Leadership in women—North America. | Christian leadership—Asia. | Christian leadership—North America. | Asian American women—Religion.
Classification: LCC BV4415 (ebook) | LCC BV4415 .L43 2017 (print) | DDC 270.8/3082—dc23
LC record available at https://lccn.loc.gov/2017042865

♾ The paper used in this publication meets the minimum requirements
of the American National Standard for Information Sciences—Permanence
of Paper for Printed Library Materials, ANSI Z39.48-1992.

Most Westminster John Knox Press books are available at special quantity discounts when purchased in bulk by corporations, organizations, and special-interest groups. For more information, please e-mail SpecialSales@wjkbooks.com.

*For our mothers
and
daughters*

Contents

Acknowledgments   ix

Introduction   1
    Jung Ha Kim and Su Yon Pak

PART 1: REMEMBERING WISDOM

1. Crumb-Gathering Wisdom Calls Out for Pacific Asian and
   North American Asian Women Historians   17
   Haruko Nawata Ward

2. Taiwanese American Women Pastors and Leaders: A Reality in
   Our Churches   29
   San Yi Lin and Grace Y. Kao

3. Neither the Suffering Servant nor the Syrophoenician Woman   43
   Hee Kyung Kim

4. Returning to the Source: A Call of a Leader in a Healthcare Setting   57
   Yoke Lye Kwong

5. "While There Is Life, There Is Hope": My Journey toward
   Leadership   69
   Elizabeth S. Tapia

Liturgical Interlude 1

"We've Come This Far by Faith": Celebrating the Thirtieth
Anniversary Annual Conference of PANAAWTM   79
Su Yon Pak

PART 2: UNSETTLING WISDOM

6. "I Shall Not Bow My Head": Ghostly Lessons for Wise Leading   89
   Mai-Anh Le Tran

7. A Letter to Friends   99
   Suk Jong Lee

8. *Phronēsis*, the Other Wisdom Sister   105
   Jin Young Choi

9. Foolishness of Wisdom   115
   Unzu Lee

10. Three Tales of Wisdom: Leadership of PANAAWTM   125
    Keun-Joo Christine Pae

Liturgical Interlude 2

"Ricing Community": Liturgy of Gathering   141
   Boyung Lee

PART 3: INCITING WISDOM

11. Becoming Wisdom Woman and Strange Woman: Asian and
    Asian American Women's Leadership in Coping with Stereotypes 151
    Min-Ah Cho

12. One-Pot Menu: Korean American Women's Wisdom Leadership   163
    Hannah Ka

13. "Working to Make the World a Little Better Place to Live":
    An Interview with Helen Kim Ho   175
    Jung Ha Kim

14. Wisdom Crying Aloud in the Street   193
    Deborah Lee

15. Fitting Nowhere: Meditation on Ministry, Wisdom, and
    Leadership   205
    Laura Mariko Cheifetz

Appendix   217

Notes   223

References   241

Contributors   251

Acknowledgments

The conversations, actual writing of chapters, presenting papers and panels on Asian and Asian North American women's leadership at various conferences, and this book would have not been possible without the support of many. The Louisville Institute's Project Grant for Researchers has enabled us to host the focus group meeting, a panel discussion at Princeton Theological Seminary and a special gathering of the Pacific, Asian and North American Asian Women in Theology and Ministry (PANAAWTM), to work on this book project. We are grateful for the Louisville Institute's continuous support and interest in inclusive leadership in the church and society. We would also like to acknowledge PANAAWTM sisters for commissioning and trusting us to work on this anthology to celebrate thirty years of shared stories of struggle and leadership. They have been our comrades, mentors, teachers, and friends. This book is a small testimony of how they have nurtured our lives.

We would especially like to thank the authors who persevered and diligently worked with us throughout the long process of making *Leading Wisdom*. We would also like to thank Robert Ratcliff and Julie Tonini at Westminster John Knox for excellent attention to administrative details and copyediting work.

The work of *Leading Wisdom* has just started, for it will continue to invite women and men to remember, unsettle, and incite wisdom in their own lives. With much anticipation, we await to hear more stories of how wisdom leads.

Introduction

JUNG HA KIM AND SU YON PAK

I was sent out from power
I came to those pondering me
And I was found among those seeking me
Look at me, all you who contemplate me
Audience, hear me
Those expecting me, receive me
. . . .

I am the silence never found
And the idea infinitely recalled
I am the voice with countless sounds
And the thousand guises of the word
I am the speaking of my name.[1]

WHEN AND WHERE WE ENTER

In March of 2015, PANAAWTM (Pacific Asian and North American Asian Women in Theology and Ministry) celebrated its thirtieth anniversary. Members—including founding members, new and not-so-new national and international members—of PANAAWTM in the presence of invited guests, ritualized and retold the *herstory* of PANAAWTM. Recalling the root stories of the network, highlighting the influence and impact that PANAAWTM members had in the academy, church, and society in song and litany, we remembered the collective wisdom of the network that held its first gathering in New Haven, Connecticut, in 1985.

As a network staffed solely through volunteer labor, commitment, and love, PANAAWTM has matured and grown in its thirty years of ceaseless work. Why participate in PANAAWTM? Among a wide range of reasons for women who came together, formed, built, led, and affiliated with PANAAWTM since its inception in 1985, they named, over and over again: friends, lifeline, comrades, mentors, just to be in the midst of Asian sisters, counseling, to put human faces to the books they are reading, home away from home, empowering, network, and movement as reasons for engaging over and over again. In the earlier years, we gathered to support and survive as we articulated our own theologies in the academy that understood neither our scholarship nor our contexts. But over the years, intentionally or unintentionally, we were forming the next generation of leaders. PANAAWTM is about sharing our battle wounds and our well-worn paths while encouraging the next generation to cultivate their own paths.

This book is a weaving of the stories of these participants who found their ways, sometimes circuitously, sometimes unexpectedly, into leadership. This book captures a cross-sectional glimpse of women who have found what they were looking for in PANAAWTM and forged their own paths as leaders in the church, academy, and society. All authors of this anthology have been participants of the annual conferences and are affiliates who continue to network. Hence, this book is yet another testimony of how the PANAAWTM movement enables women leaders to experience the nurturing and empowerment necessary to define their calling and ministry on their own terms.

Ten years ago, as a way to celebrate twenty years of PANAAWTM, four coeditors published *Off the Menu: Asian and Asian North American Women's Religion and Theology*.[2] And as a way to celebrate its thirty years of history, we, two coeditors, embarked on another anthology: *Leading Wisdom: Asian and Asian North American Women Leaders* (2017). While *Off the Menu* showcases significant contributions that the PANAAWTM network has accomplished in many different disciplines, mostly in the academy, *Leading Wisdom* lifts up the women themselves as they struggled, challenged, transformed, and further built relationships and positions of leadership in the church, academy, and community.

When an organization or a movement celebrates a thirtieth anniversary, it often reassesses the mission and accomplishments to plan for future sustainability. Likewise, PANAAWTM reassessed at its annual conferences and meetings during the annual meetings of the American Academy of Religion (AAR) and the Society of Biblical Literature (SBL). We discussed the status, accomplishments, future directions, and projects of PANAAWTM. How do we meaningfully mark thirty years of Pacific Asian and Asian North American women coming together across lines of generation, ethnicity, sexual orientation, social class, language, discipline, age, family experience, religious sensibility, and geography?

To date, there are a few timely and much-needed attempts to recollect selected first-generation members of PANAAWTM as pioneers, trailblazers, and cultural workers. For example, Kwok Pui-lan and Rachel A. R. Bundang's article "PANAAWTM Lives!" in the *Journal of Feminist Studies in Religion*,[3] documents both the history and the key people who led the Pacific Asian and Asian North American women's movement. Rita Nakashima Brock and Nami Kim's "Asian Pacific American Protestant Women," in the *Encyclopedia of Women and Religion in North America*,[4] also names and describes Asian American women's historic contributions in the church and society. Both articles mentioned many first-generation PANAAWTM members, such as Rita Nakashima Brock, Jung Ha Kim, Kwok Pui-lan, Nantawan Boonprasat Lewis, and Naomi Southard, and subsequent generation PANAAWTM members such as Jane Naomi Iwamura, Nami Kim, Lai Ling Elizabeth Ngan, Seung-Ai Yang, and Gale Yee, as they all contributed to making respected fields of studies and professions stronger. The twentieth anniversary of PANAAWTM was marked by *Off the Menu*, edited by Rita Nakashima Brock, Jung Ha Kim, Kwok Pui-lan, and Seung Ai Yang. *Off the Menu* showcased sixteen PANAAWTM authors, along with Mary Foskett, Damayanthi Niles, and Su Yon Pak, who participated in the process of making the anthology. More recently, Laura Mariko Cheifetz and Stacy D. Kitahata authored the chapter "Forming Asian Leaders for North American Churches" in *Religious Leadership: A Reference Handbook*; their work highlighted "the complex trajectory of Asian American Christian leader formation" that, by and large, goes unnoticed and "under the radar of the mainstream."[5] In this article, the authors recognize the key role PANAAWTM has played, and continues to play, in the formation of individual women leaders as well as in shaping the academy as a whole.

These and other attempts to recollect leadership of Pacific Asian and Asian North American women served as "bridges called my back"[6] as we worked on this anthology. As coeditors, we worked on this anthology for two years; we facilitated many conversations, conducted a focus group of the regional New York and New Jersey chapter of PANAAWTM, cohosted a conference around the theme of "Wisdom Leadership," made presentations about the anthology project at conferences, and engaged in numerous informal interviews. By the time the call for chapters went out to PANAAWTM network, most of the chapter contributors had already heard about plans for this anthology and had participated in some form of conversation and critical reflection on themselves as leaders in their own fields.

We would like to first confess that not all women who initially committed were able to contribute. There are a few others who we wished very much to include in this anthology for their leadership in the areas of racial reconciliation and sexual justice work but who could not contribute at this time, mostly due to personal circumstances. This project, like all things that are PAN-AAWTM, was voluntary. Life took place alongside our collective efforts and commitments to work on this project. We are grateful to all chapter contributors for their willingness to persevere and share experiences, stories, lessons, and testimonies of their life journeys in this volume.

Unlike anthology projects that begin with the editors' preconceived themes and chapter contents and then fit writers into a given outline, this project began with much conversation about how to meaningfully mark thirty years of PANAAWTM and to celebrate its women leaders. Out of these conversations, we have decided to put women at the center of the inquiry and provided a list of questions to further consider as the authors reflected on leadership. (See the appendix for the process and list of questions.) We also identified "wisdom leadership" as a possible organizing theme of the anthology, which itself was contested and challenged by some of the writers. They were given permission and freedom to write what matters to them. As editors, we had the task of shaping and curating the chapters that came out of this organic process of the writers' engagement with and interpretation of their experiences.

Once we started to receive the chapters to be edited and revised, we realized that many authors expressed ambivalence in claiming themselves as conscious and intentional leaders. Some used the expressions such as "reluctant," "resistant" or "accidental" leaders, "tricked by God" to take on various leadership opportunities and responsibilities. We found this shared reluctance and ambivalence intriguing and asked authors to further unpack and probe the issues related to perceiving and claiming themselves as leaders. We also noticed articulations of wisdom as embodied, practiced, and born out of experience. (For some, wisdom was gained by doing things for others, by going to the well of their mothers', sisters', and grandmothers' wisdom.) We asked authors to wrestle with the notion of wisdom and what qualities and criteria are often assumed of leaders to be wise in the Asian and Asian North American context. After numerous rounds of revisions, we decided to keep the chapters mostly as they are: for we believe that what the authors say and don't say in their own words are utmost important.

We are also aware of something missing in most of the chapters in this anthology: mentors and mentoring aspects of leadership. This absence comes even after we specifically included the significance of having a mentor(s) in the prompts for writers to reflect. The importance and relevance of mentoring, especially for women in leadership positions, has been documented in many spheres. Numerous studies show that mentoring helps to alleviate stressful and anxious conditions at work and thereby guide people in the right path to accomplish career goals and objectives.[7] Research also suggests that mentoring is especially effective for individuals vulnerable to severe stress and burnout, such as those in racial and gender minorities.[8] Yet only a handful of authors in this anthology mentioned informal mentoring in their profession. Most authors, instead, identified and drew on foremothers—both biological and cultural—as their lifeline resources and sisters in solidarity. Only one author mentioned formalized or organizational mentors as her lifeline.

What we offer in this volume are Asian and Asian North American women's first-hand life narratives of leadership experiences in the fields of social activism, parish ministry, teaching, U.S. Army chaplaincy, religious history, Christian denominational work, theology, nonprofit organization, theological social ethics, clinical spiritual care education in healthcare systems, and community organizing. Just as educator Parker J. Palmer reminds us that "we teach who we are"[9] and that our teaching can be experienced as the embodied self, so too we realize that the authors wrote who they are, each in their own distinctive and particular way.

While unique in its own right, Asian and Asian North American women's wisdom leadership is also part of the larger conversation around how women lead in the twenty-first century. What follows, then, is a brief overview of the discourses on leadership and women's leadership in particular and the salience of wisdom when referring to Asian and Asian North American women's experience of leadership.

ON LEADERSHIP

The landscape of literature and methods of leadership and leadership formation is vast and varied. From self-help books to a cognitive scientific approach, organizational management models and leadership academies, there is a deep hunger to understand and to learn authentic and transformative leadership. A brief survey of this growing field portrays a complex picture of the key components of leadership from different disciplines: personhood of a leader (e.g., personal traits and competencies), the context of leadership (e.g., organizational management and change management models), and models of leadership (e.g., adaptive leadership, authentic leadership, transformative leadership, servant leadership, leader-member exchange and change leadership, and shared, collective, and distributed leadership.) And more recently, the topic of women and leadership has been popularized by Sheryl Sandberg's *Lean In: Women, Work, and the Will to Lead*;[10] Ariana Huffington's *Thrive: The Third Metric to Redefining Success and Creating a Life of Well-being, Wisdom, and Wonder*;[11] and Sheri Parks' *Fierce Angels: Living with a Legacy from the Sacred Dark Feminine to the Strong Black Women*;[12] all of these books have revitalized the discourse on strategies for women in leadership.

On religious leadership, Sharon Callahan's two-volume work *Religious Leadership: A Reference Handbook* portrays a "snapshot of religious leadership in the United States in 2013."[13] This snapshot is panoramic; it begins with the history and development of religions on U.S. soil and offers perspectives on leadership from many religious and spiritual traditions. Religious leadership, however, is not only the purview of the clerics or the formally recognized leaders of the faith communities. If we only focus on strategies to "lean in" in the boardrooms, the session, or the vestry, we lose the opportunities to change the rules of engagement and opportunities to adequately capture the varied and imaginative ways Asian and Asian North American women lead and transform churches, academy, and communities.

Many pages have been devoted to identifying formal and informal barriers to leadership for Asian and Asian North American women. Patriarchy, Confucianism, sexism, homophobia, racism, and culture as external and internal pressures have prevented many women from breaking the "stained-glass" ceiling. But what if our metaphor of leadership was not that of a vertical ladder or a ceiling but a labyrinth[14] or a web? What if we looked for Asian and Asian North American women in leadership, not only on the rungs of ladders but also in the recessed places of a labyrinth or in the interstices between connective fibers of a web? If we place Asian and Asian North American women's experiences at the center of our inquiry, would their stories change the way we think about leadership in faith communities and society? Can this exploration help imagine other ways of "being" and "doing" church, community, and academy?

Expanding our horizon around leadership is crucial as the demographic and religious landscapes of Asian Americans are shifting. According to the Pew study on Religion and Public Life, Asian Americans scored the highest rate of religiously "unaffiliated" and "not religious" among all racial-ethnic populations in the United States.[15] Taking seriously the "spiritual but not religious" sensibility of Asian American communities, the anthology identifies spiritual and other cultural/ethnic practices that ground one's convictions and commitments in the community. Moreover, since the trend of "not religious but spiritual" is also reflected in the larger U.S. population, examining and showcasing Asian and Asian North American women leaders in various institutional settings can offer an invitation for others to explore nonconventional religious leadership as well. This anthology is an invitation to reimagine community, ministry, and leadership.

ON WISDOM

As Asian and Asian North American women, our formation as individuals and as leaders has been shaped by the wisdom and the wisdom traditions of Buddhism, Confucianism, Taoism, and other Asian religions. For example, whether or not we actively and intentionally embrace and live according to the Confucian precepts of filial piety, benevolence or the ritual consciousness/propriety, many of us have been shaped (both positively and negatively) by these precepts. These everyday practices were cultivated by our forebearers. Furthermore, as (mostly) Christian women, the wisdom tradition of the Bible grounds our living and leading. As an example, we highlight the Wisdom literature of the Hebrew Bible (Proverbs, Job, Ecclesiastes, Ecclesiasticus, and Wisdom of Solomon); it is a rich source of instruction for folk wisdom (instructions on how to live) and for theological wisdom (for example, reflections on the nature of God, human beings, and the meaning of suffering). In the New Testament, Jesus' many parables offer unconventional wisdom and an invitation to see the world from a different vantage point.

Some writers in this anthology intentionally engaged and dug deeply into some of the wisdom texts. Others have used it as the North Star for finding their way home or as a home base from which to journey. As a result, wisdom, articulated and found in these chapters, is not a static entity or quality that individuals possess. Rather, Asian and Asian North American women point to remembering, witnessing, and cultivating wisdom in between and among various human relationships: in friendships; in intergenerational relationships among grandmother, mother, and daughter; among members and leaders of the community; among comrades; and in student-teacher exchanges as coeducators. Wisdom is the very root of sustaining relationships and resources in Asian and Asian North American women's life journey as leaders. Put differently, what makes a person wise does not come from *within or without* but *betwixt and between* engaged relationships. As Rita Brock articulates, it is living with "interstitial integrity" recognizing that we are "constituted by these complex relationships." Our lives are imprinted with the lives of others. Wisdom is "being present while being aware of being present and examining what we hold together as we weave it."[16] Wisdom is holding together what is seen and unseen in an interstitial integrity, refusing to let go of either seemingly different worlds. As a result, wisdom is connective, integrative, and restorative.

STRUCTURE

The book is organized around three emerging themes: remembering wisdom, unsettling wisdom, and inciting wisdom. Part 1, "Remembering Wisdom," provides five chapters that are historical and autobiographical in nature that trace the journeys of wise leaders in the context of Asia and Asian North America. Part 2, "Unsettling Wisdom," examines why and how Asian and Asian North American women's experiences of leadership have been historically and culturally framed as "wise" rather than "strong," as in the African American women leadership context, or "strategic," as in the white American women leadership context. In this section, authors probe, evaluate, reassess, and lift up the wisdom framework and tradition as both expected and unexpected in the context of Asian and Asian North America. In part 3, "Inciting Wisdom," the writers examine ways that wisdom is made anew in their contexts and in their time. Many of the writers have found themselves as a leader in unlikely places, places they do not seem to fit. There is also a sense of temporariness and homelessness in their place and nature of leadership; and yet, that is where they find and claim home. In these places, wisdom is made anew, kindling and rekindling their call to lead.

Part 1: Remembering Wisdom

Haruko Natawa Ward's chapter, "Crumb-Gathering Wisdom Calls Out for Pacific Asian and North American Asian Women Historians," remembers three Asian Christian women leaders in sixteenth-century India and Japan and seventeenth-century China. Their stories are ones of perseverance "despite forced migration, the violence of colonialism, war, inquisition, expulsion, torture, and martyrdom," which Ward asserts many Asian and Asian North American women have also experienced in recent history. While separated by space and centuries of time, she offers these women's faith journeys as wise resources for all to draw from.

San Yi Lin and Grace Kao's chapter, "Taiwanese American Women Pastors and Leaders: A Reality in Our Churches," highlights the importance of disaggregating race and gender categories such as "Asian" and "women" by sharing four Taiwanese American clergywomen's experiences. Deeply rooted in the "aboriginal matriarchal culture," the authors argue that these clergywomen do not experience the Taiwanese ethnic church as a site of patriarchal oppression. By selectively and consciously remembering indigenous Taiwanese history and culture—rather than comparing and contrasting themselves with other ethnic Asian American clergywomen's experiences—Taiwanese American clergywomen further empower their status and roles in the church.

Remembering her own parents as two different models of leadership, Hee Kyung Kim sets out to find a more balanced and ideal wisdom leader for herself and other Asian and Asian North American women in her chapter titled, "Neither the Suffering Servant nor the Syrophoenocian Woman." "While my father was a stern, authoritative, and rather distant figure whose commands loomed powerfully over us, and often against us, my mother was a self-sacrificing servant-leader type" who she also saw as "the unofficial yet real leader." Hee Kyung Kim then critically examines two biblical models of leadership: the suffering servant and the Syrophoenician woman in the New Testament. And she argues that both models fall short for more communally oriented Asian and Asian American women to emulate. What makes a leader wise is her almost intuitive discernment of what's needed for whom and when, like that of a seasoned cook, "who serves the community with love and care, preparing just the right well-balanced and delicious dish for just the right occasion."

Yoke Lye Kwong remembers her grandmother's Daoist teaching, "Having received, give back in return," in the chapter "Returning to the Source: A Call of a Leader in a Healthcare Setting." She traces her multiple im/migrations—from China to Malaysia to Canada to the United States—and the arduous journey that led her to the field of Clinical Pastoral Education. Despite obstacles, Kwong held fast to her grandmother's teaching. She became the first woman to be approved for ordination in Christian ministry in her church, the Subang Jaya Baptist Church in Malaysia, in 1995, and became the first Chinese Malaysian American woman to be certified as a Clinical Pastoral Education (CPE) supervisor by the Association for Clinical Pastoral Education in 2001. Kwong also remembers her grandmother's wisdom to care for the less healthy and less able in her daily life.

Elizabeth Tapia's deeply autobiographic chapter, "'While There Is Life, There Is Hope': My Journey toward Leadership," takes us back to a small fishing village in central Philippines where she remembers and reconnects all her leadership experiences based on the RICE principles: Respect and responsibility; Integration and Intellectual curiosity; Compassion and Companionship Skills; and Enthusiasm and Ecofeminist praxis. Tapia connects this RICE principle with what she remembers from how she grew up, *Haban may buhay, may pa-asa*, "while there is life, there is hope." Wise leaders are informed by the RICE principles and people who help us to remember the power of hope.

Part 2: Unsettling Wisdom

In "'I Shall Not Bow My Head': Ghostly Lessons for Wise Leading," Mai-Anh Le Tran narrates three wisdom tales: first her mother's wisdom and wisdom's survival during and after the Vietnam War; second, a mythical tale of the Truang sisters in 40 CE who led an army of eighty thousand against the military forces of the colonizing Chinese Han Empire; and third, a story from Ferguson and the public protest after the killing of an unarmed African American teenager, Michael Brown, by a police officer. She draws attention to how leaders' bodies are teaching bodies, both mnemonically and mimetically. There are many lessons garnered from the wisdom tales in this chapter. From these three wisdom tales, a notion of inheritance or legacy bubbles up to the surface. Relationships are about the past in its ghostly forms reappearing to give us lessons on wise living and wise leading. It is also about mining the wisdom that we have inherited, whether they be tales of s/heroism or of trauma and suffering; these ghostly tales are embodied and re-embodied in the present, creating links and relationships to the past-present-future.

To think of Chaplain (Lt. Col.) Suk Jong Lee as a leader is not a challenge, particularly when you see her in uniform. However, understanding how she claimed and experienced leadership in the U.S. Army, as a Korean American Presbyterian minister with a petite physical stature, requires attentive imagination. She insists that "God tricked" her; she did not plan on becoming a U.S. Army chaplain. "One thing led to another" after immigrating to New York at the age of fifteen, she reiterates that chaplaincy is not her career choice even after serving the army for more than twenty years. She sees herself as a "reluctant leader" who was "tricked" into a vocation that requires her to demonstrate an explicit and masculine style of leadership. What she shares in her chapter, which is a letter to coeditors, is how she deciphers the dissonance between what the Army dictates about leadership and "what the Lord requires" her to do. Whether at various Army posts in the United States or deployed in Iraq, she tried first and foremost to uphold the Chaplain Corp motto, *Pro Deo et Patria*, "For God and Country," even when soldiers "look down" on her or see her as the women they met at bars while they were stationed in Korea. In her chapter, "A Letter to Friends," Lee shares how she straddled two ongoing conversations: with her God who "tricked" her into the vocation and with soldiers who cause both pain and joy as she learns to care deeply for them.

Jin Young Choi problematizes cultural assumptions of Asian and Asian North American women leaders as wise and offers culturally contextualized exegesis on the Greek words *sophia* and *phronēsis* as two different types of wisdom. In her chapter, "*Phronēsis*, the Other Wisdom Sister," she argues that while the Western feminist's understanding and representation of *sophia* tend to prioritize and essentialize women's experiences, *phronēsis* resists a singular or essential formulation of wisdom. The difference in their denotation of wisdom is akin to how silence is understood differently in Western culture and in Asian American culture. By highlighting several Asian American women writers' usage of silence as examples, Jin Young Choi illustrates that silence is not merely an absence of sound but "a figure of speech [that] signifies tacit understanding." And she observes that most of Asian and Asian North American women's leadership experiences and leadership styles are based on *phronēsis*—embodied wisdom.

Unzu Lee argues that "leaders are not born but are made." Growing up in the politically and economically unstable South Korea, Unzu Lee reflects on her distrust of public leaders as a way of self-protection in her chapter "Foolishness of Wisdom." She reclaims the quieter and less visible leaders in her own family whose wisdom is neither learned in school nor formed in public: wisdom of her mother and her paternal grandmother. She tells the story of her paternal grandmother who rescued one of her sons during the Korean War. This story becomes her "root" story; she returns to it over and over again, especially during challenging times as an immigrant woman and as a leader in a mainline Protestant denomination. The story of her grandmother's "foolish" wisdom enacted with such courage that saved her father's life during wartime in Korea became a *phronēsis* of the paradox of leadership. It is grandmother-like individuals whom Unzu Lee seeks to recognize as unlikely wisdom leaders in her work.

For Keun-Joo Christine Pae, relationships form the foundation for the leadership of PANAAWTM. In her chapter, "Three Tales of Wisdom: Leadership of PANAAWTM," Pae begins by critiquing the conventional Eurocentric American ways of using "wisdom" to feminize and "Orientalize" leadership for Asian Pacific American women. By situating "wisdom" in a concrete PANAAWTM historical context, she draws out the hard-earned "survival wisdom and open-ended legacy of a diasporic community" and its desires to hand that wisdom down to new generations. From "organic" relationships to "peripheral" relationships, Pae's interviews with twelve PANAAWTM members across generations highlight community building based on friendships. These friendships are dialogical relationships between the individual and the community. However, an overreliance on friendships can keep some people out. Pae suggests that the future of PANAAWTM depends on moving from "closed friendship" to "engaged friendship." She calls for the PANAAWTM leadership and network to intentionally embrace multiplicity, fluidity, and engaged diversity.

Part 3: Inciting Wisdom

Min-Ah Cho's "Becoming Wisdom Woman and Strange Woman: Asian and Asian American Women's Leadership in Coping with Stereotypes" illustrates how she navigates her identity as a Korean feminist theology professor at a predominantly white Catholic woman's college in the Midwest. While at times she is seen as a "wise woman" who can bring her "otherness" as a flair or flavor, to most of her students she is seen as "a strange woman" who has no respect for their beliefs or threatens their culture with "yellow peril" and who does "not look like a theologian." To that end as she encounters everyday sexism and orientalism in classrooms and draws on postcolonial readings of wisdom literature as resources to create more reflective community with her students. By using these stereotypes strategically, she works to disclose her marginality as an Asian woman and invites students to reflect on their own marginality. This act of teaching-learning can "resist the forces that displaces and depoliticizes them." As such, her classroom becomes a reflective community where people (strange and wise) are encouraged to acknowledge multiple contradictions and to create mutually liberating opportunities.

Hannah Ka offers a model of leadership that is circular and shared in a nonhierarchical and horizontal way. In her chapter, "One-Pot Menu: Korean American Women's Wisdom Leadership," she works with a small group of Korean American women in a Korean American church where top-down hierarchy prevails. With them, she articulates that wisdom is "engrained in their hearts and embodied in their life experiences." Wise leaders have the insight to recognize and embrace others' diverse gifts, the ability to organize others' gifts toward a purpose. And above all, a wise leader regards people's presence, rather than their gifts, as the most valuable gift of the community. She draws on Korean cultural and religious "ingredients" of Confucianism and Taoism to reach this conclusion. She proposes a one-dish menu, *kimbap* (Korean seaweed roll) or *bibimbap* (one rice bowl dish with mixed seasoned meats and vegetables) as a metaphor for leadership where different people bring ingredients to make one communal meal. Unlike a potluck, where each brings her signature dish to the gathering, in making *bibimbap*, different people bring different ingredients but make one dish. She writes, "We are radically indebted to each other because we cannot make the dish without others' participation, yet unequally indebted because we bring disparate gifts to make the dish communally."

Jung Ha Kim's interview with Helen Kim Ho, "Working to Make the World a Little Better Place to Live," lifts up issues of leadership and community building in the nonprofit world. By consciously and intentionally situating her own politics of identity to advocate the civil rights of the immigrants and their descendants, Helen Kim Ho shares stories of both successful and challenging experiences of community organizing. As she moves from leading a local organization to being a regional leader of a national organization, she critically assesses the daily work of collaborating with other national partners. What sustains her throughout various challenges is the faces of empowered and committed community members who have realized their own potential to bring about necessary social changes. She also emphasizes the importance of being reconnected to stories and dreams of her first generation immigrant parents. She reflects, "I am living their dreams" to some extent, but also, "I have duties and responsibilities to care for" people in the community who are like her parents.

Deborah Lee, in her chapter, "Wisdom Crying Aloud in the Street," begins in the street. She writes, "I am a pastor, that is true. But pastoring thus far hasn't landed me in a church." In the last ten years as an ordained minister, she has presided over interfaith prayer services outside immigration detention centers, in front of courthouses or banks, or on the steps of the state capitol or the Pentagon. "I have learned to invoke the Spirit through traffic and honking horn," she attests. Her work is to reclaim contested public spaces as holy and sacred. She does this with the people of God, particularly, undocumented youth, the homeless, immigrant families, and peace activists. Her ministry is an embodied exegesis of Proverbs 1:20–21, "Wisdom shouts in the streets." The street is holy because that is where the suffering people are.

In Laura Mariko Cheifetz's semiautobiographical chapter, "Fitting Nowhere: Meditation on Ministry, Wisdom, and Leadership," the reader is invited into a poetic reflection on wisdom. Drawing on her own experiences in leadership as well as the experience of other Asian American women leaders in the church, she articulates the nature of wisdom that is varied and pluriform. Wisdom, for Cheifetz, lives in communities of sisterhood and friends. Wisdom surrounds her. She writes, "Wisdom is my mother. My colleague. My friend. My classmate. My rival. My sister in Christ." Sometimes, Wisdom creates accidental leaders. And other times, leaders are cultivated to receive wisdom. Wisdom, in her many ways, asks leaders not to fashion leadership after someone else's but rather to find a unique voice and model of leadership. Cheifetz surveyed Asian American leaders in the church who speak about "fitting nowhere." Her leadership, she attests, also "fits nowhere." But by fitting nowhere, these leaders can minister to a multitude of communities; they can find ways to serve others who "fit nowhere." It is in this community of women leaders who fit nowhere that she finds wisdom.

In between this three-part structure of these wisdom stories are liturgical wisdom interludes of different genres that serve to connect the three parts. The first is a liturgy, "We've Come This Far by Faith: Celebrating the Thirtieth Anniversary Annual Conference of PANAAWTM," written by Su Yon Pak, which was presented at the thirtieth anniversary celebration at Garrett Evangelical Seminary. The second interlude is a liturgy, "'Ricing Community': Liturgy of Gathering," written and adapted by Boyung Lee, that ritualized the gathering of Pacific Asian and North American Asian women at a conference. During this conference Pacific Asian and North American Asian women brought their wisdom to set the eucharistic table.

CONFOUNDING WISDOM

We began this introduction with an excerpt from "The Thunder: Perfect Mind," an ancient poem from the Nag Hammadi documents. Thunder, which dates back as early as the first century BCE and as late as the third century CE, is thought to have been used by Egyptian Christians. It is a series of mostly feminine, divine, self-proclaiming "I-am" statements that vocalize identity, gender, violence, social struggle and cultural prejudice. Bringing together what do not belong together, Thunder disrupts socially constructed categories and binaries and suggests a third space with multiple centers that themselves are destabilized in the text.[17] In a certain sense, this anthology is like that. And we find leadership is like that too. These multiple voices and silences brought together disrupt our construction of what it means to lead. It resists easy categorization. It is stubborn and unruly and not easily tamed, if at all. We let their voices speak for themselves in this text in its multiplicity of experiences and identifications.

> Finally, a voice from *Thunder*:
> I am she who is revered and adored
> And she who is reviled with contempt
> I am peace and war exists because of me
> I am a foreigner and a citizen of the city
> I am being
> I am she who is nothing
> . . . .
>
> Hear me, audience, and learn from my words, you who know me
> I am what everyone can hear and no one can say
> I am the name of the sound and the sound of the name
> I am the speaking of my name.[18]

PART I

Remembering Wisdom

1

Crumb-Gathering Wisdom Calls Out for Pacific Asian and North American Asian Women Historians

HARUKO NAWATA WARD

From there he set out and went away to the region of Tyre. He entered a house and did not want anyone to know he was there. Yet he could not escape notice, but a woman whose little daughter had an unclean spirit immediately heard about him, and she came and bowed down at his feet. Now the woman was a Gentile, of Syrophoenician origin. She begged him to cast the demon out of her daughter. He said to her, "Let the children be fed first, for it is not fair to take the children's food and throw it to the dogs." But she answered him, "Sir, even the dogs under the table eat the children's crumbs." Then he said to her, "For saying that, you may go—the demon has left your daughter." So she went home, found the child lying on the bed, and the demon gone. (Mark 7:24–30)

The exchange between the Syrophoenician woman and Jesus in Mark 7:24–30 can empower and aggravate at the same time, especially for Pacific Asian and North American Asian women. Jesus' words reflect a racist, nationalist, imperial-colonist, and chauvinist worldview that is rather familiar to Pacific Asian and North American Asian women even today. At the same time, the story points to the woman's potent wisdom as she responds, "Sir, even the dogs under the table eat the children's crumbs." In the face of humiliation and rejection, she remains cordial, composed, and firm; she teaches the unwise. Jesus yields to her: "For saying that, you may go—the demon has left your daughter."

Pacific Asian and North American Asian women who are pursuing a vocation in helping those who lack both resources and ecclesiastical recognition can find a model of wise leadership in the Syrophoenician woman.[1] She, like the Woman Wisdom in Proverbs, cries out for justice. She also represents many oppressed racial-ethnic and religious minority women. She resists politico-military, socioeconomic, ethno-cultural, religio-patriarchal dominant structures, which constantly relegate her to the subhuman status. She courageously speaks up when Jesus mocks her even as she prostrates before him. She is singularly focused on liberating her daughter from the demon and determined to gain access to Jesus' resources.

Until very recently, the study of early histories of Asian women has been dismissed as unimportant despite their evident wise leadership. A historian's painstaking task of gathering evidence to recover their stories is not unlike the Syrophoenician woman's gleaning the fragments that have been swept off the table. I offer this chapter in the hope that we come to see such tedious historical gathering and examination as worthwhile endeavors. Furthermore, such historical knowledge can empower us to deliver our next generation from the demonic possession of marginalization and invisibility.

I, a revisionist historian for Pacific Asian and North American Asian women, speak autobiographically as an Asian American woman historian in order to invite Pacific Asian and North American Asian women to unearth their own histories. In *Postcolonial Imagination and Feminist Theology*, Kwok Pui-lan reflects on the interconnectedness of individual and global histories: "I want to conjure a female diasporic subject as multiply located, always doubly displaced, and having to negotiate an ambivalent past, while holding on to fragments of memories, cultures, and histories in order to dream of a different future."[2] I, together with other Asian women, try to make sense of these ambivalent histories by embodying, remembering, and appreciating. We embody communal ancestral memories of voluntary and involuntary exiles, multiple dislocations, diverse cultures, ethnicities, languages, customs, societies, nations, continents, traditional religions, and missionary and indigenous Christianities. We also remember the violent traditions of patriarchy, many wars fought in Asia, lasting influence of Orientalism, and misogyny and antagonism in North America. And we appreciate our deep heritage in Asian wisdom and spirituality. I am a member of this collective identity.

I am also an academic historian who seeks to lift up women's voices. For centuries, the predominant mode of writing history was that of a grand narrative of the male winners of wars; this mode neglected women's presence throughout. Serious scholarship on women's history began only recently. In January 2013, an obituary section of the *New York Times* published the legacy of Gerda Lerner, who in the 1970s "helped make the study of women and their lives a legitimate subject for historians."[3] In a 1981 booklet titled *Teaching Women's History*, Lerner notes the gap in research and writes, "Women of racial and ethnic minorities have been doubly victimized by scholarly neglect and by racist assumptions," and alerts the invisibility of "women of Asian American groups" in particular.[4] Since then, hundreds of works on women's history and source collections of women's writings in modern America have been published, but Pacific Asian and North American Asian women's work in the area remains scanty.[5]

My professional identity is that of a revisionist, postcolonial, and globally connected historian of women in Reformation studies. While the church history textbooks repeat the erroneously simplified grand narratives of "great (men) Reformers," many revisionist historians today define the whole period as "the Reformations," noting the diversity of Reform visions and ideas, locations and practices, historical agents and leaders, including women. In 1977, Joan Kelly-Gadol asked if women participated at all in the creation of Renaissance culture.[6] Although writings of Christine de Pizan were rediscovered, she lamented that women in premodern society lacked public voices. A generation of historians following Kelly-Gadol has gathered massive evidence of numerous women who contributed not only to the Renaissance but also to reformation of the church. In the 1980s Merry E. Wiesner-Hanks, who spearheaded the recovery of women in the Reformations, published her twin works *Women and Gender in Early Modern Europe* and *Christianity and Sexuality in the Early Modern World*.[7] Kirsi Stjerna, in her *Women and the Reformation*, argues, "Teaching courses on the Reformation is no longer feasible without the inclusion of women as subjects in the story of the Reformation and . . . the exploration of the lives, thoughts, and contributions of women in different Reformation contexts."[8] While her work includes women from Lutheran, Reformed, Anabaptist, English, and Catholic camps, they are all Europeans. In the recent essay, Wiesner-Hanks notes an important shift of scholarship in women's contributions to the Reformations in early modern European colonies and missions in Asia, Africa, and the Americas.[9]

Between the sixteenth and eighteenth centuries, numerous Asian women became active leaders in Catholic missions in Asia. According to the Treaty of Tordesillas (1492), by the early 1500s missionaries under the Portuguese royal patronage reached Asia via Africa while missionaries under the Spanish patronage arrived in the Philippines via the Americas. Founded in 1540, the Jesuits soon became the major global missionary order. In addition to the Catholic orders, the papal institution of the Propaganda Fide sent missionaries to Asia from 1622. Protestant missions did not begin in Asia until the modern era, even though the English and the Dutch East India Companies established trading settlements also in the seventeenth century. There were also constant intra-negotiations between empires and kingdoms in Asia, and "reformations" of Buddhism, Confucianism, Islam, and other Asian religions took place during the time.

In such a turbulent period of history, Asian Catholic women leaders cultivated their wise venues of ministry. Like the Syrophoenician woman in Mark,
they were told no. They were not eligible to hold ecclesiastical positions. Furthermore, the church vehemently criticized their unofficial leadership. Patriarchal cultures hindered the preservation of women's writings and images.
Nevertheless, it is possible to string together "crumbs" found in missionary
records, which contain some words spoken and written by women as well as
descriptions of their activities. In scrutinizing these texts written by men, I
endeavor to lift up Asian women's voices. Below, I introduce a few such wise
women ancestor leaders in early modern Asia.

CATHARINA OF FERÃO AND ETHIOPIAN WOMEN CATECHISTS IN GOA

In 1542 Francis Xavier founded the Jesuit mission in Goa, India, a Portuguese
colonial post in the Vijayanagar kingdom. Goa was religiously, ethnically,
culturally, and linguistically diverse. Portuguese colonial laws and sixteenth-
century Catholicism dictated all aspects of the everyday life of natives. The
Jesuit *Constitutions*, as an order of clergy, excluded women's membership. In
the Jesuit records, however, Catharina of Ferão appears as one of their leading evangelists. Luís Fróis describes her as "a widow, a native of Ethiopia, big
in stature and bigger in grace and virtue," "manly in zeal and constancy"; her
ministries were "most outstanding in all of India."[10] He also remarks that "she
teaches Christian doctrine and preaches the faith in the [superior] manner
which baffles us [the Jesuits] all." This big African-born immigrant woman
preached in Goa's Konkani language and cared for new converts. Pero
Almeida praises her as "a great servant of God, and great converter" of non-
Christians.[11] In the Jesuit-led massive conversion campaign that took place in
1559, Catharina helped hundreds of villagers to turn to Christianity. In doing
so Catharina shielded them from the confiscation of their farms, for there was
a colonial regulation allowing the confiscation of farms from people that did
not convert to Christianity. Fróis invoked the story of the Syrophoenician
woman in Mark when he described Catharina's dedication to gather even the
"left-over crumbs" of the bountiful harvest.[12] She invited these new converts
to her house, fed them, and prepared them before sending them to the House
of Catechumens in the Jesuit quarters. Later these converts requested Catharina's presence at their baptism, even though she most likely did not have
permission to administer the sacrament.

Like the Syrophoenician woman, Catharina was a healer. When a woman
convert experienced difficulty in delivery, her family summoned the traditional

healers. But none of their methods worked. As the story goes, when Catharina came in she threw out these healers and started to pray: "Lord, in order that all these Christians, so young in faith, and these non-Christians, know you and understand that the life of this woman does not depend on their industry or human medicine, but that we depend totally in your mercy, Lord, lighten their eyes . . . with the light of your clemency and pity."[13] Even before she concluded her prayer, the woman gave birth to healthy twin girls to the great amazement of all.

And like the Syrophoenician woman, Catharina liberated the enslaved and oppressed women as her spiritual daughters.[14] In 1562 Catharina saw one hundred Ethiopian women in an Arab merchant caravan. During this period, Muslim merchants often raided Christian villages in Ethiopia, force-fully taking women to be sold at the slave markets in India. After Catharina informed the Jesuits, she ran after the caravan and caught up with it just out-side the city. She argued with the merchant in Arabic. She then talked to the women in Ethiopian and brought several of them to the highest religious authority in Goa, Archbishop Gaspar Leão Pereira (1560–67). She explained to him in Portuguese that Ethiopians are all Christians, that these women were kidnapped by the slave traders, and that the church forbade enslave-ment of Christians. The Jesuits had to support her arguments. The arch-bishop ordered that all one hundred women be protected at the Jesuit House of Catechumens. Soon after Viceroy Francisco Coutinho (1561–64) declared them to be legally free.

Catharina established a network of several other Ethiopian-born women catechists at the Jesuit House of Catechumens.[15] These women catechists provided further spiritual and physical care for Indian and Ethiopian women whom Catharina helped convert and liberate. The Jesuits noted that between 1558 and 1566 these woman catechists annually served seventy to one hun-dred women. These recovered historical recordings clearly point to how Catharina empowered women across boundaries of language, culture, ethnic-ity, and religion.

NAITŌ JULIA AND THE MIYACO NO BICUNI

After laboring in Goa, Francis Xavier went on to Sri Lanka, Malacca, the Spice Islands, and Japan, where he founded the first Christian mission in 1549. Unlike Goa, Japan was not a Portuguese colony. Nonetheless, people experi-enced violence and oppression as warrior strongmen fought to increase their control over the sixty-six fiefdoms. Oda Nobunaga and Toyotomi Hideyoshi, the First and Second Unifiers, benefited from European trades by obtaining guns but remained suspicious toward Christianity and Western colonialism. The church in Japan grew as the Jesuits adopted the missionary method of cultural accommodation by studying Japanese language and culture and soon published Christian texts in Japanese with the help of Japanese converts. They recruited numerous Japanese male converts as their members. As in Goa, many Japanese women became their "missionaries" even though, as noted before, the Jesuit *Constitutions* did not allow women to be an official part of their Society. After Hideyoshi issued his *Edict of Expulsion of Foreign Priests* in 1587, the Jesuits had to increasingly rely on native catechists. Hideyoshi also executed twenty-six missionaries and Japanese male catechists in 1597.

The most prominent catechist was Naitō Julia, a noble widow and a former abbess of a Pure Land Buddhist convent in Kyoto.[16] According to the Jesuit records, Julia received a "divine light" through studying Christian literature and attending Jesuit sermons around 1596. After her conversion, she staged religious debates with her former fellow Buddhist clerics.[17] Even before her baptism, the Jesuits had great expectations for her leadership, and she became their most effective Christian apologist. Already a notable Buddhist preacher, she was able to convince many Buddhists to accept Christianity.

Julia wisely applied her experiences as a Buddhist abbess to the Mother Superior of her Christian daughters. Around 1600, she founded a society of women catechists, named Miyaco no bicuni (Nuns of Kyoto).[18] She and other women took monastic vows under Jesuit supervision, lived in a house next to the Jesuit house, dressed in black, and went about preaching, catechizing, teaching, baptizing, promoting Ignatian *Spiritual Exercises*, and occasionally hearing confessions, so that their converts may be able to receive the Eucharist.[19] They also engaged in vigorous disputations with Buddhist monks, who sometimes became enraged and physically attacked the nuns. In 1603, Tokugawa Ieyasu, the last unifier who became Shogun, adopted Confucianism as the national ideology and began to tighten anti-Christian measures. Even so, between 1601 and 1611, Naitō Julia and her catechists persuaded about 60,000 women and men to Christianity across social ranks, from the aristocracy to the poor. Because of her success, the Jesuits called Julia their "Apostle."[20]

In 1612, the Second Shogun Hidetada issued the total ban of Christianity. The authorities arrested foreign missionaries and Christian leaders, including members of the Miyaco no bicuni, and publically humiliated and tortured them. In the Great Expulsion of 1614, Julia and fourteen members of her community were deported from Nagasaki, along with the Jesuits. It is significant to note that the government felt such a strong threat from this small group of women who freely associated with the foreigners and men that they had to be deported. Violating the government's ban of Christianity, they rebelled against Confucian social demands for women to be subservient to their lords, fathers, husbands, and sons.

After a horrid sea voyage, the exiles resettled in Spanish Manila in early 1615. While the Jesuits from Japan began to integrate into their community there, Julia and the women with her chose total enclosure. In stark contrast to their active life in Japan, Julia's "*beatas*" (holy women) devoted themselves to a reclusive life of contemplation, intercessory prayer, visions, and writing. The people in Manila sought their wise counsel and prophetic messages, which were delivered only through their Jesuit confessors. Having exercised her wise leadership successfully in very different religious vocations and under the difficult situations of persecution in Japan and in the diaspora of Manila, Naitō Julia died in 1627. In 1656, after forty years in exile, the community dissipated with the death of its last two members. The Jesuits gave them a solemn Mass and buried them in their own cemetery as if they were official members of the order. Although Julia and her beatas did not recruit novices in the Philippines, they may have inspired Ignacia del Espiritu Santo of Binondo (c. 1663–1748). In 1684 Ignacia founded the first congregation of native Filipina women, called the Beatas de la Compañía de Jesús.[21] Ignacia's society pursued an active apostolate and became "missionaries" for the Jesuits in Manila.

ŌTA JULIA, KOREAN CONFESSORS AND MARTYRS IN JAPANESE PERSECUTION

The first conversions of quite a few Koreans to Christianity began during Hideyoshi's invasions of Korea and China between 1592 and 1598. Hideyoshi's soldiers took many Koreans back to Japan. The Jesuits ordered the Christian lords and ladies to free these hostages. A group of Japanese Christian women in Nagasaki rescued some captive Korean women in 1593.[22] On Christmas, while the governor of Nagasaki forbade the church assembly, they gathered in one woman's home, where about one hundred Korean women were baptized. In 1610, Korean Christians built São Lourenço Church, which lasted until 1619, when the authorities tore it down as they did all other churches in Nagasaki.[23]

Records of some notable Korean-native Christian women leaders appear in the Jesuit accounts. Pak Marina (c. 1572–1636) was one of the core members of the Miyaco no bicuni.[24] She became blind in her exile in Manila but received many spiritual visions and delivered messages of encouragement.

Another Korean woman, named Ōta Julia (n.d.), was brought to Japan during Hideyoshi's invasion of Korea in 1592.[25] She was baptized in 1596 while

serving a Japanese Christian noblewoman, Sō Konishi Maria (1575–1605), in
Tsushima. In 1600, Unifier Ieyasu executed Maria's father, and her husband,
Sō Yoshitomo Dario, sent Maria away. Ieyasu then took Julia to his court in
eastern Japan. Julia maintained her deep Christian devotion; she cared for
the poor and, having taken a vow of chastity, rejected men's sexual advances.
In 1611 Shogun Hidetada ordered the interrogation of the Christian women
at his courts. Julia refused to renounce her faith. Though exiled three times,
from one desolate island to another, Julia still claimed her vocation as a catechist. According to the record, she persuaded two fellow women exiles to
become Christians. But because she did not know the words of the baptis-
mal liturgy, she instead held a Christian naming ceremony. At another time,
she sent letters to the Jesuits in hiding and asked them to send her liturgical
paraphernalia for celebrating the Eucharist. Legends say that Julia perished
on one of these islands where she was exiled. In 1970 the Japanese Tourist
Bureau built a memorial of her on an island and still sponsors a "Julia Festi-
val" every May. There is also a memorial to Julia in Seoul, Korea. But according to the Jesuit records, she eventually went to Nagasaki and then to Osaka,
where she ministered to young Christian women. There are no records of her
whereabouts after 1622.

Under the third Shogun Iemitsu (1623–50), the persecution of Christians
escalated. An estimated forty thousand Christians became martyrs. Records
of about eighty women martyrs, including several Korean women, are available for further investigation. In 1629, the authorities arrested Christian villagers in Shimabara and tortured them to extract the public recantation of
their belief in Christianity. The officials dipped them in the boiling volcanic
magma of Mt. Unzen, little by little each day, so that they suffered the pain of
burns and fear of more torture. Among the group was Isabel, a Korean, whom
a Jesuit writer praised as "a valiant woman. Neither the apostasy of other
Christians, nor her husband's weakness, nor the persuasion of non-Christians,
nor cruel torture would move her away from her constancy."[26] When the
authorities told her that Japanese law demanded a wife to follow her husband,
Isabel answered: "In all other matters a woman may follow her husband, but
when it comes to the matter of salvation, this [law] does not apply. I have
another spouse in heaven whom I follow." Frustrated, the officials threatened
that they would torture her until she apostatized. Isabel laughed at them,
saying, "I will suffer as much torture as you give me for another 100 years
or more whether you end up killing me or not. I will not deny my faith,
so whether I live or die is no concern to me." The officials dragged Isabel
through the rugged mountains for three days until she fell unconscious, and
they forced her thumbprint on a paper of recantation. Nevertheless, the Jesuits recognized Isabel as a martyr. Choosing the foolishness of the cross, Isabel

and other martyrs demonstrated the wisdom of God in courage, bravery, and hope (1 Cor. 1:18).

CANDIDA XU AND PIONEER CHINESE CHRISTIAN WOMEN LEADERS

In Ming-Qing China, women faced deeply gendered laws. Both their seclusion to homes and the prohibition of direct contact with men other than their husbands limited their interactions with the missionaries, priests, and other Christians. Yet Christian women leaders devised indirect ways of receiving the sacraments and exercised their vocation widely as teachers and evangelists without ever leaving home. They maneuvered the difficult situations of arranged marriage and concubinage to non-Christian men without compromising their faith.

Philippe Couplet (1622–93), a Jesuit missionary, published two biographies of Candida Xu (1607–80).[27] Couplet's main agenda was to defend the Jesuit cultural accommodation against Franciscan/Dominican charges of syncretism. He also aimed to solicit European noblewomen as patrons for the China mission. For this purpose, he depicted Candida, a new Chinese convert, as an exemplary embodiment of both Confucian and Catholic virtuous widowhood. Yet Candida was more than a pious and chaste widow. Born as a granddaughter of Paul Xu Guangqi (1562–1633), a notable member of the Chinese literati converted by the mission of Mateo Ricci, Candida got married to a non-Christian husband and bore him eight children. Because she was a good wife and Christian witness, her husband died as a new convert in 1653. Freed from household duties at age forty-six, Candida took up the role of the mother of all Christians. She financed thirty-nine churches, not with the inherited wealth but by marketing embroidered silk weaving made by her female relatives and by investing the profits. She also provided for the missionaries regardless of their order. She aided the Jesuits' outreach in publishing "eighty-nine books on astronomy, philosophy . . . and one hundred and six books about theology and religion," especially for women readers who could not leave their house.[28] She sent around blind itinerant storytellers to recite the Gospel accounts. She trained midwives to give emergency baptisms for babies at risk of death and managed an orphanage to discourage female infanticide. Because the Chinese regarded proper funeral and burial as important, she commissioned her agents to provide such ceremonies not only to Christians but also to the poor who could not afford proper rituals. She supported lay sodalities and congregations of catechists, who carried out major tasks of education and pastoral care of Christians because priests were always in short supply. She organized devotional gatherings at her house and continued to persuade her female relatives to accept Christianity.

According to Gail King, who first introduced Candida Xu to English readers, there were many devotional gatherings at other Chinese women leaders' homes. In addition, special chapels and separate churches were built for women in nearly all the provinces. While such gender-segregation may seem like an impediment for women's ministry, in these women's spheres, women "chose their own leaders" who cultivated creative ways of ministry.[29] Dominicans and Franciscans too worked with consecrated nuns, who became teachers, catechists, preachers and counselors for women and who also took care of the orphans and the poor.[30]

In addition to these pioneer women in China, there were Chinese-speaking women leaders in Southeast Asia, including a mother-daughter team, both named Catharine, who served as catechists in Vietnam.[31] Stories of diaspora Asian women in Latin America during the early modern period also need to be explored.[32] These and many other studies can illustrate how Pacific Asian and North American Asian women are historically and globally connected to their Asian ancestral women leaders.

HISTORIES FOR ENVISIONING
A DIFFERENT FUTURE

These women leaders exercised crumb-gathering wisdom in early modern Asia for the liberation of their spiritual daughters from the oppressive demons of imperial, colonial, religious, and state authorities. Even in the midst of wars, forced seclusion, torture, expulsion, and execution, they ventured out to share their vocational journeys with others.[33] They even established collegial relationships with those whom their societies labeled as their enemies. Practicing their new vocations, they did not totally abandon all of their traditional religions, which the church often labeled as heretical. Instead they gained spiritual nourishment and leadership skills from them. While those in power regarded these women as nobodies, their wise eyes looked to Jesus, who was despised, humiliated, beaten, criminalized, spat upon like a dog—like the Syrophoenecian woman and like them—crucified and resurrected for the liberation of humanity. They contributed this new vision of wisdom leadership to the church of the Reformations in the early modern world.

I believe that Pacific Asian and North American Asian women today must claim the wisdom from these women ancestors so that our children can envision a different future. As one of the very few women of color historians of women of colors, I would also like to see more Pacific Asian and North

American Asian women scholars join me in re-visioning the history of the Reformations and beyond. We must continue to gather crumbs of historical knowledge about these and other women to rediscover full stories of our diasporas. Pacific Asian and North American Asian women pastors also must proclaim these newly framed church histories from pulpits and at communion tables. Teaching the stories of crumb-gathering wisdom will help our children to imagine the full loaf and create wise leadership in their own contexts.

2

Taiwanese American Women Pastors and Leaders

A Reality in Our Churches

SAN YI LIN AND GRACE Y. KAO

"Would you tell us about the difficulties of being an Asian American woman in your ordination journey?" asked a pastor on an all-white panel for Shirley's readiness committee for ordination in the Reformed Church in America (RCA). Shirley rolled her eyes in her mind, sighed, and answered the question she had heard countless times before with something she knew they would find hard to believe: "I am Taiwanese American. My family and church have been completely supportive of my ministry and my call."

Those well-intentioned pastors are not unlike the scholars and progressive church leaders who bemoan the second-class treatment of women in Asian American Christian communities. They lament that leadership positions for women are either discouraged or permitted only under the "stained glass ceiling" (i.e., women can head the kitchen and food service, choir, nursery, children's ministry, youth group, or women's ministries but can't lead the congregation as the senior pastor). Several theories have been offered to explain the patriarchal traditionalism of East Asian churches in particular, chief among them the fusion of Confucian family values with conservative evangelical Christian views about gender that Western missionaries originally taught them.

As Taiwanese Americans who have been raised in Taiwanese American church contexts, we have found generalizations about women's subordination in Asian American churches untrue to our experiences: Grace grew up in a Taiwanese American evangelical church whose founding and senior pastor of twenty-plus years was a woman and where women were represented among other authority figures; Shirley is an ordained RCA clergywoman who has received ample support for her ministry from her family and community and whose experience in the Taiwanese American Church largely mirrors Grace's. While as Asian Americans we stand in solidarity with our sisters who struggle with sexism in ministry, the disconnect we have felt as Taiwanese Americans about wholly patriarchal characterizations of Asian American churches led us to ascertain if our experiences were anomalous from or continuous with those of other Taiwanese Americans. We thus offer in our chapter reflections on the reality of women's leadership in our churches through qualitative interviews we conducted with four Taiwanese American female church leaders, a snowball sampling of churches with their leadership (i.e., session/consistory/board) information, and our review of the existing literature on gender relations in Taiwanese American contexts.

Based on our study, we conclude that Taiwanese American churches respect women as spiritual leaders and accordingly offer them opportunities to serve God, the church, and other people in ministry. We speculate that this honoring of Taiwanese American women leaders is connected to two factors: (1) our cultural tradition of men and women working together in partnership in their workplace and in the home and (2) the way Taiwanese people have understood their Reformed heritage, including on matters of biblical interpretation.[1] Since our intention is neither to suggest that our environments were bereft of any traditional gendered norms nor that Taiwanese American women leaders encounter no gender-specific ministerial challenges, we also explore the ways in which the gender of Taiwanese women does and does not make a difference in their practice of ministry.

Our chapter proceeds in three sections. In the first we provide a brief overview of the scholarship on women in Asian American church contexts. In the second we present our findings from our interviews and recall our own Taiwanese American church experiences. In the third we speculate as to why the Taiwanese American case differs from the portrait of women's inferior treatment that emerges in other Asian American churches. Since little scholarship exists on Taiwanese American Christians, our aim here is to add more Taiwanese American perspectives to the growing literature on Asian American Christianity and thereby make a scholarly contribution for the church and academy.

GENERALIZING ABOUT "SEXIST" ASIAN AMERICAN CHURCHES

Women make up the majority of the church faithful according to the growing literature on the "feminization" of Christianity. The representation of Asian American women in church leadership, however, tells a different story.

Scholars, including historian Timothy Tseng and practical theologian Su Yon Pak, report that Asian American churches generally find it "difficult, if not impossible, for Asian American women to be in traditional pastoral leadership where they have authority over men."[2] Their observations that "male leadership is normative"[3] is further substantiated by the comparatively well-documented experiences of Korean American women who are prevented from exercising the full range of their ministerial gifts and abilities in either first or second generation Korean American churches because of the "overtly genderized church culture."[4] Leading Korean American male theologians have also been vocal about condemning disordered and inegalitarian gender relations in Korean contexts as sins from which congregations must immediately repent.[5]

This depiction of sexism in Asian American churches is so common in the literature on Asian America Christianity that it has become conventional wisdom. Since that sketch has largely been drawn from studies of *Korean* American churches, however, the question remains whether it holds true for *Taiwanese* American contexts.

While not much scholarship exists on Taiwanese or Taiwanese American Christian women, the research we found on the former has been consistent with the larger characterization of marginalized women.[6] In the Taiwanese *American* context, however, some sociological studies suggest that women are using their faith as a source of empowerment. Sociologist Carolyn Chen found that Taiwanese immigrant women in the United States were not only more likely than their Taiwanese counterparts to be religious and to report experiencing an "enlarge[ment] . . . of women's traditional sphere of authority" whether they worked outside or inside the home,[7] but also more able to use their newfound Christian faith to "negotiate old traditions and to construct new traditions of gender and selfhood."[8] That is, the immigrants' conversion to Christianity allowed them to use their new identities as daughters of God to individuate themselves from their traditional households and accordingly break out of the "Confucian ideals" of "womanly virtues of obedience to and dependence on male relatives" with which they had been raised.[9]

Another sociologist, Chien-Juh Gu, presents findings about Taiwanese American women in the workplace and the home consistent with some of the observations we make in sections 1 and 3. At work, Taiwanese American women seem to have "subverted" popular images of Asian women "as passive, subservient, quiet, and docile."[10] At home, slightly less than half of her informants (47 percent) reported an equal division of housework labor.[11] In decision making about children's education and family finances—what Taiwanese American couples regard as the "two most important decisions in the family"[12]—the most common pattern of decision making was joint (46 percent), followed by mother-alone (36 percent) and father-alone (18 percent).

Women's authority was most pronounced in the arena of family finances: nearly half (41 percent) of the wives "were independently in charge of financial decisions," even if it was their husbands who earned all or most of the income; many husbands even report being given an "allowance" and having to account for every dollar they spent.[13] While women and men might have fulfilled traditional roles in other ways, we see here that Taiwanese American women have been able to exert power in the workplace and in the home that defy simple stereotypes.

The scant literature that exists on gender relations among Taiwanese Americans begins to correct the depiction of Asian American women as uniformly oppressed in private and public spaces. It does not, however, address the role of women in Taiwanese American *churches*—the topic to which we next turn.

OUR FINDINGS: HEARING FROM TAIWANESE AMERICAN CLERGYWOMEN

For our study, we conducted hour-long interviews with four Taiwanese American Christian women ministers in 2014: three ordained pastors and one seminarian.[14] We also informally surveyed Taiwanese American church pastors and congregants about their church leadership structure during the 2014 Taiwanese Christian Church Council of North America (TCCCNA) conference and obtained other information through personal connections and through statistics gleaned from various websites.[15] What follows is a sampling of the experiences of the clergywomen we interviewed, particularly those experiences they identified as gendered.

A Senior Pastor: Sarah

"Sarah,"[16] a recent immigrant from Taiwan, was officially installed in April 2014 as the senior and sole pastor of a Taiwanese American church after a difficult two-and-a-half year job search in the early 2010s. Sarah had initially experienced gender-based discrimination in the United States in a way that she had not in Taiwan. Sarah not only recalls approximately equal numbers of women and men enrolled in seminaries affiliated with the Presbyterian Church in Taiwan (PCT), including at her alma mater, Taiwan Theological Seminary, but also no overt gender discrimination for job placements among her classmates postgraduation. For example, if a church wanted to apply for an intern, they would have to be open to receiving either a man or a woman and accept whomever the General Synod of the PCT appointed through a lottery system. When she was living in Keelung, she was not the first woman to have served at her church; seven out of fourteen churches were currently pastored by women or had been in the recent past.

Sarah's experience in the United States was not the same. Because she can speak Mandarin in addition to Taiwanese, Sarah looked for positions in both Taiwanese American churches and Chinese American churches, regardless of denominational affiliation. She found that most of the Chinese churches to which she had applied took issue with women in leadership. Those early experiences of being dismissed out-of-hand led Sarah to conclude that the *Taiwanese* church had progressed on gender equity matters where *Chinese* American churches had not. In her words:

> [These Chinese churches in the United States are] may be like [Tai-wan was] 30 years ago. It's like they stayed where we were 30 years ago. . . . So [these] churches here [in the United States] are not as progressive. . . . Chinese churches . . . have been very influenced by the conservative Biblical interpretation, so when they don't accept female pastors . . . they [also] don't accept women elders and deacons, but they accept women . . . [as] Sunday School teachers.

Sarah credits a mentor, a Taiwanese woman pastor currently serving at the PC(USA) denominational level, who guided her to a more egalitarian PC(USA) church where she was finally hired.

An English Pastor: Jane

Our English Ministry pastor, "Jane," received her call when she was a junior in high school. Like many upwardly mobile Taiwanese people, she initially wanted to become a doctor—a brain surgeon to be exact—to help others. A few weeks after that initial thought, however, a different idea popped into her mind: "Why be a medical doctor when I could be a spiritual one?" Her parents were very encouraging of her vocational path and her father, a pastor himself, responded to her early concerns about the propriety of women in church leadership with gentle instruction about how to contextualize patriar-chal Bible verses about women's submission in light of the egalitarian thrust of other passages. Additionally, members of her community have regarded her ministry not only in terms of divine vocation but also as a positive reflec-tion on her family and particularly her father's ministry, with one church member telling her that her father must have been a very good pastor for her to want to follow in his footsteps.

Jane has now been working as the English ministry pastor for over a decade. While the English Ministry pastor is not considered the senior pastor of the church, Jane does not feel that she is the subordinate youth or children's pastor—a role traditionally viewed as more acceptable for women pastors in Asian American churches, as discussed in section 1. Instead, Jane regards herself as the senior pastor of the English-speaking side of the church, not only because she does all the work that a senior pastor would do, including meeting with her three worship leaders on a regular basis, but also because she does not have any oversight from the consistory (church board), which traditionally assigns a deacon to oversee any ministry under its control. Not having a deacon signifies to Jane autonomy in her ministry to serve her congregants as the Spirit leads and as she sees fit.

When pressed to describe the ways in which her gender has affected her leadership, Jane reports never having been "second guessed because [she is] female and in a leadership role." She does acknowledge, however, her gender "mak[ing] a difference" with her relationship with the (male) senior pastor. When they meet, she must wait for the pastor's wife to arrive before they can commence with business. We coauthors understand this arrangement as connected to two factors: (1) Taiwanese cultural understandings of the possible inappropriateness of frequent, private meetings between a man and a woman who are neither married to each other nor in the same family, and (2) an example of spouses sharing ministerial responsibilities (to be discussed further in section 3), even if only one of them technically holds the office, for the pastor's spouse is to provide her own insights—not simply to be present to preclude gossip from others.

A Hospital Chaplain: Shirley

The third ordained pastor and coauthor of this essay ("Shirley") is a hospital chaplain. As we recounted earlier, Shirley's family has always been receptive to her work in ministry. Indeed, Shirley credits her mother for encouraging her toward ordination, even before she had discerned that path for herself. Shirley had enrolled in divinity school without a call to ministry. When Shirley eventually came to see herself as her mother did and completed the ordination process, her father, who had simultaneously been in process, completed all steps as well. Shirley and her father were thus ordained together in the same service—a source of pride for him and something he continues to brag about as a unique blessing from God.

Shirley has yet to serve as a church pastor, though she has never experienced difficulties taking on other church leadership roles. In fact, she has been invited to be the keynote speaker for various conferences and retreats and has also received unofficial job offers even while not actively looking for a ministry position. As a hospital chaplain, she finds that others have perceived her gender as an asset, not a liability, due to traditional gendered norms and societal expectations of women being more understanding, caring, and physically affectionate. In her own words, "I have been able to hold their hands, touch their arms, or give them hugs to offer comfort [in ways] that a male chaplain may not have been able to give."

A Seminarian: Rebecca

The fourth person we interviewed, "Rebecca," is in the midst of the ordination process. She currently serves as an elder in her church and has held other leadership positions in the past, including Sunday School teacher and nominations committee member. Though Rebecca has been a member of her current Taiwanese American church since elementary school, her presence there had been sporadic while in seminary due to course and internship requirements. For this reason, she was surprised to find herself recently nominated as an elder candidate in her church: during the church meeting, someone shouted out her name to nominate her from the floor (n.b., her name had not been on the ballot). Once her name was called out, however, a majority of congregants voted for her. Given her extensive years of service as a lay leader in the church, Rebecca does not anticipate encountering any major gender-based obstacles to securing more significant leadership positions in the future since she believes, and has seen, the Taiwanese American church assess her and others' leadership abilities based on their merits.

A Pioneering Role Model: Pastor Chou

While we were not able to interview our fifth research subject, we would like to present as a case study the senior leadership of the Taiwanese American church in which Grace was raised. Evangelical Formosan Church of Orange County (EFC OC) was founded as a church plant (from the parent church, EFC of Los Angeles) in the early 1980s by Pastor Chou, a woman who held the position of senior pastor until some years into the first decade of the new millennium. Pastor Chou was a constant presence in EFC OC the entire time that Grace was a member, as her church had two different (male) English ministry pastors serving under her during that same time. Pastor Chou also tangentially fits the "spouses as partners in ministry" model in that her husband was simultaneously pastoring a different church plant (EFC of South Bay). Over the course of about twenty years, Grace has asked her parents, who have served as respected leaders in the church,[17] her church friends, and their parents if there have been objections to Pastor Chou's status as the senior leader on the basis of her gender. The answer she has received, to her surprise, has consistently been the same: save for one instance in the late 1980s when one male church member could not accept the prospect of senior female leadership and left, the issue of Pastor Chou's gender has never prevented the church body as a whole from respecting her wisdom and authority. Yes, various church members have disagreed with her on one matter or another throughout the years (as parishioners in any given church community are wont to do), but her gender on its own has never been a point of contention. In Grace's view, the acceptance of a woman senior pastor was not tied to her home church teaching progressive or feminist theology—it was a typical conservative evangelical church on other matters[18]—but due to other factors to be explained below in section III.

Summary of Our Findings

Each of the women we interviewed has had different experiences in ministry. We nonetheless found significant commonalities among them. All four found support for their call to ministry in their families and congregations from the beginning of their journey. All four had calls early on in their lives and acted upon them, rather than in middle age as second-career pastors. All four also reported in their own ways that gender has been less of a hurdle for them or for others to deal with than their (youthful) age: all of the women we interviewed are younger than forty years old, with ministry being their first and only career. They have felt that they are still learning on the job and thus have not yet experienced the full range of challenges they may eventually encounter.

While there may not be many female senior pastors in the Taiwanese American church, we believe it is premature to conclude that the cause is sexism per se. Just as Pak cautions against viewing leadership solely in terms of "hierarchical, vertical models of one-pastor or senior pastor leadership,"[19] so we find significant women's representation as church leaders in other ways. According to our snowball sampling of twenty-one Taiwanese American churches, all of them either currently have or have had women elders or deacons or both, with the number of women deacons outweighing those who were men. This latter statistic is significant, for if our interviewee Rebecca is correct that there is an "unofficial rule" in Taiwanese American churches that one must serve as a deacon first before serving as an elder, then these women who have been deacons have positioned themselves to take on more responsibilities in the future.

To be sure, our interviewees who reported having few or no women serving as elders in their churches were quick to note that more women have served in the past or that the lone woman currently on the board held the most powerful position. According to the website of the National Taiwanese Presbyterian Council (NTPC), the moderator, vice moderator, and treasurer are women—only the secretary is a man. We have also discovered in our interview with Rebecca that getting elected after being nominated is not more difficult for women than for men. Still, Rebecca reports a concern about how to navigate "serving in the church [when] your husband is not," which suggests anxiety about creating family disharmony if the woman is perceived to be more publicly committed to the church than her husband. This issue, in our judgment, merits further reflection and study.

Based on our own experiences and interviews with others, we conclude that Taiwanese American women do not experience the same problems, or the same magnitude of problems, of being recognized as trustworthy and competent leaders in the church simply because they are women. Indeed, in one of our surveys, a Taiwanese American pastor who headed a second-generation Korean American church for many years spontaneously compared his experiences of having served these two different ethnic communities. In his words,

> [The] Taiwanese have a much different experience from the Korean churches. We are much more egalitarian. In my experience with Taiwanese Presbyterian churches, women leadership has always been encouraged and facilitated. . . . [T]he women leaders do not play a secondary or subordinate role next to a male leader of same level or capacity. While we may not have equal numbers of male and female leadership, I haven't seen at any level [whether local or national] . . . where Taiwanese women have been reduced and subjugated by another male leader.[20]

Accounting for the Disconnect: Some Explanations

As scholars we recognize that we should not generalize about women in church leadership across all Taiwanese American Christian communities on the basis of the interviews we conducted. Even so, our findings leave unresolved a question animating our study: Why do at least some Taiwanese American churches value women as leaders in ways that differ markedly from the conversation about the diminished status of women in other Asian American churches? We offer two possible explanations in the space remaining: (1) our longstanding cultural practice of men and women sharing responsibilities in the home and partnering together in work even if only one spouse holds the job or office, and (2) the Reformed tradition's history of women's education and leadership development in Taiwan.

Our first hypothesis is that Taiwanese people are familiar with the model of de facto marital egalitarianism in the workplace and at home, even under a de jure presumption of patriarchy. Taiwanese people have been influenced not only by patriarchal Chinese (Confucian) culture but also by two additional factors: the sociocultural structure of many aboriginal tribes in Taiwan and the modernizing influences of the Western and Japanese powers who have exerted various forms of control over Taiwan since the late sixteenth century.[21] More specifically, scholars have long described most Taiwanese aboriginal (Austronesian) cultures as matriarchal.[22] Though Taiwan later inherited the patriarchal Confucianism of "traditional Chinese culture" through Chinese emigration beginning in the mid-sixteenth century (when the Han Chinese mostly from Fujian and Guandong began to mix with the aborigines), Taiwan's later history of being colonized by the Dutch, modernized and formally educated by the Japanese,[23] and subsidized by the United States during its period of industrialization beginning in the 1960s, has resulted in the infusion of a "variety of cultural elements into tradition" into Taiwanese society.[24] More specifically, not only did Taiwan under Japanese rule experience what one scholar has coined its first wave of feminism,[25] but the increase of women working outside of the home and the fight against colonialism also propelled Taiwanese intellectuals and other elites to rethink women's issues as well.[26] In light of these factors, we concur with the scholarly consensus that Taiwan can appropriately be characterized as "both traditional and progressive; a continuity of the past and discontinuity from that legacy," such that there remains a "constant ambivalent struggle between convention and modernity, native and foreign, and local and cosmopolitan."[27]

We coauthors, who can trace our ancestors in Taiwan for many generations (i.e., we are *běngshěngrén* or "people of this province"),[28] know intimately the ways in which our families can be paradoxically described as patriarchal, matriarchal, and egalitarian. Shirley's mother may have been the cook, but it was her father who did the dishes. Grace's father was a physician, but it was her mother—a college graduate in accounting—who did the bookkeeping, managed her father's medical staff, and served as vice president of his private practice. Shirley's grandfather, also a pastor, emphasized repeatedly that his ministry would not have been as successful as it was had it not been for his wife (Shirley's grandmother), who provided the bulk of the pastoral care to their parishioners. Grace's maternal grandfather was also a physician, but it was her grandmother who likewise ran his office, cared for his patients emotionally, and acted as an unofficial nurse. Our families also directly confirm one of the sociological findings of Chien-Juh Gu considered earlier, that women in our households were the ones who controlled the purse, even if it was the men who made the money. While these are only four examples in two generations of our two families, it is clear to us and in the stories of our extended family and friends that Taiwanese people have long separated "respect" and "honor" from "office" in the sense that the former two have long been possible without the latter. That is, it may have been the fathers and grandfathers who are or were the titled doctors or reverends, but everyone understood that the esteem, responsibilities, and accomplishments fell just as much to their wives.

Our second hypothesis has to do with the Reformed heritage of Taiwanese Christians.[29] The first missionaries to Taiwan in the late part of the nineteenth century were Presbyterian and evangelized to a Taiwanese people culturally rooted in patriarchy and matriarchy. The Taiwanese people specifically requested female missionaries and encouraged women to become educated and to evangelize. The first school to train women to become evangelists opened in Tainan in 1884 by Rev. George MacKay.[30] After 1901, the school was reorganized by Rev. William Gauld (1840–1922) to meet more modern goals and educational standards for women. Not to be outdone, his wife, Margaret Mellis Gauld, is equally revered among Taiwanese Christians as the mother of Taiwanese church music, as she pioneered piano teaching in Taiwan and otherwise supported "Taiwan's first generation [of] most talented musicians and composers."[31]

The first ordination of a Taiwanese woman occurred in 1950 by a foreign missionary in the Presbyterian Church in Taiwan.[32] During this dangerous time in Taiwanese history (known as the "white terror"), she could minister to people in ways that men could not without fearing for their lives under martial law (1949–1987). Though the church began to officially ordain women as pastors in the mid-1950s,[33] this pattern of women as spiritual authority figures had already been established during the missionary period. Thus the longstanding presence of women in church leadership in Taiwan helped to normalize the reality of women ministers both in Taiwan and in Taiwanese American churches, the latter due to outmigration following the 1965 Immigration Act, and this continues today to provide positive examples to the next generations of women and men.

We invoke not only the tradition of strong women leaders in the Presbyterian Church in Taiwan to explain the more progressive gender relations we find in Taiwanese American churches but also the larger Reformed emphasis on the importance of context for biblical interpretation. Based on what our research subjects reported and our reflections on our own experiences in Taiwanese American churches, we theorize that Taiwanese and Taiwanese American Christians have long been taught to regard the Bible as the Holy Word of God whose meaning must be understood in context. When asked to comment on those passages in the New Testament suggestive of women's subordinate role to men, all four of our interviewees stated the importance of understanding Paul's social-cultural context: Paul wrote to specific churches about particular matters involving the behavior of women and thus was offering context-specific solutions to their context-specific problems in ways that might not have universal application. We conclude, then, that as Taiwanese American Christians have been taught to contextualize "problematic" passages, they have become more comfortable with seeing both women and men in the pulpit. In short, they appreciate talented, dedicated, and visionary spiritual leaders wherever they are to be found, whether men or women. We acknowledge, however, that when less than five percent of the total population of Taiwan is Christian, the Taiwanese honoring of both women and men leaders might be attributable as much to practical necessity as to their aforementioned theological egalitarianism and longstanding cultural norms.[34]

CONCLUSION

Our goal in this chapter has been to add Taiwanese American voices to the larger discussion in Asian American Christian circles about women in ministry. We neither seek to generalize about all Taiwanese American Christian communities nor claim that Taiwanese American Christians are superior to other Asian American Christian communities because of gender issues. Our study and historical research has nevertheless led us to postulate a few reasons why the Taiwanese American church we know and serve respects women leadership. Those of us who are active in the Taiwanese American church recognize that it is far from perfect. We do, however, have profound appreciation for the model of strong women we have received, for the support we have experienced in our vocational paths, and for the ways in which we have not felt marginalized on account of our gender.

INTERVIEW QUESTIONS

We asked each interviewee the following questions, in addition to discrete follow-up questions based upon the answers they provided.

1. How long have you served in your present leadership capacity? What are your responsibilities? What previous jobs or experiences prepared you for this position?
2. Who do you understand yourself to be serving in your ministry? What do you understand your ministry to be principally about?
3. Please share your "call" story—was your family supportive? Your church? If not, how did you know God was calling you?
4. How do you understand your gender as affecting your leadership? How do you think OTHERS see your gender as affecting your leadership?

   a. Sometimes women can be the biggest critics of other women leaders. Have you found this to be the case? Have other women supported your ministry/leadership? Have they seen you as a competitor or as someone who is doing a "man's" job instead?

   b. How do you interpret passages in the Bible (e.g., Pauline letters) that say that women should be silent and not have authority over men?

   c. Growing up, what kind of models of women's leadership did you have? Did you think certain roles or positions were closed to you because of your gender?

5. What do you think are the factors that have played into your "success" in church leadership? For example, did you have a mentor or a "sponsor" encouraging you or making it possible for you to be known?

6. Women in positions of authority, either in church or in industry, face scrutiny about their abilities to be successful in their work *and* responsible in the home. Have you struggled with the desire or expectation to "have it all?" Have you faced questions or suspicions about your marriage or "singleness" because you are so dedicated to ministry?

7. One stereotypical image of Asian American women in the church is that they are treated like second-class citizens in that they are never to "take authority" over men or become senior pastor. Does your experience in church fit this stereotype? Do you think there is anything about being Taiwanese and working among Taiwanese people that either would confirm or push against this stereotype?

Neither the Suffering Servant nor the Syrophoenician Woman

HEE KYUNG KIM

INTRODUCTION

When I think of leadership, I think of my parents, who showed me two very different ways of being a leader. My father, a well-meaning, patriarchal, and conservative Christian, ruled over my mother and his five children at home with "God-given" power as a father, believing that only unconditional obedience and submission to his authority would keep our family strong and prosperous. If my father was the official charismatic leader of our family, then my mother was the unofficial yet real leader who would handle the day-to-day challenges and various dramas of her five children. While my father was a stern, authoritative, and rather distant figure whose commands loomed powerfully over us, and often against us, my mother was a self-sacrificing servant-leader type. In her relationship with my father, my mother rarely asserted herself, and she always put herself last, sacrificing so many things for my father and for us. When she took up a leadership role as the president of the Women's Mission Club in our church, I remember her being a humble servant. In contrast to my father, who enjoyed giving public speeches and was often seen shaking hands with important people in the church, my mother was usually behind the scenes, cleaning and cooking for others in the kitchen.

Both of my parents taught me virtues necessary for leadership, including authority, confidence, sacrifice, service, and humility. At the same time, they also created some obstacles for me by deeply engraving two stereotypical images of leaders in my mind: the authoritative leader of self-assertion, power, and authority on the one hand, and the self-emptying servant leader of self-sacrifice and submission on the other. Intellectually, I recognize that this categorization of the traits of leadership into two groups is rather artificial and unrealistic, but old habits are hard to break. I still find myself limited by these two images of leadership, thus struggling to envision myself as a leader. I am too shy to become an authoritative leader like my father and too selfish to become a self-sacrificial servant leader like my mother. I simply do not fit into either of these engrained types of leaders.

Still, I have to ask myself, "Aren't I a leader?" Well, indeed I am. I am a director of children's ministry at my local Korean immigrant church, leading children and their parents toward a vision of a Christian life and education. I am also an adjunct professor at a few Boston area colleges, leading students toward the world of diverse and interesting perspectives on religion and philosophy. Despite my occupation and leadership positions, I have never consciously thought of myself as a leader. Being neither authoritative and charismatic nor self-sacrificial and humble, I have had trouble embracing myself as a leader. This hinders my becoming a better leader, which is indeed problematic.

In this chapter, I will examine some of the stereotypical characteristics and images of leaders while searching for a more liberating model of leadership. For this task, I will explore the biblical symbols of the suffering servant and the story of the Syrophoenician woman that together convey the importance of self-sacrifice and self-assertion, respectively. Through my exploration, I will identify some strengths and weaknesses of these models and see whether they may point me in the direction of another, less problematic and more liberating model of leadership.

THE SYMBOL OF SUFFERING SERVANT AND KOREAN AMERICAN WOMEN LEADERS

For both Korean Christian men and women, the symbol of the suffering servant has been very important. Growing up in Korea, I often heard male pastors calling themselves the "Lord's suffering servants," pledging to live a life of sacrifice and service to others. Many Korean Christian women also identify themselves as the suffering servant, placing high value on this symbol. Observing the resonance many Korean women feel with the image of the suffering servant, scholar Sun Ai Lee Park has identified the suffering servant as a powerful and influential symbol for many oppressed Korean women. She asserts that throughout Korea's long history of oppression and suffering, including civil war and the division of the North and the South, Korean women became the "most suffering of the suffering lambs, carrying out the role of imminent and potential eschatological redemption for all."[1] Chung

Hyun Kyung also states that the symbol of the suffering servant is the "most prevailing image of Jesus among Asian women's theological expression," and says that the experience of suffering is one in which Asian women most easily and closely experience Jesus.[2]

This endearment of the symbol of the suffering servant by many Korean Christians must have affected me quite profoundly in my youth, as I imagined the path of the pastor, until fairly recently, as a thorny road where one has to nail oneself to the cross and carry it for others. Surely, there is a dimension of self-sacrifice and service in the path of leaders, especially for religious leaders. But I see now that this excessive emphasis on virtues like sacrifice, obedience, and humility is not helpful for leaders, especially for Korean American women leaders, when we consider their cultural and historical context.

As is well known, East Asian culture is deeply influenced by a Confucian notion of patriarchy with its dualistic understanding of character and roles for men and women. According to these notions of gender, men are considered superior to women and are usually responsible for public work outside the home, while women are primarily defined as mothers, confined to the domestic sphere. Surely, these gender concepts have lost some contemporary influence, and few people would openly accept discriminative Confucian gender ideas such as "*namjon yeobi* (honored men, abased women)" or "*Samjongjido* (a woman must follow three men in her lifetime: her father, her husband, and finally her eldest son)."[3] However, Confucian patriarchal culture's influence still remains strong in Asian culture, as does the understanding of women as obedient and self-sacrificial mothers.

Across various cultures, mothers are usually associated with a nurturing, loving, and care-giving role. In addition to these characteristics, Korean culture has traditionally highlighted the sacrificial nature of maternal love. In a study conducted by Elain H. Kim, many male interviewees, when asked about their mothers, noted that a woman's sacrifice for her family is a necessary and sublime one.[4] Kim reported that "love, [the male interviewees] said, means sacrifice, and sacrifice develops character. Besides, a woman's patience is usually rewarded."[5] One male interviewee's comment is indeed revealing: "women are best at home; a wife must serve others, not herself."[6] Although a contemporary Korean audience might criticize this comment, the image of a self-sacrificial mother who always puts her children first is still widely accepted in Korean culture.

In fact, I do not deny that motherhood involves a certain level of self-sacrifice for others. To sacrifice oneself for others is indeed one of the most noble, sublime, and ethical human actions. It becomes problematic, however, when society creates certain norms and ideals about motherhood and imposes these so-called norms on women. While the virtues such as sacrifice, self-emptying love, and service to the others are a real and important part of motherhood, they are also noble ideals for all of humanity, including men. These virtues lose their innocence when they are fixed according to gender and enforced as imperatives.

When the cultural expectations of motherhood are combined with ecclesial expectations of a leader (those associated with the suffering servant), a more difficult situation arises in which women are expected to become a kind of self-sacrificial mother and servant for the whole congregation. In this context, women leaders are expected to serve and help others even to the point where they lose themselves. In many cases, the symbol of the suffering servant is not an option women can freely accept or deny; rather, the suffering servant and the sacrificial mother become ideals imposed upon Korean American women leaders. When women leaders deviate from these ideals and exhibit so-called unwomanly natures—being assertive, strong, or firm on their boundaries—they receive criticism. In such contexts where self-sacrifice and suffering for others are expected of Korean American women, the theological symbol of the suffering servant can exacerbate the situation, rather than liberating them.

In fact, many feminist theologians have pointed out the problems and dangers latent in the theological symbol of the suffering servant. One criticism of the symbol of the suffering servant is that this symbol unfairly glorifies suffering and the traditionally "feminine" virtues of vulnerability and self-sacrifice, creating false ideals and norms for women who have already sacrificed too much for others. Rita Nakashima Brock thus criticizes an excessive theological emphasis on Jesus' suffering and self-sacrifice and says that this emphasis can encourage us to glorify innocent suffering and death.[7] She further says that the glorification of suffering naturally leads us to lose our ability to "be angry about unnecessary suffering" and "dulls the acuteness of our caring."[8] Elisabeth Schüssler Fiorenza also asserts that "the notion of innocent victimhood and redemption as freely chosen suffering" persuaded people to "accept suffering, war, and death as important ideals."[9] Cautioning us not to overemphasize Jesus' suffering and death, she warns that notions of self-sacrifice and freely chosen suffering can function as a religious warrant to "render the exploitation of all women."[10]

These feminist insights may also be applied to the situations of Korean American women in leadership roles. If women pastors see their role as a suffering servant and sacrificial mother responsible for the care of their congregations, they will accept and endure unfair expectations, demands, and even exploitation. Although the suffering servant is a powerful symbol that helps many women to make sense of their hardship and suffering, this symbol is not without problems. When combined with the cultural norms and expectations toward women in Confucian culture, this model can idealize unfair suffering, imposing these values on Korean American women leaders.

Additionally, the suffering servant leadership model can reinforce some of the female gender stereotypes, namely the idea that women must be submissive and obedient helpers. Traditionally, women have been confined to the roles of supporters rather than leaders, and this cultural stereotype is still alive even in contemporary American culture. Many children's cartoons still describe female characters as more supportive, helping, and serving than male leading characters. According to the Geena Davis Institute on Gender in Media, there is normally only one female character for every three male characters, and this ratio has remained the same since 1946. Also, female characters are often passive and monotonous, ready to be saved by the more active and complex male leading roles.[11] The dominant image of the suffering servant as the submissive and obedient helper of God, when combined with the engrained cultural expectation of women as submissive helpers, can indeed be negative for Korean American women leaders.

Lastly, the suffering servant leadership model, which depicts a grim and unhappy picture of leadership, can hinder Korean American women as they try to envision positive pictures of multiple leadership forms. A leadership path does not have to be a gloomy and thorny road of suffering. In fact, many women leaders choose this path because it offers fulfillment and happiness, despite some hardship and difficulties. Instead of an emphasis on excessive self-sacrifice, a healthy emphasis on self-assertion and care for oneself would serve as a more helpful message for many Korean American women leaders.

Despite this negative impact of the symbol of the suffering servant, we do not have to completely abandon it. In fact, the suffering servant symbol can teach us a very important characteristic of the wisdom leader, and that is *the awareness of the interconnectedness* of the leader and her community. The Christian understanding of the suffering servant traces its origin to the Hebrew Scriptures. Here, from Isaiah 53:5–6, the innocent Servant of Yahweh suffers for others, thus redeeming their sin: ". . . he was wounded for our transgressions, crushed for our iniquities; upon him was the punishment that made us whole, and by his bruises we are healed. All we like sheep have gone astray; we have all turned to our own way and the Lord has laid on him the iniquity of us all."

Many scholars who interpret this passage note the closely *intertwined relationship* between the suffering servant and the community as a distinctive theme. Henning Graf Reventlow, for instance, says that the suffering servant can be viewed as the "representative of the whole community," as it is the case in the royal psalms of complaint and thanksgiving.[12] Although the speaker in the psalms may be viewed as if he is isolated in suffering, his experience is in fact not a private one because the person always calls to his brothers and fellow worshipers in his thanksgiving and praise.[13] Refreshing the biblical thought in which "individual and community belong together."[14] Reventlow says that the destiny of a single person—the king in the royal psalm—and the larger community are closely intertwined.

R. E. Clements also points out the communal dimension of the suffering servant's fate. Although the Servant and the community she serves are not exactly identical, the "representational role" of the suffering servant is important.[15] In this picture, Clements says, "the fate of one individual in some way both embodies, yet redeems, the fate of the larger group."[16] Thus, he examines other figures in Hebrew Scripture, such as the Royal Servant, the prophets, and even Moses, and draws parallels between them and the suffering servant. What he finds in his examination is the way in which a single figure's fate is connected to the existence, well-being, and destiny of the whole community. For example, although Moses led the people to the promised land, he himself could not enter. Moses was a righteous person and an intercessor between his people and God; however, the sins of the community affected him, making him a victim. Moses's fate was in this sense intertwined with that of his people. Moses, a righteous individual who sometimes "stood over against his people," eventually "suffered with them on their account."[17] This interconnectedness is indeed important when understanding the relationship of the leader to his or her community. A leader is never a lonely individual, but an integral part of the community where the two share the same fate. Without the profound awareness of this interwoven relationship between the individual and the community, a person cannot become a true leader. The symbol of the suffering servant has the potential to illuminate this insight well.

While there is value in reflecting on the image of the suffering servant as a model of leadership, it remains true that the image is problematic and even dangerous, as outlined by the aforementioned difficulties. Thus, I will now consider an alternative biblical symbol—that of the Syrophoenician woman—in hopes that she offers a different, less oppressive conception of leadership for women from that of the suffering servant.

THE SYROPHOENICIAN WOMAN AND
KOREAN AMERICAN WOMEN LEADERS

The Syrophoenician woman of Mark 7:24–30 and Matthew 15:21–28 is known for her bold character and fearlessness. Where the symbol of the suffering servant fails to inspire leadership in its overemphasis on self-sacrifice, the Syrophoenician woman steps in—at least at first glance—as an alternative model of leadership. She is assertive, wise, and remains in relationship even as she exercises her autonomy.

The Syrophoenician woman belongs to the lowest class of individuals within her social contexts; she was a pagan and a single mother and was further stigmatized by the unclean spirit of her daughter. Some have even suggested that she may have been a prostitute, given that she was in public without any male escort. With this status, it may have been expected of her to act docile, submissive, and obedient as she quietly accepted her victimization. And yet, the Syrophoenician woman refuses to linger on the margins of society, stuck in stigma. She boldly approaches Jesus and speaks to him, unbothered by social convention prohibiting a woman to approach a man and initiate conversation. In fact, she actively struggles to come to Jesus, making quite a scene as she fights to reach him. The disciples' effort to silence her fail; they complain directly to Jesus about her presence and her loud cries. Jesus harshly remarks, calling her and her daughter "dogs." She is not deterred. Instead of being ashamed by Jesus' insults, she engages in an argument with him and illuminates a point that was ignored by Jesus before, that dogs also deserve some attention. In this scene, we can see that the Syrophoenician woman is not a passive victim but a strong, bold, and brave master of her own destiny; she is not afraid to ask for what she needs. Her strong will and determination shine through despite the harsh social conditions. In her self-assertion Pacific, Asian, and North American Asian women can indeed find inspiration for leadership.

Furthermore, the Syrophoenician woman is a viable candidate for leadership because she is exceptionally wise. In the story, she wisely reappropriates Jesus' remark, turning the phrase to remind Jesus that even the dogs are fed from the master's table. Many scholars in fact have praised her wisdom and intelligence. Stephenson Humphries-Brooks highlights the fact that Jesus almost always wins theological debates in the gospels and the Canaanite woman is the only one who wins a theological debate with Jesus.[18] Surekha Nelavala also points out that the Syrophoenician woman's remark demonstrates her "wisdom," probably accumulated through a wealth of experiences, rather than "knowledge, per se."[19] I agree with Nelavala. In fact, the Syrophoenician woman exhibits wisdom similar to Aristotle's concept of practical reason. Aristotelian practical reason is differentiated from theoretical reasoning, which impersonally reflects on facts and their explanation.

According to Aristotle, practical reason is always situated in particular contexts and is connected with concrete actions. It is a moral capacity to reflect upon good, right actions and their values and has the power to motivate action: "[reason] urges [people] aright and towards the best objects."[20] In other words, reason leads people toward the right direction and exhorts them for the good. If we think of these aspects of practical reason, we can see that the Syrophoenician woman is indeed exercising practical reasoning here, thus making her wise in practice. She remains situated in a concrete context and thus helps Jesus re-orient toward the good. Her reply also had the moral force to motivate Jesus' moral action; it helped Jesus to recognize the good and thus immediately let him desire the good by virtue of its persuading force. If her response to Jesus was formulated with theoretical reasoning and intellect alone, it would not have had the moral force to persuade Jesus, since "thought by itself moves nothing," as Aristotle insisted.[21] But since her reflection is rooted in a concrete situation that ignites the desire for the good and moral action, her remark had sufficient power to move Jesus, thus allowing him to do the right thing in the given context.

Lastly, the Syrophoenician woman is indeed a promising candidate for leadership because she demonstrates the relational aspect of autonomy that is crucial for Korean American women leaders. The term "relational autonomy" at first may seem paradoxical. After all, autonomy is self-determination belonging primarily to one's own will. However, to think of autonomy as an exclusive possession of the self, and thus viewing it as purely individualistic, is problematic. Yes, there are solitary and individual aspects to autonomy, and autonomy at times includes confrontation with others and even the disruption of one's relationship with others. However, the tendency to view autonomy as belonging to the isolated and even disembodied self ignores the deeply social and interpersonal nature of the self. To say the least, this view of autonomy generated by an unencumbered and self-sufficient self simply does not account for the experiences and daily reality of many Korean American women. Autonomy and interpersonal relationships are in fact compatible, and we need to find a way to explain both autonomy and relationality, together. The Syrophoenician woman illustrates the compatibility of autonomy and relationships, thus providing an enlightening image for relational autonomy. Let me explain this point a little further.

As I have already noted, the Syrophoenician woman demonstrated a strong form of autonomy that confronted her culture and the oppressive relations around her. And I think that this autonomy comes not solely from herself as a lonely and isolated individual but from the healthy and right sort of relationships with the people around her and her community, including her daughter. Although we do not hear any story of her own community in the gospels, if we exercise the hermeneutics of imagination as Elisabeth Schüssler Fiorenza once urged us, we can imagine that she must have had a community of her own where she received positive influence and empowerment from others. One of the hints we get about this community, I think, is through a consideration of her daughter.

In the story, the Syrophoenician woman approaches Jesus not out of her own well-being or desire, but for her daughter. Her courage to approach Jesus in public despite the harsh treatment from the disciples and Jesus himself may have arisen in her because of her relation to, interdependence with, and love for her daughter. I myself, as a young mother, can imagine how the Syrophoenician woman would have been encouraged and empowered by her ill daughter. Although one may think that an infant is completely dependent on her caregiver, I feel that the reverse may be also true. In fact, I find myself already so dependent on my infant daughter. From her I receive energy and power to go on with my daily life; I want to be a better member of a society and a healthier person, both physically and emotionally, when I see her. I imagine that maybe the Syrophoenician woman could have overcome some of the negative influences of the larger culture because her daughter both empowered and comforted her. I think that the autonomy and assertiveness of the Syrophoenician woman was not indeed a solitary product of her own self-consciousness or theoretical reason; instead, it probably emerged as the result of the right relationship and mutual interdependence with her daughter.

This idea that interdependence and relations with others are essential for autonomy, agency, and self-assertion is well explained by Susan Brison, who discusses her own experience of trauma and the process of recovering her sense of autonomy. She discusses how trauma victims who lose their self-control and the will for self-determination as a result of trauma may ultimately recover their autonomy through relationships with empathetic others. According to her, trauma victims recover autonomy and a sense of self only when they are engaged in "the right sort of interaction with others."[22] Particularly, relationships with those who are willing to listen to their stories of victimization are essential to their recovery of autonomy.[23] Although we have to only imagine the Syrophoenician woman's relationship with her daughter and others in her intimate community, it is easy to picture these women embracing one another, comforting and being comforted in their loving relationship. Perhaps the Syrophoenician woman went home after the encounter with Jesus and told her exciting story to those who were taking care of her daughter while she was out. That community of empathetic listeners was perhaps the precise site where the Syrophoenician woman constituted and strengthened her autonomy.

Understood this way, the Syrophoenician woman demonstrates an important quality of a good leader: the ability to form her autonomy and power through right relationships within a community. Such a leader then is not an authoritative figure with a strong ego whose knowledge, power, and exceptional quality triumphs over the members of the community. Rather, she is a wise and humble leader who is situated within a community, being nourished and empowered by members of the community. Even as an assertive, wise, and relationally autonomous leader, reservations of her model of leadership remain, particularly when thought of in light of Korean American women's experiences.

The first difficulty with the Syrophoenician women model of leadership for Korean American women is a difference in context. While my social location as an immigrant Korean woman in the United States may resonate with her marginalization, a significant power differential remains. I am an educated middle-class woman who yields power in places like classrooms and church pulpits; she is a desperate and downtrodden woman who could not even afford to be angered by Jesus' insult. Surely, there must be Korean American women leaders who can identify with the experience of social oppression embedded in the story of the Syrophoenician woman, and they can surely take great comfort in her story as she becomes empowered in spite of her position of social marginalization. However, I do not regard the experiences of marginalization and oppression as the primary and defining experiences of Korean American woman leaders. We need to go beyond the stereotypical image of the docile oppressed Asian woman and embrace and express the diverse and vibrant images of Korean American women more realistically.

The second difficulty lies in the fact that the Syrophoenician woman does not completely overcome the negative influence of the larger culture around her; she ultimately falls short of becoming the ideal model of the leader. Although she challenges Jesus initially, she comes to accept Jesus' designation of her and her child as dogs, thereby accepting the logic of exclusion and marginalization initially held by Jesus. Musa Dube argues that the Syrophoenician woman who accepts the unjust logic of imperialism is a victim of colonization rather than a hero.[24] Other scholars like Nelavala also point out the limits of the Syrophoenician woman, saying that she is only a "trickster" who uses tricks—useful perhaps, but still a rather passive way of resistance.[25] These limits, in my view, actually make her character more realistic and human. She does not completely rise above her social relations, and thus her story indirectly teaches the influence of the larger culture upon the self. Recognizing her failures only serves to underscore the importance of transforming the negative and oppressive social discourses and symbols for women in society.

Still, it is problematic to cast her as an ideal figure. We may sympathize with the Syrophoenician woman, but her failure to transcend her culture becomes an obstacle for us as we seek to embrace her as a positive leadership symbol. Good symbols allow us to imagine ourselves in new and desirable ways, but the Syrophoenician woman, with all her imperfection, lacks the power to carry Korean American women to the new vision for a leader.

The third difficulty comes from the hostile setting of her story. She is an uninvited guest and a belligerent stranger, entrenched in a battle for good surrounded by a rather hostile audience, if not enemies. However, not every setting calls for a warrior leader, and this setting limits her symbolism as an ideal leader. There are metaphorical battles to fight as a leader, and Korean American women certainly have adverse situations to overcome concerning culture and ethnicity. I am a leader as a teacher and minister, and I am surrounded not by my enemies but by my fellow learners and pursuers of God's love and wisdom. True leadership does not always require the existence of overwhelming adversity.

Moreover, the Syrophoenician woman's strong personality may not resonate with some Korean American women. Imposing a bold character on Korean American women can be just as oppressive as the imposition of the stereotype of Asian women as shy and quiet, suffering servants. True leadership should play to the natural personality of an individual, accommodating and accepting their strengths—be it their boldness or their shyness.

The final difficulty that arises in the symbol of the Syrophoenician woman as a leader lies in the fact that, in truth, she is not completely free from the image of the sacrificial mother. After all, the Syrophoenician woman enters the hostile land uninvited, enduring insult and harsh treatment, solely for benefit of her daughter. She is there to ask Jesus to heal her daughter, not herself. The self-sacrifice that the Syrophoenician woman exhibits is clearly a great virtue, and there is nothing wrong with this noble act. However, it can also be used to reinforce the social and cultural image of the self-sacrificial mother, which no longer functions as an innocent image for Korean American women, as examined in the previous section.

Acknowledging these difficulties, the story of the Syrophoenician woman still holds lessons on leadership: the importance of self-assertion, the courage to speak, and the power and wisdom in finding one's voice. The Syrophoenician woman also demonstrated that autonomy is and should be always relational and has its origins in the right relationships with others. All of these qualities are indeed crucial, and Korean women leaders can learn much from these insights as they create their own symbols of leaders based on their diverse experiences, social locations, and individual tastes.

A MODEL OF A LEADER FOR KOREAN AMERICAN WOMEN: A WISE COOK

Having reflected on both the symbol of the suffering servant and the story of the Syrophoenician woman, highlighting the inspiration and pitfalls of each model, I now offer my model of a leader for Korean women: a wise cook serving a delicious dish. These images of a great leader as a wise cook and leadership as a delicious dish come partly from my fond memories of my mother's food. Although my mother was probably not the best chef in the world, with flamboyant knife skills or unusually creative recipes, she was certainly a wise and talented cook. Her dishes were always simple yet delicious, bringing various ingredients together with delicate harmony and balance. She cooked with love and care, and her food always brought our family together.

More important, I remember my mother always serving the perfect dish for every occasion and situation, perceptively discerning both our physical and mental states at the time. She would make us sizzling seafood scallion pancakes on a rainy day or spicy pork *kim-chi* stew on a cold night. After school, my mother would give me a cup of milk with honey and mashed fresh strawberries, knowing that I had surely run around with my friends just before getting home, and must be thirsty and craving something sweet. I also can never forget the soft tofu stew and a warm rice bowl she brought to the library one evening when I was a senior in high school. I was embarrassed when my mother brought a homemade meal to the library because it was unusual to bring a big pot of steaming stew there. Most of my friends hastily ate instant snacks from convenience stores or simply packed dinner. Feeling embarrassed, I, an immature adolescent youth, almost rejected the meal. But despite my initial grumbling, I remember the hot homemade meal tasting very good and comforting. What I received from my mother that night was more than simply food—it was a warm and meaningful expression of her love, care, and concern for me.

A good leader is like this wise and talented cook who serves the community with love and care, preparing just the right well-balanced and delicious dish for just the right occasion. The true leader discerns the setting of each meal, its complex context and circumstances, and the various needs of her community members, and then crafts accordingly. True leadership then is the product of a wise cook—a well-cooked dish, prepared with care and love and served to the right person in the right situation. The ability to balance various components of taste and texture is, of course, a significant virtue of a cook, and the well-cooked dish, like leadership, must provide balance and resolution to social situations.

This image of a leader as a good cook resonates more with the image of my mother than that of my father, who was never around the kitchen. To state this, however, is not to say that I choose my mother's leadership example over my father's. In fact, I believe that it is important to negate both tropes of leadership, namely the over-emphasis on sacrifice and humility on the one hand and top-down authoritarian style on the other hand, just as I have negated the uncritical acceptance of the images of Suffering Servant and the Syrophoenician woman. Moreover, I believe that the symbol of a great leader as a wise cook emerges as a creative synthesis only after the process of deconstruction; we are well served by the grateful appreciation of the positive and an honest acknowledgment of the negatives that exist at both poles.

Thus, unlike my mother who was cooking behind the scene often out of social expectation and forced duty as a woman and mother even when she was hungry and tired, a wise cook does not starve herself or hide silently out of sight. Instead, a wise cook's kitchen is full of her own voice—humble yet authoritative—always in conversation with others helping in the kitchen. The wise cook would cook not only for others, but also for herself, thus balancing self-assertion and care for others. The dish would be shared with all, and the abundant food will bring together all community members, including herself.

Unlike my mother, who took up all the preparation, cooking, and cleaning tasks herself, a wise cook invites others to participate in the process. Others provide fresh ingredients, equipment, and even extra hands in the kitchen. This cooking process resembles *kim-jang* in Korean culture—the communal cooking process of making *kim-chi*. It is not a solo performance by a single chef. When doing *kim-jang*, people gather together to prepare, cook, and clean; the finished product is fresh *kim-chi* and side dishes enjoyed by everyone together. *Kim-chi* made through *kim-jang*, then, is not a product of one great cook but the result of hard yet festive communal labor and collaboration.

Leadership should be created through a process similar to *kim-jang*. The leader, like a wise cook, invites and even relies on other people in the community. She is an active but not sole creator; the entire community contributes to the creative process. And as they share the fruits of their labor, the lives of the wise cook and the members of the community are deeply connected. The wise cook shares the table with all and in all times, be they times of joy or sorrow.

To become a good leader, like the wise cook, is surely not an easy task; it takes experience, discernment, strength, and trust to build deep relationships with the community, and the wisdom to take care of oneself as well as others. Though leadership does not come easily, it is not impossible if one receives encouragement and nourishment from all—oneself, others, and God. Until one becomes a great leader, she does not have to suffer along the rough and thorny path to leadership alone. Instead, one can have fun with herself and others, cooking, eating, and sharing her dishes with all in her kitchen. In so doing, the one who cooks and shares with others will become wiser every day, and one day, perhaps without even recognizing it herself, she will share true and wise leadership with all around her.

4

Returning to the Source

A Call of a Leader in a Healthcare Setting

YOKE LYE KWONG

THE FORMATION

"When one drinks water, one should remember the source."
—*A Chinese Proverb*

I left Malaysia in 1982 for a university education in Canada, and I was fully aware as I did so that this opportunity was afforded to me as a result of my parents' unconditional love. After all, no woman in my family—either on the maternal or paternal side—had, at that time, even attended a school, much less a university. My parents' love was manifest in their willingness to break from traditional cultural expectations. In our village, firstborn daughters were expected to take care of their younger siblings and to keep the house; going to school was primarily the privilege of sons. Yet I, the firstborn of nine, was allowed to go to school; moreover, my parents respected my decision to become a Christian at around seventeen years of age. Their continual willingness to yield space for me to discover and claim my hopes, dreams, and spirituality offered me the inner freedom necessary to embrace the call on my life to be a trailblazer in my field; today, because of their unconditional love, I am able to work as a Chinese female clinical pastoral education (CPE) supervisor.

Being the first wave of immigrants to Malaysia from China, my grandparents and parents endured the hardships of dislocation to raise a new generation in a new land, knowing nothing of its native languages and cultures. They courageously faced extreme political, social, and economic challenges in multiple contexts. Grace emerged to sustain them, and they returned the same grace. My family and our neighbors became each other's source of life, living in community in that humble village. They passed on to me the wisest of all wisdom, that I too would follow in their footsteps and raise my own family in the United States of America—a country far away from my motherland. It was an open journey. I did not know that I would be called to a ministry where crisis would be the "norm"; just as dislocation, hardships, and crisis are known by immigrant families, so too are they known by people in the healthcare context. I minister to people in crisis, faced with illness and disease, caught in the paradoxical moments between death and life. My childhood equipped me for and sustains me in this work.

Growing up in a multigenerational family with my parents, grandparents, aunt, uncle, and my younger siblings under the same roof, we kept nothing from each other. Together, we ate every meal.[1] We shared a common water well and a tap water source which was provided to us by the government. We were an agricultural community. Our farms were plotted next to each other. My grandmother, Ah Po, took care of our neighbor who was saddled with illness. Graciously, she helped water the neighbor's farm without being asked. When Ah Po became too weak to work the farm on her own, she gave the farm to her neighbor. In gratitude, from time to time, this neighbor brought produce to Ah Po. As a young girl observing this relational exchange of care, I was deeply affected by it, even to this day. As a pastoral educator and leader, I have yet to fully comprehend its richness. At that time, I saw this wonderful social exchange between my grandmother and her neighbor as the practice of the Tao: having received, she gave back in return.[2]

Now I understand how growing up in such a community was, for me, a process of spiritual formation. While my pastoral theories and practice were shaped by seminary professors, certification committees, students, clients, patients, theologians, educators, and theorists many years later in the United States, Ah Po, who was invisible to the world, was always my teacher and the cultivator of my soul. Her caring acts challenge North American individualistic models of care and community. We need to move from independence to interdependence, from self-sufficiency to neighborly richness to develop a more supportive and community-based paradigm of spiritual care.

A culture focused solely on the individual dehumanizes. Individualism is seductive because it justifies one's own consumerism at the expense of others. There is an ethical tension between consumerism and communal relationships worth examining. For example, a study done by *Scientific American* in 2012 indicates that the average American drains as many resources as thirty-five natives of India and consumes fifty-three times more goods and services than someone from China. Such inequalities in consumption give pause, causing us to look at critical issues such as the global oppression of humanity's right to resources, denying some the right while allowing others to abuse the privilege, leading to the environmental exploitation of our mother earth.

Perhaps a return to love-of-neighbor in these trying times of social, economic, ecological, political, and unspeakable unrest is the way to experience abundance. To actualize abundance in the midst of our dominant narrative of scarcity requires us collectively to examine the meanings and implications of boundaries, dominance, competition, consumerism, and power in the contexts of social responsibility, transformation, and justice. We must take a step back to reflect on the essence of who we are as human beings created in the image of the Creator. We have gone too far. It is time to return to the Source.

THE SEEKING

"One written word is worth a thousand pieces of gold."
—A Chinese Proverb

At the age of ten, I published my first article in a local Chinese newspaper. The article was "Why I love my school?" It declared my passion for school and joy I felt for having the opportunity to attend school, and it was certainly the highlight of my life. The school principal, having read the article and received a payment from the newspaper company for my writing, publicly handed it to me in a school assembly. It was a total surprise that turned my life around. In that moment, I discovered the power of finding my authentic voice through writing in Chinese—especially as a young female in a patriarchal society. It was the beginning of a quest for liberation and authenticity in my work and in my life.

Yet this process of liberation was complicated geographically and culturally with moves from country to country. Along the journey, I found myself letting go of my Chinese identity, heritage, culture, and memory of my village in order to find a place of "belonging." I stopped speaking and writing in Chinese—including my own name. By the time I began my college education in Canada in 1982, I was using a Western name, "Jerrymia." My intention in employing this name was to relieve my Canadian classmates, professors, and anyone in my social circle the embarrassment in saying my Chinese name incorrectly. It was to relieve my own embarrassment as well. In what I thought was a comfort zone, I was losing my Chinese heritage, voice, language, and identity. Acquiring a new language (Canadian English) and a new culture became the urgent task to secure my devastating need to belong. Years later, studying in the United States, my American professor gave me an "F" on a French test; his justification for this failing grade was that I translated the work using Canadian English instead of American English. The trauma of my journey to belong suddenly became clear. I felt despair, as though written words were worth a thousand pieces of gold and I could write them in neither Chinese nor American English.

I was drifting further and further from my roots and my source and found no water to drink. By the time I arrived in America in pursuit of my call—the difficulty had only just begun. To overcome obstacles on my journey, I learned to redefine and to reclaim my identity over and over again. This is a costly process that continually situates me as an outsider, even in my current outward success—being one of only eight hundred clinical pastoral educators in the nation. For example, I was asked recently by a task force to provide feedback on the current certification model of clinical pastoral education. What are the skills identified for trainers to supervise the supervisory education students (SES)? I took a risk to offer my original and yet seemingly provoking responses by asserting that it takes more than "skills"; one needs also to be current and well versed in theological scholarships and theories from communities of color. Our current practices, pedagogies, theologies, and methodology are still largely Eurocentric. This curriculum has the power *to colonize* not only Asians/Asian Americans but other minority supervisory education students (SES).

Eurocentric curriculum leads to a larger ethical issue of health disparities. In my experience as a chaplain for over twenty years, I have witnessed many pastoral care situations where patients from the minority cultures received inadequate spiritual care. This has direct relationship with our current models of practice and theory. The body of Asian and Asian American scholarship remains invisible, unrecognized. An educator from any ethnic cultural background would not be considered incompetent if she/he did not know the work of Asian/Asian American theologians. To be recognized as competent, employable and certifiable, an educator must pay attention to the scholarship "endorsed" by the Western and theological academic world. In the process of doing so, and arriving at this place, an Asian/Asian American SES often has to put aside, if not altogether abandon, her/his indigenous original self, cultural heritage, and racial-ethnic identities.

In this context, I learned to lead. Out of it, I emerged with my own voice, vision, and dignity. Despite these challenges, I was the first woman to be approved for ordination in Christian ministry in my church, Subang Jaya Baptist Church, Malaysia, in 1995. I was the first Chinese-Malaysian-American female to be certified as a Clinical Pastoral Education (CPE) supervisor in the Association for Clinical Pastoral Education, Inc. in 2001. The theme of "firsts" followed my path of ministry wherever I settled. An interesting note: whenever I moved into a new office space at a new job, the person who occupied the office before me was always a white male Clinical Pastoral Education supervisor.

THE CALL, HEARD AND TESTED

Upon finishing a Master of Arts in Theology in 1991, the graduating class was charged by the president of the university to "Go to places of ministry where God's light is dim, God's voice is heard small, and God's power is not known, even to the utter most bounds of the earth." As a young seminary graduate with a faith so innocent and so eager to serve, I was very certain that my president's charge to me was to pastor a dying church in some godforsaken place. In 1993, after about four years of ministry at a Chinese American church serving side-by-side with my husband as the unpaid pastor's wife, I came face to face with my own sense of inadequacy in ministry. I quickly realized that not only was I in the way of my husband's ministry, complicating his job, but I was also dying inside. What should I have said and what could I have done when parishioners' wives came to me as though I had the answers to their spouses' employment issues and their teenage children's "rebellion"? How could I have helped with their ongoing yet unnamed grief and profound losses?

In that spirit of despair, I learned about Clinical Pastoral Education. The promise of this year-long CPE residency program was attractive as it outlined what a student would learn upon graduation: counseling techniques and interpersonal skills for ministry. That was what I needed, so I thought. Upon acceptance and enrollment into the program, I became one of a nine member cohort of CPE students. These peers came from different ministry contexts. I had two white male CPE supervisors who appeared to be invested in us. I was their *first* CPE student who was Chinese and spoke English as her fourth language. Several months into the program, I soon learned that I was accepted into the program because they needed "cultural diversity" in the department to credit its openness to cultural differences. Hence, I became the "token" student of cultural diversity in their CPE program. I often experienced my supervisor's frustration with me. They questioned why I was spending so much time with international patients and was told "Jerrymia, you live in North America, not Asia!" In one instance, I wrote a ministry encounter verbatim with a patient who spoke only Chinese, in which I used both English *and* Chinese to convey its cultural nuances. When discussing it with my CPE supervisors, they were frustrated with me. They concluded that my use of "foreign" language was to challenge their ability to accurately evaluate my ministry. While the stated goal of the program was to empower students to claim their voice, identity, and authority, I soon felt disempowered and as though I did not fit in the program. The process of invalidation was too pain-ful to endure. I began to question why I was in it. I wondered if I could go on.

One particular morning when I was making rounds in the hospital, I noted an Asian woman sitting in the outpatient waiting area. Later in the day, at about four p.m., I noticed that same woman was still there when I made after-noon rounds through the outpatient area again. At this instance, I decided to approach her to see if I could be of any assistance to her. Unfortunately, I could not speak her language. When I noticed that she was holding what appeared to be an appointment slip, I gestured with my hands to ask if I could look at it. She was glad to see me and handed the slip to me immediately. After reading the piece of paper, I tried to explain to her that her appoint-ment was actually scheduled for the next day. I gestured to her to come with me to see the receptionist to clarify her appointment. I saw tiredness on this woman's face. I signaled to her to wait for me while I returned with a cup of hot tea and a biscuit for her. She offered a soft smile and tears flowed down on her face. Touched by her feelings, I joined her in tears. At that moment I realized why I was in clinical pastoral education. Indeed, I was answering my university president's charge and God's call to go to the "utter most bounds of the earth."

On the last day of this CPE program, I was called into my CPE supervi-sor's office. He concluded that after all, I was not so bad in providing care to patients. He then showed me a check with a large amount of money donated to the Spiritual Care department. It came from another family that I minis-tered to just a week before. However, the CPE supervisor concluded that I was not CPE "qualified" because CPE was a Eurocentric model of learning that could not be used by a person like me. It was then that he made a decision to turn me down from continuing into a second year of the CPE training. To compensate for this "loss," he asked me to take the check and to "move on." Taken aback by what he said, I stopped for a moment to gather my thoughts. I said, "Keep the check. It is not over yet. I will see you in the future." The family that I ministered to reminded me of how my grandmother's neighbor returned with produce from the farm to give to my grandmother out of a sense of gratitude. In that moment of humiliation in the CPE supervisor's office I sensed the presence of the Holy. Yes, I moved on. Ten years later, by some unplanned circumstances, I sat next to this supervisor as his colleague. I looked into his eyes and smiled.

Looking back, it was the moment of humiliation in my encounter with the CPE supervisor on that last day that clarified the call on my life to become a CPE supervisor. No, it was not an experience like Jesus at his baptism when he heard a voice out of the heavens say, "This is my Son, the Beloved, with whom I am well pleased" (Matt. 3:17). Neither like Moses when he was attending his sheep on a good day and saw the burning bush when God came forth to call him for a mission, "the angel of the Lord appeared to him in a flame of fire out of a bush; he looked, and the bush was blazing, yet it was not consumed" (Exod. 3:2). My experience being in the presence of the Holy came at the darkest moment of humiliation felt in my being. The darkness did not drown me; neither did I run away from it. I was called by God then to trust God for the journey with its unknowns. The Presence experienced was the grace and empowerment needed for me to face the darkness—like what Hannah needed to transcend her humiliation in childlessness. When she turned to God to intercede, the priest Eli accused her of being a drunkard. She rose to her dignity and defended herself by correcting him: "I have drunk neither wine nor strong drink, but I have been pouring out my soul before the LORD. . . for I have been speaking out of my great anxiety and vexation all this time" (1 Sam. 1:15–16). In the end, the priest blessed her. In responding to my call and the journey with many trials that took, the Holy guided me out of the darkness and into the light to see my call actualized as a CPE supervisor.

It was during the CPE supervisory training process that I began to reclaim my voice and identity. I reclaimed my original name, given to me by my father, Yoke Lye, which means *a beautiful jade*. In Chinese culture, jade embodies the meanings of humanity—justice, purity, and transparency. The beauty my father would have hoped for me—if he knew it would take the hardship of leaving my homeland and relational comforts, perhaps he would have changed his mind. I named the suffering I went through in my first CPE residency training. I articulated the alienation and disconnection I experienced as an Asian student trying to navigate race, ethnicity, gender, and institutional polices. I had to pave my own path in the absence of an Asian woman mentor. Despite these challenges, I was certified as a CPE supervisor a few years later. And now, I am privileged to journey with and support other Asian women CPE supervisory education students in their certification process.

In 1997, Paula Ellen Buford wrote a doctoral dissertation titled, "The Lost Tradition of Women Pastoral Caregivers from 1925–1967: A Dangerous Memory." She dedicated her work to the "female and male pioneers who established the field of pastoral theology, care and counseling, often in a hostile environment."[3] She challenges contemporary caregivers to emulate their courage and openness to new ideas. Her research highlights obstacles women face when claiming their visibility, voices, and calling in the context of their profession:

> "The personal is political" resounded throughout the nation in the late 1960's and 1970's as women sought empowerment. I write with suspicion from the margins, questioning the silence of women in

previous histories . . . Interpreted "dangerous memories" function as a mirror and hold the promise for agitation, reflection, and social change. As in therapy, once this "dangerous" interpretation is made, it has the power to impact the intertwining links of self-identity and praxis, with an energy and a direction that is limited only by human imagination and courage.[4]

Buford's work was a powerful confirmation of my experience and educational process. I was "interpreting" dangerous memories and claiming my "self-identity and praxis."

THE CALL REALIZED

With renewed energy and direction, I supervise CPE students. It's the place of my greatest creativity. Many have journeyed near and far, both geographically and vocationally with a goal to lessen spiritual and emotional pain and to bring comfort to the patients. It is an important goal of spiritual care and requires critical reflection on human "doing" and human "being." The following pedagogical questions frame my work: How can I be with my CPE students or another human being in such a way that they might discover and embrace their humanity? How can I be present with my students or another human being who might be in the darkest night of their soul? How do I listen to my students in order that they might listen to the voices of lament from their patients *without* saying, "I understand"? How do I refrain from naming their struggles and provide quick solutions, when physicians have yet to come up with names to the diseases of their patient? Where is the sacred and holy in the midst of suffering and death? How do I introduce to them healthcare disparity when they often come from places of privilege?

Self-identity and praxis—human "being" and human "doing"—in chaplaincy is about more than providing spiritual care. It is also about advocacy, about naming injustices and inequalities. Advocacy has always been an important element in my leadership. As I wrote in a chapter in *Professional Spiritual and Pastoral Care: A Practical Clergy and Chaplaincy Handbook* (2012), "a chaplain in health care must take on new ethical dimensions: 1- as an advocate for immigrants in accessing health care, and 2- as a cultural broker between the health care system and the patient/resident and family whose culture is different from ours."[5]

Living out the call over the years certainly has brought much joy and fulfillment. Nevertheless, there are seasons of vulnerability and fragility with these questions of my call: How does healing continue when one struggles for social justice? How can I connect social justice with individual healing? How do I practice justice from my position, as one who is privileged (in some contexts) and underprivileged (in other contexts)? How do I sustain my call—to be the source (to provide water to those who need a drink)—and at the same time find sources I can drink from? It takes wisdom to know the balance of these two spaces.

NURTURING THE CALL

> Wisdom has built her house,
>   she has hewn her seven pillars.
>
> *Proverbs 9:1*

In the institution where I serve, its mission is built on six pillars: service, quality, people, finance, growth, and community. Using this metaphor of a pillar, I offer my five pillars that nurture my vocation and work: community, presence, education, advocacy, and renewal.

COMMUNITY

In her book *Church in the Round: Feminist Interpretation of the Church*, Letty Russell helps us to think about issues of relational connection and inclusiveness, power and authority, and the practice of hospitality and justice faced by the women in the church in North America.[6] Today, these issues are still faced by women, and especially by minority women. Russell's conviction is that until women are given a place at the round table, they will not experience hospitality, shared power, and freedom. For Russell, the round table is a symbol and a metaphor of communal life where welcome, partnership, dialogue, and inclusiveness take place. However, for minority women, having a place at the round table is not enough. It does not automatically open up the same privilege, respect, and power as women from the dominant culture. Hence, a different community needs to be created. For me, this need remains a process of its own and is yet to be fully discovered, found, and experienced deeply.

PRESENCE

Change is always around us. When change happens, the basic human need for security is threatened, and the soul becomes restless and fearful. I am reminded of the Chinese word *wei-ji*, which mean *crisis*. These two characters simultaneously convey a moment of danger and opportunity—dynamically speaking of relational conflicts. Instead of becoming reactive, I need to learn from the perennial plant during the winter season. It naturally engages an inner rhythm called dormancy that promises growth in the season to come. When threatened or faced with unease, instead of reacting and finding ways to run away, I learn to respond with a non-anxious and hopeful presence as opportunities for service.

EDUCATION

What is the difference between spirituality and religion? This question represents an underexplored field of education. The role of a chaplain is often misunderstood, and this misunderstanding is compounded by the fact that few professional chaplains are willing to study, research, write, and publish. This work is necessary to make known the inextricable connections between the spiritual, biological, psychological, and sociological dimensions of the human experience in the time of illness. How can we better articulate the interconnectedness of spirituality and medicine? Following the pillar of education, I research, write, and publish the theory, theology, and praxis of spiritual care in Clinical Pastoral Education programs and my vision of the ministry of chaplaincy.

ADVOCACY

Healthcare is the right of every individual human being. However, access to healthcare is not equal within our healthcare system. The "haves" and "have-nots" are divided by socioeconomic and cultural factors, among others, leaving a disparity in insurance coverage. Now serving from a place of privilege, I am mindful to advocate each day through my call and ministry.

RENEWAL

Renewal is what *saves* my life. A mindful practice of self-care and self-compassion is a daily discipline that sustains my call to ministry and service. Compassionate service to others is cultivated through mindful practice of self-care. As a chaplain, I am exposed to the grief and despair of my patients and their families. As a clinical pastoral educator, I am exposed to my students' pains as they encounter their own unhealed and traumatized past, entangled in the stories of their patients. Journeying with them on their way to becoming wounded healers is an emotional commitment. Creating a ritual of self-care takes me to a space of Sabbath, reclaiming the freshness of life forces that restore, heal, and replenish me so I may return to them once again, and love them for who they are.

REMEMBERING THE CALL

Faced with an increasingly complex landscape of ministry in the healthcare setting as a Clinical Pastoral Education Supervisor and chaplain, hardly a day goes by without remembering my grandmother, Ah Po, and her farm.[7] I see her perseverance, hard work, and quiet strength in turning a hard ground filled with brush and weeds with her bare hands into a fertile garden. I remember her endurance to survive even in the midst of a bare amount of food. I used to bring her lunch every day. I handed her a container of rice, peanuts, and a few strands of preserved vegetables. From the tree branches, Ah Po carved a pair of chopsticks with a knife. I watched her closely with admiration. Her hands were so worn from work and yet so gentle handling the chopsticks, playing through the rice and picking up peanuts, one by one. Call it faith at work, call it imagination, or call it magical. It is the source of wisdom I drink from. In the end, she gave it away simply knowing that her neighbors needed it more than she did. Her generosity of heart continues to capture me afresh each time my memory recalls her, the farm she transformed and then happily passed on to someone who needed it more than her. When I drink, I remember the water source, my grandmother, Ah Po.

I believe these cultural traits shaped my capacity for wisdom leadership as an Asian woman, as a Filipina Christian leader.

The Philippines, still a developing country of 100 million people, is the country of my birth, childhood, youth, and early adulthood. It was there that my leadership in church was formed, tested, and grew. I was born and raised in Bulacan where I experienced economic poverty first hand. My Roman Catholic father, David Tapia, was converted to Protestantism after attending evangelistic meetings conducted by Protestant missionaries and Filipino lay evangelists. Eventually, he himself became a lay evangelist while mending his fishing nets with men in the village. *Amang* (father) David instilled discipline at home and obedience to authority. He also taught me how to read, how to respect elders, and how to be brave. My Methodist mother, Lydia Santiago, who home-birthed ten children, taught me how to pray, cook rice, and sell fish in the market while I was still in grade school. She repeatedly told me (out of all children): "You will be a leader. So go to school and stay close to Jesus."

When I was seven years old, I dreamt of becoming a medical doctor because there were many sick people around, but we had only one doctor and one midwife in the whole town. I have always admired the village's only midwife, Aling Tikang, who helped my mother and other women give birth at home. Though she was only five feet tall and slender, she walked fast, and she could lift heavy things. Another trait I admired in her was her ability to connect with people. She listened as well as advised. The menfolk in the village respected her as well. Every morning, I would watch this petite leader walk with dignity and joy. She was indeed a wise woman. But my dream to become a medical doctor never materialized because of a lack of financial resources.

When I turned seventeen, I felt the call to Christian ministry. This call came to me not abruptly, but gradually through the years. Family love, confirmation class, attending Christmas institutes for youth, my grandmother's faith, and a desire to serve Christ by serving people, especially the poor, made me commit myself to full-time Christian service. But since there were no role models for women clergy in my district, I was trained as a deaconess— a lay full-time church worker. At age twenty, I finished my studies at Harris Memorial College in the Philippines and was appointed by the Bishop as Deaconess in the largest local congregation then in the district. After two years, I was appointed as the District Deaconess, supervising seventeen deaconesses, training youth workers, and visiting thirty-six congregations each year. Both a combination of a great need for leadership in the district and my skills and commitment were reasons for my appointment. They needed leadership to coordinate and supervise the Christian education work in the district after the previous District Deaconess left. My God-given gifts and talents, people skills, excellent training, and my love for the work made me a perfect candidate. With this responsibility entrusted to me, I was even more enthusiastic and committed. I wanted to show folks that women can be leaders and supervisors. I wanted to demonstrate that unmarried young women can and should have a place in the church. I traveled in public buses and accepted parishioners' hospitality. Although my salary was small, working with the people gave me much joy.

I was enjoying my work in the district when Dr. Prudencia Fabro, president of my alma mater, Harris Memorial College, recruited me to be a faculty member. She advised me to go and get a graduate education. Of course, I was very happy that she thought of me for this position. I needed to earn a master's degree in religious education. But in Manila at that time, neither the degree nor a scholarship was available to me. Then Leah Hattrick, an American missionary at Harris College and my teacher in Creative Dramatics, a course I excelled in, told me about scholarship possibilities in the United States. So I applied and was accepted at Pacific School of Religion in Berkeley, California. I was twice refused a student visa by staff in the Consular Office at the U.S. Embassy in Manila; I almost gave up this dream of furthering my education. However, I kept thinking *habang may buhay, may pagasa,* "if there's a will, there's a way." While there's life, there's hope. So I applied for a student visa the third time. I asked the consul why I could not be given a student visa when all my papers and scholarship were secured. "Young lady, he said, there are many young women who go abroad, marry there, and don't come back." I said, "Sir, I am going to California for graduate studies, not to get married there. I will have a teaching job when I return here in Manila in two years. So I hope I can get this visa soon, as I am already late for September orientation." Did he see determination in my young face? Did he realize how angry I was inside? When I finally got my visa, I was exhausted. Even still, on the following day, I said farewell to my family, packed my one suitcase, changed my peso salary into a hundred dollar bill, and I flew to the United States. I was the first in my family to travel abroad.

When I arrived at the campus of Pacific School of Religion in late August, 1974, I was shown my dormitory in Anderson Hall. Everything looked huge to me, the buildings, the roads, the library, classrooms, and food in the cafeteria. I was freezing though fully clothed, while students wore shorts and complained of an "Indian summer." It was a culture shock almost every day, but I survived! I excelled in my studies and became active in the anti-Marcos dictatorship while I was in the Bay Area. For rest and renewal, I would take the Bay Area Rapid Transit (BART) to San Francisco. It was lovely!

When I learned that the degree program I had enrolled in would be terminated, I was devastated. My adviser remarked that my one year could be credited to a Master of Divinity degree since I took many courses with MDiv students. But MDiv was a three-year program and I had a two-year visa for two years of scholarship. I prayed. I strategized. I consulted some folks. I finished the Master of Divinity degree from PSR in two years and two summers. I also followed my dream to become an ordained clergy.

I became an ordained pastor in June 1976 in the United Methodist Church through the California Nevada Annual Conference. In the same month, I returned home to the Philippines to teach at Harris Memorial College. People were curious about a female pastor. Many male pastors did not invite me to their meetings. Teaching at Harris Memorial College gave me opportunities to mentor young women who would become deaconesses and leaders in church and community. I taught courses in biblical theology, Christian education, leadership formation, youth and adult education, and worship. I enjoyed teaching and mentoring future women leaders. I decided to forgo getting married.

I was encouraged again by the college president, Dr. Prudencia L. Fabro, to take up a doctoral degree. Again, if there were no scholarships, there would be no graduate studies for me. Fortunately, I was granted a full scholarship by the Leadership Program of the General Board of Global Ministries. So after several years of teaching in Manila, and still unmarried, I took off again. I would have liked to take up PhD studies in Manila, but there was no guaranteed scholarship. I completed my PhD studies at Claremont Graduate University at age thirty-nine. While in California, I joined the Asian Women Theologians (later PANAAWTM) network and became a founding member. And in my last year of the PhD program I met my future husband, Rev. Alan Cogswell, while speaking at the Jubilee Youth Conference in St. Louis, Missouri. The following year, we got married in Ohio where his parents lived. Alan joined me in California and subsequently in Manila in 1989. We taught at Harris Memorial College for a year. In 1991, we joined the faculty of Union Theological Seminary in Cavite, Philippines. Alan taught biblical languages while I taught systematic theology. We tended a vegetable garden near our faculty housing. We lived a simple lifestyle. Our fellow teachers respected us. Our students loved us. It was good to be home.

By the time I turned forty-seven, I had been teaching in an ecumenical seminary—Union Theological Seminary in Cavite—for seven years. I was the first woman to teach systematic theology. Asian Women's theology courses also made it into the curriculum, and I served as Academic Dean at the Union Seminary Cavite for four years. I was the first woman dean in this hundred-year-old seminary. While it was never easy to be a leader in patriarchal institutions, I took these leadership responsibilities believing that I could make a difference. I did not seek this position. The faculty and board of trustees of the seminary saw me fit for this leadership. I accepted with gratitude and joy.

My teaching and leadership roles took me outside the Philippines from 2002 to 2005. I was offered a teaching job at the prestigious Bossey Ecumenical Institute, part of the World Council of Churches, in Geneva, Switzerland. The graduate students at Bossey came from different countries and from Protestant, Roman Catholic, and Orthodox churches. I was the only Asian and the only woman faculty in residence. I held the Chair of Missiology position, funded by The United Methodist Church. Outside the institute, I met several undocumented migrant Filipinas who became my friends. This broader ecumenical experience further cultivated my wisdom leadership. It taught me how to honor diversity while pursuing Christian unity.

Then my journey took me back to the United States. After the long process of acquiring legal permanent residence, in 2007, I began work at Drew University's theological school, directing their new Center for Christianities in Global Contexts. I organized regular fora and lectures on global Christianities, worked with international students, co-led two travel seminars for MDiv students (one in Mexico with Dr. Arthur Pressley; the other in the Philippines, co-led by the late Dr. Ada María Isasi-Díaz). When the Luce Foundation salary grant could not be renewed after three years, I lost this job. Sadly, I needed to move on. But I won't forget the vibrant and loving academic community at Drew University's theological school, led by Dean Maxine Beach.

I had hoped to find a job, but jobs eluded me. So I joined Alan in his rural church in Porter, Maine. I went from academia to the rural congregation of Riverside United Methodist Church. I sang in the choir, joined my husband on visitations, cooked meals, tended a small garden, and took long hikes in the beautiful woods and beaches of Maine and New Hampshire. The migratory birds came back and they reminded me to sing with hope. I frequented the library of Boston University's theological school where Alan was pursuing a master's degree in pastoral care and counseling.

Then, in 2011, I was offered a job that was an extension of my ministry. From 2011 to March 2015, I served as Director of Mission Theology at the Global Ministries of the United Methodist Church in New York City. I stood at the intersection of global mission and local mission. It was amazing to witness how God's mission is alive in a diverse, interconnected world. I preached, taught mission seminars, organized theological fora, and worked with committed staff. Traveling and meeting people in and outside the United States provided me with opportunities to encounter wise leaders in local and global mission. Learning does not stop.

At age sixty-five, I became a missionary in my own country. After missionary training (in Nashville) and commissioning in the New York Annual Conference on June 12, 2015, I was sent as a missionary teacher at John Wesley

College in Tuguegarao City, Cagayan. Bishop Pete Torio Jr. of the Baguio Episcopal Area appointed me as dean of the newly formed graduate program of the College, offering MDiv and Doctor of Ministry programs. I had to recruit teachers and students. I am the first full-time teacher in residence; the seven other faculty are part-time teachers. Our students are local pastors serving in rural and mountain area churches. Our daily challenge is to spread the gospel in a multicultural context, to learn a new language/dialect, to mentor the next generation of leaders and pastors, and to participate in God's mission in diverse and depressed contexts. In the midst of these challenges, I celebrate the wisdom and commitment of the people of Cagayan Valley. To God be the glory!

ESSENTIAL TRAITS FOR WISDOM LEADERS

What I have learned from diverse people and contexts can be summarized with an acronym, RICE, or what I call the RICE principle. Rice is the staple food for many Asians. I personally can't live without rice, though I need to moderate my rice intake nowadays. As rice can nourish my body, these "RICE" principles nourish and guide my spiritual journey. It represents my compass to wisdom leadership. Let me share the RICE principle that I have experienced in my life.

R—Respect and Responsibility
A wise leader respects all persons. It also means taking responsibility for what I say and do and left unsaid and undone.
I—Integrity and Intellectual Curiosity
A wise leader has integrity. She is keenly curious, a critical thinker, and humble.
C—Compassion and Care Skills
A wise leader is compassionate at heart and caring. Her listening skills and ability to relate with all kinds of people exude a nonjudgmental attitude. Her caring is not only for humans but also for the four-legged creatures, and all of creation.
E—Enthusiasm and Ecofeminist Praxis
A wise leader is in love with herself as a part of the nature, enthusiastic about life with its many sunrises and sunsets. Caring for creation, she practices ecofeminist principles of non-harm, peace with justice, equity, and gender parity. Wisdom leadership must address the climate justice issue of our time.

At present, the Philippines is experiencing drought due to an El Niño. I stand in solidarity with the farmers in Kidapawan, Mindanao, who are also experiencing hunger and human rights abuse. The saying, "Live simply so others may simply live" still rings true to me. Fullness of life is what Jesus the Christ has promised. I believe the power to lead is a privilege and serious responsibility. I take RICE principles in navigating power and responsibility. We all need spiritual practices, such as RICE principles, that can sustain us.

ROLE MODELS AS AFFIRMATIONS IN OUR JOURNEY

Grateful for the life and leadership opportunities I have, I want to lift up three wise Filipina women who touched my life. I am grateful for their affirmation of my journey in wisdom leadership.

Norma Dollaga of Manila, Philippines. She is a former student of mine who became one of my close friends. Norma, a deaconess in the United Methodist Church, is a powerful leader in the church and society. She organizes church meetings as well as protest demonstrations in front of the presidential palace or at the Philippine Congress. She works with the poor while "speaking truth to power." For me, she embodies wisdom leadership.

Norma, a wise leader, leads the KASIMBAYAN, Churches for the Country, an NGO church-wide organization working for peace, justice, and people's empowerment. Though always working on serious issues, Norma would delight you with her infectious laughter, poetry reading, and fashionable blouses with indigenous jewelries. She is one of the leading Pinays doing theology. Her work and leadership is documented in a recent book, *Pinays Doing Theology*, published in 2015 by the National Council of Churches in the Philippines.

Mother Mary John Mananzan, OSB. She is an incredibly wise, Filipina leader who mentored me to gain both a political consciousness and a feminist spirit. She chaired GABRIELA, the umbrella organization of over two hundred women's organizations for social change. She also served as Mother Prioress of the Benedictine Sisters in the Philippines, as well as President of St. Scholastica's College, Manila. We have been friends for more than thirty years. A woman of wisdom and courage, Sr. Mary John embodies wisdom leadership and ecofeminist spirituality. She has influenced many lives and given birth to hundreds of projects that benefited and transformed lives of the poor. Mary John has inspired me as a leader. She taught me not to take myself too seriously. From her I learned to do *Shibashi* (like tai chi), consciously slow bodily movement exercise to achieve mindfulness. Recently, when my husband was hospitalized in Manila, she was the first one to visit. Her compassionate presence filled the room.

A world traveler-pilgrim, she documented her insights and values in her book, *Nun Stop: A Pilgrim's Tale*. She writes, "When one travels, one gets rid of absolutes. . . . One cannot be dogmatic about one's beliefs, one's practices and one's point of view. One learns how to really listen, to learn from others, to integrate new learning into one's treasure trove of experiences."[1]

Finally, I pay loving tribute to my dear mother, *Lydia Santiago Tapia*. I owe my life to her. Without formal schooling, she was full of wisdom and insight. She raised ten children in an impoverished community. She never made public speeches like Norma Dollaga or Sr. Mary John Mananzan. She never wrote a book, preached, or traveled abroad. Yet her innate wisdom, love, and faith have been great inspiration for me and my siblings. My mother did set the table with simplicity, hospitality, and full of RICE—respect, integrity, compassion, and enthusiasm—in her life. A woman of faith, she taught her children and grandchildren to have reverence toward God and to have confidence in what they can be and what they can do. My mother, my dear *Inang*, now deceased, is my guardian angel. I dedicate this article to her beautiful memory.

CONCLUDING THOUGHTS

While there's life, there is hope. While there is hope, there is also wisdom leadership. Wise leaders speak from their hearts and work with their feet deeply grounded in the Spirit as they walk alongside their people. Wisdom leadership should be grounded in reverence toward God and in celebration of life.

For me, the core principles of Respect and Responsibility, Integrity and Intellectual curiosity, Compassion and Care skills, Enthusiasm and Ecofeminist praxis (RICE) are essential traits and skills needed for a nourishing and sustainable leadership. May the community of Pacific Asian North American Asian Women in Theology and Ministry continue to be blessed with abundant life and RICE. May they celebrate wisdom leadership and set the RICE table wide and open to nurture future women leadership.

Liturgical Interlude 1

"We've Come This Far by Faith"

Celebrating the Thirtieth Anniversary Annual Conference of PANAAWTM

SU YON PAK

On March 12, 2015, Pacific Asian and North American Asian Women in Theology and Ministry (PANAAWTM) held a banquet to celebrate its thirtieth anniversary. In a beautifully transformed chapel at Garrett Evangelical Theological Seminary, many invited guests and PANAAWTM network members settled in to witness the retelling and re-membering of the thirty-year work of building community, sharing wisdom, and developing theology. Fierce Korean drumming and soulful singing were woven in throughout the ceremony.

This is the liturgy of celebration enacted on that evening.

DINNER

We asked the members, "What brings you to PANAAWTM year after year? What does PANAAWTM mean to you?" These responses were collected and shared with the group gathered that evening.

Korean Drumming	**Min-Ah Cho &** **Jung Ha Kim**
Song of Gathering "I Want Jesus to Walk with Me"	**Reiko Yuge**

WELCOME

Welcome to the thirtieth anniversary of PANAAWTM. My name is Su Yon Pak. I am a long-time member and an advisory board member of PAN-AAWTM. I am honored to be emceeing the event tonight. I am sure that many of us in the PANAAWTM network can remember our first PAN-AAWTM experience. Mine was in 1985. As a student at Princeton Theological Seminary, I accompanied Dr. In Sook Lee to the conference. Not knowing what I did not know, I was surrounded by Asian women, powerful, beautiful, assertive, and passionate. Scales fell from my eyes and I was able to see. I was presented with a new vision of who I am and who I can be. My story is not unique. Thirty years of transformative journey—many of my sisters are here tonight as a witness to the power of PANAAWTM in our lives.

Let me first recognize all of us, all of you, who are in this space. Some of you come from across the street, and some, from across the world.

First, from across the world:

Japan, India, Vietnam, Malaysia, China, South Korea, and Canada

There are thirteen states represented here. So please stand as I call out your state. Please remain standing:

California
Minnesota
Illinois
Georgia
Texas
New York
Ohio
Arizona
Missouri
Pennsylvania
New Jersey
Massachusetts
Connecticut

I want to also recognize our special guests who came from California, New Jersey, and Illinois. And to the faculty and staff of Garrett Evangelical Seminary who are celebrating with us tonight. Thank you.

Each year, the PANAAWTM conference has moved from one city to another. Except, three years ago, with the hospitality of Garrett Evangelical Seminary and the support of President Lallene Rector, PANAAWTM was able to hold our annual conference, three years in a row, right here. Thank you, President Rector. And thank you, Dr. Anne Joh, for your hard work and commitment to make this feel like coming home. I know that she does not sleep about a month before the conference to make things just right. Her generosity of spirit and her desire to "set a table" for us is such a gift. Thank you. I also want to acknowledge the local committee and the steering committee for the planning and taking care of all the nitty-gritty details to make our time together a success.

Song for the Community "We Have Come This Far by Faith"

HISTORY OF PANAAWTM

On October 5, 1984, thirteen women gathered at the home of Professor Letty Russell of Yale University. It was a gathering of Asian women graduate students in theological education and several women working in ministry in the United States. This meeting was convened by the Women's Theological Center in Boston and the Ad Hoc Group on Racism, Sexism, and Classism in New York.

Out of this small gathering, the network called Asian Women Theologians, Northeast U.S. Group was formed. Within a year, a small group of Asian American women affiliated with PACTS (the Pacific and Asian Center for Theology and Strategy) from the West Coast, were added to the group.

The first annual conference of the Asian Women Theologians, Northeast U.S. Group, was held on February 22–23, 1985, in Madison, Connecticut.

During the initial years, local small groups would meet in Boston, New Haven, New York, Princeton and Madison, New Jersey, and Claremont, California, and the annual conferences were held in the Northeast.

To connect with theological movements spearheaded by women of color, representatives from womanist and mujerista theologies were invited to these early meetings. The support of Katie Cannon, Ada María Isasi-Díaz, and Elsa Tamez was invaluable. As the network expanded, seminarians, faculty, graduate students, and clergywomen in other cities, including Atlanta, New York, Cambridge, Toronto, Chicago, and Berkeley, took turns hosting the conferences. The Thursday evening plenary sessions were made open to the public to share and showcase the rich and fertile theological work being done by PANAAWTM members.

As the network has matured, its concerns have organically evolved and changed. From a more academic, theological focus, the orientation has broadened to include the concerns of those preparing for ministry in church and community contexts. The membership has also broadened to include Asian American sisters as well as Asian Canadian sisters. These changes have been reflected in the change of our name from Asian Women Theologians (AWT) in 1985 to Asian and Asian American Women Theologians in 1986 to Asian and Asian American Women in Theology and Ministry (AAWTM) in 1991 to finally Pacific, Asian and North American Asian Women in Theology in Ministry (PANAAWTM) in 1996.[1]

We've come this far by faith.

Sung Refrain "We've come this far by faith."

CREATING A NEW FIELD

Since 1985, the women of PANAAWTM have been cultivating a field, a new field of study.[2] The members of PANAAWTM have contributed to the new and emerging discourse on Asian and Asian North American feminist theology and religious studies through research, teaching, and publications; through creating institutional spaces and public forums; and through mentoring the upcoming generation. You will notice that some of the books published by PANAAWTM members are on display in the United Library at Garrett Evangelical Seminary. And you will find a full list in your program booklet and on the PANAAWTM website: www.panaawtm.org.

In 2007, in celebration of PANAAWTM's twentieth year of our network, we published an anthology, *Off the Menu: Asian and Asian North American Women's Religion and Theology*. This volume brought together women who were searching for authentic Christian dialogue in a world of hybridity and changing context. It represented one of the most significant areas of growth and vitality in contemporary Christianity.

To celebrate PANAAWTM's thirtieth year, we are now working on our second anthology, *Leading Wisdom: Asian and Asian North American Women Leaders*. This volume focuses on the topic of leadership. Through theological reflection on experiences of Asian and North American Asian women leaders in church and community, it explores the variety of forms and contexts that leadership takes root and blossoms.

Speaking of leadership, PANAAWTM members have played a critical role in the leadership of other guilds:

American Academy of Religion
Society of Biblical Literature
Asian Pacific Americans and Religion Research Institute (APARRI)
Institute for Leadership Development and Study of Pacific and Asian North
    American Religion (PANA)
Congress of Asian Theologians

Ecumenical Association of Third World Theologians (EATWOT)
Society of Christian Ethics
Religious Education Association
Foundation for Theological Education in Southeast Asia
Association for Asian American Studies
United Methodist Women of Color Doctoral Scholars Program
Asian North Americans in Theological Education
and Association of Theological Schools

PANAAWTM has played and still plays an important role in forming Pacific, Asian, and North American Asian women to be scholar-pastors, activist-scholars, and pastor-activists.

PANAAWTM has cultivated leadership in the academy, the church, and the society. Not only do we have among us the president of the American Academy of Religion, the recipient of United Way Women's Legacy Award, the founder and director of the Soul Repair Center but also the "firsts" and the "onlys" in many of our locations of work who blazed the trail for others to follow. The first Asian American woman to pastor an African American congregation, the first and only Asian woman to be teaching in a predominantly white school, the first Asian American clinical pastoral education supervisor, the first Asian American community organizer to create a leadership program in a seminary, and many more firsts and onlys. Every time an Asian female body enters a pulpit, a classroom, or a rally, we are, you are making the path by walking. We are looking toward to the next and new generation of leaders who will blaze their own trails.

We've come this far by faith.

Sung Refrain "We've come this far by faith"

Thirty years of holding an annual conference is a major accomplishment. It requires dedication, work, and time from this volunteer body. And we keep coming back year after year because it is meaningful to be with each other. I did an informal sampling of our members about why they keep coming back year after year. At the risk of our sociologist-in-residence, Dr. Jung Ha Kim, chastising me for my tautological sampling, here are some of the responses.

I come to PANAAWTM:

because of the rigorous theological inquiry and exploration
because of mentoring by world class scholars
because of support and solidarity
because it's like coming home
because it is my much needed mental health break

because I miss my friends
because here, I can breathe out and breathe in
because this is my family

I want to invite you to speak your thoughts and desires into this space. Why do you come to PANAAWTM? What does PANAAWTM mean to you?

[Responses from the audience.]

Thirty continuous years of hosting a conference requires not only programmatic and logistical planning but also fundraising. We have institutional support and funding from foundations. The full list you will see in your program. But what we want to highlight tonight is the commitment of PANAAWTM members who donated their speakers' fees, royalties from book sales, travel and lodging costs, award moneys, goods for auction, and their precious time to this important work. Thank you.

To get you a taste of what we've been engaging for the last thirty years, here is a selection of themes from the past PANAAWTM conferences:

1985	Total Liberation from Asian Women's Perspective
1990	Asian and Asian American Women: Survival in Patriarchal Culture
1994	Asian Women and the Body
2000	Sacred Belonging: Re-membering the Past, Shaping the Present, Re-envisioning the Future
2001	Building Wisdom's House: Asian and North American Asian Women and the Church
2004	Embodying the Spirit: Culture, Justice, Wholeness
2006	Off the Menu: Cultures, Practices, and Theologies of Asian and Asian North American Women
2008	For Such a Time as This: Empire, Globalization, and the Church
2009	Freeing Creation: Hope and Labor in Asian and Asian North American Feminist Theology
2011	Immigration, Borders, Boundaries
2012	Abundant Life and Unjust Prosperity
2013	Dangerous Memories: Theologies in a Time of War and Healing
2015	Transformative Journey with PANAAWTM: Thirty Years and Beyond

A full list can be found on the website: www.panaawtm.org.

We've come this far by faith.

Sung Refrain: "We've come this far by faith."

And our allies, some of you who are here tonight, I want to recognize you. I asked them to bring a brief word of solidarity, support, and work toward our future together.

Joanne Rodriguez, Director of the Hispanic Theological Initiative
Frank Yamada, the President of McCormick Theological Seminary
Carolyn Roncolado, representing the Committee on Status of Women in
    the Profession of the AAR
Jeffrey Kuan, the President of Claremont School of Theology

We've come this far by faith.

Sung Refrain: "We've come this far by faith."

I want to borrow a word from our West African brothers and sisters: *sankofa. Sankofa*, literal meaning is "reach back and get it." It symbolizes the necessity for us to look back and get the past in order to move toward a future. And this evening has been a way of reaching back to get and claim our history, in order to dream dreams for our future together.

We will end this portion of the celebration with a song of benediction and a charge for us to "move on."

Song of Benediction "Move On"   **Reiko Yuge**

Drumming   **Min-Ah Cho &**
                Jung Ha Kim

PART 2

Unsettling Wisdom

6

"I Shall Not Bow My Head"

Ghostly Lessons for Wise Leading

MAI-ANH LE TRAN

I live and teach in Webster Groves, a suburban forest roughly fifteen miles south of Ferguson, Missouri, the city that burst into international news in the aftermath of the shooting death of a young man named Michael Brown. It was an event in which political and religious leaders quickly realized that they needed new lessons on how to be not only instantaneously savvy but also enduringly wise. When the earth is quaking from human tantrums, the public sphere is polluted with cacophonies of discord, communities are fractured by manufactured fear and insecurity, individuals feel bereft of moral agency and imagination, and religious leadership is quick to admit that there are no "easy answers."[1] How do we, then, lead *wisely* in such turbulent times?

In the Vietnamese lexicon, the most common rendering of *wisdom* is *khôn ngoan*—sagaciousness.[2] It is distinct from a cognate compound word *khôn khéo*—clever, cunning. What differentiates a clever, cunning leader from a wise one? Ruminations on the ways of the wise led me to three story worlds replete with ghostly lessons. Their juxtapositions may very well be a stretch, but the stories selected for reflection here reveal elements of the "magico-religious"[3] habits, dispositions, and actions of wise leading—at once ephemeral yet ever so palpable in the face of human struggle.

The *first* lesson comes from #Ferguson. The popular Twitter hashtag format is used here to mark how Ferguson, a city of around twenty-one thousand residents, has become a figurative and virtual world of still-evolving woeful tales. Leaving political analysis to those more abreast, I draw attention to how bodies became public pedagogies in a surging movement of leader-full actions. There are lessons to be learned from the way leaders' bodies served as buffers between human and natural elements: between frustrated citizens and weary law enforcers, between principled protesters and disruptive saboteurs, between enflamed properties and torrential skies. The *second* lesson comes from the mytho-historical world of Vietnam—specifically, from the stories of two first-century she-rebels who exuded supra-human guile and gumption against outrageous odds, uncanny third-eye onlookers peering into the horizons with deep attunement to the rhythms of the ground upon which they stood. For the *third* set of lessons, I take an indulgent turn to a trove of autobiographical memories: the inherited tales of a black-and-white photo hidden in a rice cake; the fractured tales of eerie nights on escape boats at sea; the sketchy tales of sashays with Communism in postwar Vietnam . . . all together self-defining narratives for my own anamnestic wavers as an alien-resident-turned-naturalized-citizen who learned to listen again to that familiar spiritual while marking time on the streets of Ferguson, *"Ain't gonna let nobody turn me 'round . . . turn me 'round . . . turn me 'round. . . ."*

I begin in reverse order.

LESSONS FROM THE DARK

They say that Asian diasporics are a people "on the way."[4] For my family and me, it has been more like being "on the run" . . . with life-forming experiences born(e) in the dark.

At the crux of the war in Vietnam, the country was bleeding people in ways inconceivable to the rest of the world. There were droves that flocked by foot into the jungles toward Laos, Cambodia, and Thailand. Swarms of bodies crammed onto flimsy fishing boats, drifting out into South China Sea. And when international (particularly U.S.) agencies began to evacuate their personnel out of the country, native bodies flung themselves into the air for a mad chance at airlift.[5]

My parents occasionally recount their escape attempts with hysterical laughter—one can only laugh at the ridiculous, and with incredulity over having out-lived that which is supposed to be *un*survivable. "I can't believe we tried to get out to sea with you expecting . . . ," Dad muttered one day. The room got quiet; they chuckled. He was referring to the occasion in which they tried to escape with Mom carrying me (instead of sanitary napkins, she added), and they got arrested. For unknown reasons, she was released a week later, but he was detained for fourteen months. To announce my arrival, Mom hid a picture of me at four months into a cake and stuck it inside a parcel of goods that was to be delivered to Dad in prison. All forms of personal communications were forbidden, so a hidden picture, if discovered, would have resulted in the confiscation of the entire package of supplies. The picture made it through, and my father saw his firstborn for the first time in a folded black-and-white photo with a name and date inscribed on the back.

I linger in this immense story-world not just for self-discovery and rebirth, and certainly not to idolize my parents as living sages. Rather, I linger here for lessons that survivors of war traumas know too well—the lessons of practical wisdom and practical reasoning, which one can only learn through living.

From this story-world, I learn the following:

A. That being "wise" is being **life-wise** . . .

A wise person is one who has *lived*. Aphorisms from diverse times and cultures remind us that wisdom is gained not from armchair theorizing but rather from having lived or outlived profound human experiences, thereby gaining facility with the multiplicity of human faculties for making sense of one's experiences and making judgments in the world. It is a combination of swift exercise of common sense and a deeply-tuned "third-eye"[6] that allows one to see the impossible into being. You cannot learn this from a book. You just have to have lived through some things—and to do so reflectively. After all, to simply undergo an experience does not necessarily make one wise.

Charles Melchert's work on wisdom teaching illumines this notion of deep attunement to life. Drawing on the repertoires of sayings found in the Hebrew Scriptures concerning *hokmah*, or "wisdom," Melchert asserts that biblical wisdom is defined as "knowledge together with the reasoning ability to apply it;"[7] or "the reasoned search for specific ways to assure well-being and the implementation of those discoveries in daily existence."[8] It is more than a skill-set, a mental aptitude, or something quaint from the good old days. Rather, it is "a broad approach to life"[9] that is "intellectually honest" and "emotionally passionate,"[10] unnerved by the raw realities of life, untethered by the rules of social conventions, playful and even irreverent about ironies and paradoxes, yet tenacious in firsthand dealings with the broad spectrum of human good and evil. To have lived—or survived (from *survivre*, "to outlive")—the vicissitudes of life, and to be able to make meaning out of such range, is to be wise.

B. That "being wise" is being able to **live in the dark** . . .

When the war ended—do wars ever really *end?*—and Vietnam became a socialist republic, our family stories took comical turns. One event—which I cannot recount in full details—involved our having to evacuate from a residence that was our temporary "home," because it was rumored that the local authorities were canvassing the area and checking authorization papers. Long story short, I have a mental image of straddling the back of my father's bike, our family's mode of transportation, arms locked tight around his waist, as he peddled silently—in the dark—to take us to his parents' house.

Diasporic subjects are fond of talking about living into ambiguity, contradictions, and paradox. Theologically, one might say it is living into *mystery*. Of that event, I'd like to think that my parents—and by inheritance, we, their children—had gained a capacity to "live in the dark" due to the sociopolitical circumstances of their/our lives. We learned not to be afraid but also learned that it is all right to be afraid. We learned that it is okay if we had to wade into murky waters, or bike in the middle of the night, or pack up and find a new place to make home. We learned that by state-imposed curfew time in the early evening, you could huddle around kerosene lamps and tell one another fantastical tales of tiger-hunting expeditions. . . . We intuited then what Barbara Brown Taylor[11] now articulates with lyricism when she learned to listen to "darkness"—that if we (had to) surrender the human tendency to manufacture and manipulate light, then we would discover that life exists even in the dark.

C. That "being wise" is being able to **work with what you've got** . . .

Life stories narrated under totalitarian regimes often attest to the fact that one has to learn very quickly the craft of constant scanning, appraising, and responding in the moment.[12] After all, citizens subjected to what Achille Mbembe calls "necropolitics"[13] learn very quickly that there are powers that determine who lives and who dies in swift measures. Under such conditions, the rules constantly change, and the means are not always available or accessible, so "making do with what you have" is not a state of passive resignation but rather a crafty life-skill that eventually metamorphosizes one's outlook on life. Work with what you have and turn it into what you need—a tin can becomes a stove; plastic becomes coal; a bottle cap becomes a knife; rice, soy sauce, and melted lard become a meal; a small house becomes an estate for three families; a banana stall in a dangerously packed indoor hawker's market becomes economic security for three generations.

To be life-wise, to be able to live in the dark, to work with what you have at hand—such are lessons from the Tran-Le sagas for a life-wise approach to life. But what qualifies life-wise people to lead? The practical wisdom, honed by lived experience in both day and night, determines how one rises to challenges expected and unexpected. For this insight, I turn to the second story-world—that of ghostly female figures who refused to "bow their heads" in the face of death-dealing circumstances.

LESSONS FROM THE BOW

> My wish is to ride the tempest, tame the waves, kill the sharks. I want to drive the enemy away to save our people. I will not resign myself to the usual lot of women who bow their heads and become concubines.
> —*Tri u Th Trinh, woman leader of a Vietnamese insurrection against the Chinese in 248 C.E.*[14]

It might be forgivable to boast that my defiant photo-sneaking mother stands in a long line of mighty women in the cultural history of Vietnam. The country's historical annals are not short of fierce women figures who instantiate precolonial and anticolonial matrilineal power. For instance, it is chronicled that in 40 CE, "She-King" Trung Trac and her sister Trung Nhi of then Nam Viet (or Mê Linh, the southern region of what is now Vietnam, the more accurate rendering of which is "Viet Nam") led a people's army of eighty thousand against the formidable military forces of the colonizing Chinese Han Empire. Eventually outnumbered, the she-rebels did what was culturally prescribed for the preservation of honor and pride, especially for women of their lot—they surrendered their bodies into the river Hat Giang. Centuries later, the spirits of these mytho-historical figures are immortalized in their people's devotional practices and emulated by a myriad of female "sheroes" who followed suit.

What do mytho-historical accounts of women-led political uprisings have to offer for reflections on wise leadership? Of the many things that could be said, the Trung Sisters were heralded for their ability to rise up to unprecedented challenge and, against odds and conventions, successfully galvanize the moral courage of their people. Co-implicated in war's miseries when their military spouses became captives, these "women warriors" were more than strong-willed heroines of Amy Tan's auto-ethnographic fictions. The violence of war makes one hesitate in claiming that it is the consequence of wise leadership. I praise not the Trung Sisters' capacities to wage war "just like men." Rather, I point to their ability to animate moral conscience in an oppressed people. Generations after them went on to declare, as Trieu Thi Trinh did in the above epigraph: we will not bow down to oppressive power. Almost two millennia later, a young Vietnamese mother defies repressive government with the same principled defiance when she snuck a photo inside a cake. One could say further that the Trung Sisters were praised in the history books for demonstration of what was considered the wiser arts of warfare, according to the ancient Chinese military philosopher Sun Tzu in *The Art of War*. Of his "five essentials for victory," we see the Trung Sisters' wisdom reflected in the third tenet: "He [*sic*] will win whose army is animated by the same spirit throughout all its ranks."[15]

If wise leadership is appraised solely in terms of wins or gains, then the Trung Sisters failed: they lost to colonial powers, and they lost their lives. So did their "western" contemporary: Jesua bar Josef of Nazareth, tortured and executed with scripted humiliation for his refusal to bow down to unjust powers. However, Jesua lives on to his followers, just as the Trung Sisters remain immortal to those who come after them. Far beyond miraculous feats, deft wit, fierce courage, or virtuous life, they are remembered for having reminded the people of their collective soul, echoing back to the people's communally-forged visions of alternative realities. "We shall not bow down." "The kingdom of God is here." The rulership of injustice shall not have the last word.

Literature on leadership often discusses "vision" and "visionary leaders" with portrayals suggesting that good leadership proffers unequivocal crystal clear imperatives for the future. In real life, as argued by Stephen Preskill and Stephen D. Brookfield in their book *Learning as a Way of Leading*,[16] visionary leaders are those who possess the ability to scan, appraise, and respond to constantly changing times and to remain open to new possibilities that are presented at each critical moment. They are reflectively and inquisitively attuned to the imperatives of time and place, adept at critical analysis of experience, open to multiplicity of perspectives, and skillful in the art of listening and asking questions.[17] Wise leaders do not have locked-in visions. What is unflappable is their ability to "sustain hope in the face of struggle."[18] Far from naive optimism, wise leaders' "critical hope" is grounded in "a concrete reality that is hard, practical, and angry"[19]—a steadfast refusal to accept an unjust status quo. Possessing that "third eye" for the longer arc of the moral universe,[20] wise leaders "create a climate of possibility, an atmosphere that anything can happen."[21] Historical records offer few details of the Trung Sister's day-to-day work, but folktales herald them as s/heroes who sustained hope and vision, who saw the pain of the people's subjugation, and who fought to resurrect deadened spirits.

Wise leaders are immortalized for their galvanizing calls for courage, honor, duty. However, a different call is equally necessary at crucial moments: the call to remember, to lament, to repent. For further illumination, we turn back to story-world of #Ferguson, Missouri.

LESSONS FROM THE GAPS

August 9, 2014, means different things to different people—maybe nothing at all to some. It was the day in which a white police officer, Darren Wilson, fatally shot an unarmed black teenager, Michael Brown, and the latter's body was left lifeless and exposed for over four hours before grief-stricken, bewildered, indifferent, vulturous eyes. As soon as news broke across the country, clergy, faith leaders, and religious organizations in metropolitan St. Louis knew that they were going to have to snap to attention and spring into action. As facts remained muddied with stories and counter-stories, feet took to the streets under the rallying cry "#PrayingWithOurFeet." Soon enough, small vigils evolved into a whirlwind of actions, eventually escalating into a national and global movement of anguished, tenacious, combustive protests.

Before the police shooting of a black teenager on one ordinary midday metamorphosed into a sensational "Ferguson event" that shook up a nation, the local activists and clergy leaders who showed up to the first prayer vigil continued to "show up": at rallies, marches, forums, town-halls, teach-ins, preach-ins, eat-ins, meetings with government officials, meetings with enraged citizens. Before a movement took shape, before commercial banners were lifted against the St. Louis skyline, before eloquent open letters by public figures made front pages, before gubernatorial leadership appointed yet another commission[22] to look into the historical arc of structural disparities and racialized animus, these local activists and religious leaders "prayed with their feet" and exercised *disciplined improvisation*. They led by learning on the go. Like the social reformers profiled by Preskill and Brookfield, these Ferguson clergy-activists exhibited reflective, inquisitive, unflappable spirits. The public will always expect messianic stars to emerge out of a movement, but even the media has to acknowledge that besides the few "grass-tops" who make the billboards, at the grassroots level this cooperative is *leader-full*. The *Huffington Post* named them, as a collective, "people of the year" at the close of 2014.[23]

As the movement is still unfolding with vigilant momentum, I refrain from singling out individual leaders. However, moments, incidents, and events do stand out. One in particular was "Moral Monday," held on October 13, 2014, the culminating event for a "Weekend of Resistance" in a series of "Ferguson October" actions.[24] On that day, I saw bodies deployed as public pedagogies— mediums and instruments of instruction for a wide-eyed public.

Teaching Bodies

The Weekend of Resistance was organized from multiple bases across St. Louis, one of which was Eden Theological Seminary, where I serve as faculty. With so many moving parts and tag-team leadership, we were receiving information from every direction and through all sorts of mediums—texts, e-mails, phone calls, word of mouth. Grand-scale marches and public forums were scheduled for Friday–Sunday, but Monday was going to be a "Moral Monday," modeled after the movement of demonstrations and civil disobedience

led by religious leadership of North Carolina in 2013, in protest against the
state's legislative actions.[25] For Ferguson's Moral Monday, faith leaders across
the religious spectrum—some who ordinarily would not have thought to
stand beside their newly allied colleagues for theological reasons—would take
to the streets of Ferguson to express public solidarity with the actions of the
entire weekend. The plan was to enact a public liturgy of *remembrance, lament,*
and *repentance.* No one knew for sure how things would unfold.

As a volunteer marshal over that weekend, I witnessed first-hand the chaos
of "crowd control" and gained a glimpse of what leadership expert Margaret
Wheatley might have meant about the creative energy of *disequilibrium.* Equilibrium, she argues, is the state in which a system has exhausted its energy for
change.[26] In contrast, a system that is open to disequilibrium finds its "stability...from a deepening center, a clarity about who it is, what it needs, what
is required to survive in its environment."[27] In this view, leaders should be
"equilibrium busters": "No longer the caretakers of control, we become the
grand disturbers."[28]

The news media have their formulaic headlines for events such as this: "*x*
number of people, led by *so and so* [insert high-profile names], were arrested
in a demonstration of *y* number of monolithic people in some disorderly
confrontation with *z* number of uniform law enforcement." But as we know,
stories from rain-soaked grounds ring multivalent notes—contradictory,
paradoxical, ironic, even self-incriminating. For four hours and thirty minutes—symbolic of the length of time Michael Brown's body lay on the ground
on Canfield Drive—plus many more hours before and after, the protesters
in Ferguson on that Moral Monday endured body-numbing torrential rain
to enact multifaith *leitourgia*—a public work of the people. They were certainly not of one mind about causes and effects, but each was impelled to use
their body to bust the equilibrium of socio-political status quo sustained by
what they believed to be unjust leadership. There lies the potency of *bodies as
public pedagogies*—bodies as means of explicit and implicit public instruction.
A body bleeding on the ground . . . a body in locked arms with another . . . a
body drenched to shivers . . . a body shielded uneasily behind riot gears . . . a
body twisted in sorrow . . . a body stiffened by anger . . . a body elongated by
the hand of a stranger . . . each teaching us lessons about the moral imperatives for leadership when communities are fractured by close contact.[29]

Mnemonic, Memetic Bodies

In her 2002 presidential address to the Religious Education Association, Anne
Streaty Wimberly dared scholars of Religious Education to envision their
vocation as one of "leadership with hope."[30] Drawing on the work of Mary

Elizabeth Mullino Moore, Wimberly conceptualizes Christian religious leadership as "sacramental," in that it is the work of "mediating the Holy" through specific educative practices: facilitating the remembrance of God's demand for justice and *shalom*; expressing such theo-ethical, theo-political imperatives through both word and deed; raising people's critical consciousness to the gaps between vision and reality; and creating opportunities for people to reemploy their lives according to God's economies of justice.[31]

From Wimberly's (and Moore's) constructions, one can extract two instructive aspects for wise leadership, both of which were exhibited by the teaching bodies of the Ferguson protestors on that Moral Monday. First, their bodies became formidable *mnemonic devices* for a public in need of serious schooling—about historic injuries suffered by enslaved peoples, about insidious systemic disparities that privilege some and diminish the livelihood of others, about complex societal technologies that manage fear and security extending far beyond what we flatly call "police brutality." Bodies on the ground, on the streets, on their knees, on their feet "urge, prod, dare, and encourage" people to not forget.[32]

Second, when a wise leader steps up, or forward, to become one such teaching body, she or he presents a *memetic opportunity* for those watching.[33] We know this through a simpler notion: lead by example, lead by modeling. Lead so as to compel parallel enactment, and lead so that people can employ actions for themselves. When the leader-full teaching bodies of Ferguson marched out into the streets, they became mnemonic devices that urged memetic reenactment elsewhere in greater St. Louis, the country, and the global community. Everywhere, people followed. And how appropriate that the encouraged action is that of remembrance, lamentation, and repentance. In a time of prevailing mistrust in authority and leadership, when arrogance is mistaken for excellence and privilege masks incompetence, we need leaders who can help us say: "Forgive us our sins. We repent. Help us to live with the consequences of our actions. Help us to make right the things we did wrong."

"I SHALL NOT BOW MY HEAD"

"Not many of you should become [*leaders*], my brothers and sisters, for you know that we who [*lead*] will be judged with greater strictness."[34] The wise warning is as foreboding to leaders as it is to teachers. It would defy sapiential instructions to bring these reflections to concluding theorems about wisdom leadership—we learn more about the ways of the wise by trying out the habits of serpents and doves.[35] That said, glancing back at ghostly lessons learned from the dark, from decisions to bow or not to bow, and from the fissures of

7

A Letter to Friends

SUK JONG LEE

Dear Jung Ha and Su,

Having served as a chaplain in the U.S. Army for over twenty years, I appreciate this opportunity to reflect on the subject of leadership and my own experience in the military.

When I am asked how I became an Army chaplain, I often reply that God had "tricked" me to prepare for the ministry in the military. If memory serves me right, the only reason I applied to seminary was to force myself to read the Bible from cover to cover; for I thought I would not read the whole Bible unless I was put in a position where I had to read it. Prior to my seminary training, I served at a Korean American church as a Sunday school teacher for about eight years. In that role, I could not escape the realization that the longer I stayed as a Sunday school teacher, the more I realized how much I did not know about the Bible.

The idea of ministry in the military was planted in my mind while I was in the seminary. I do not recall the details of the context, but for some reason I decided to write a research paper on "interracial marriages in the military" during my senior year of seminary. When I discussed my paper in the class, one of my classmates suggested that I should go into the military to minister if that was my passion or calling. I dismissed his suggestion at the time, thinking that ministry and military did not go together. But here I am, over twenty years later, ministering to soldiers and their families in the Army.

I consider myself as a reluctant leader, "tricked" into a vocation in the military, where the role of leadership seems to be especially pronounced and explicit. As I ponder whose call among the biblical characters was similar to my own, a few figures came to mind. Moses was drawn to the burning bush, but when he was called to lead the people out from bondage in Egypt, Moses tried to convince God that he was not the right person. Then there was Isaiah, who responded to God's call by saying, "Here am I. Send me!" Perhaps my call is a combination of both. I was drawn to seminary education with my own reason; and when it was time for me to choose a vocation, I decided to join the Army not knowing what this decision would entail. I reported to the first Army Reserve unit without knowing what my role would be; I was assigned to the unit before I attended the basic training of Army chaplaincy. I remember asking one of the senior enlisted soldiers in the unit what chaplains do in the military. The advice I received was, "Do as Father Mulcahy in the television series *M*A*S*H* did."

An Army chaplain is expected to carry out a dual role: religious leader and religious support staff officer. As a religious leader, a chaplain provides similar ministry to soldiers and their families as a local pastor would do for her/his congregation. And as a religious support staff officer, a chaplain advises his or her commander and staff on matters of religion, morals, and morale. As an officer in the military rank structure, a chaplain is a leader who manages and prioritizes her or his religious support mission.

The Army Doctrine Publication 6-22 states, "*Leadership* is the process of influencing people by providing purpose, direction, and motivation to accomplish the mission and improve the organization." As a religious leader, then, my role is to influence military personnel by providing purpose, direction, and motivation to improve relationships with their "God(s)," regardless of their religious preferences. My role is not to convert others to my own religion but to accommodate and strengthen their own faith. That means I must remain nonjudgmental toward other religious groups. Proverbs 3:5–6, "Trust in the LORD with all your heart, and do not rely on your own insight. In all your ways acknowledge him, and he will make straight your paths," guided me whenever I experienced the urge to argue against other religious beliefs. I had to put my trust in my God to grant me wisdom to know when to stand up for my faith and when to remain quiet.

As a "Protestant" chaplain in the Army, I was once assigned to serve as the pastor of the "Gospel Service," which follows the Pentecostal tradition. Its worship services are usually filled with heightened emotions and energy—lots of singing, clapping, and loud prayers. Initially, I found myself being critical of their worship style and focused on what needs to be changed to fit my own understanding of what an appropriate worship service should be. After three years of pastoral relationship with them, however, I learned to appreciate their tradition and also had some opportunity to share my tradition. Rather than indulging my urge to change their worship style, I had to learn to be still and listen. This lesson brought home the lesson found in Philippians 2:3: "Do nothing from selfish ambition or conceit, but in humility regard others as better than yourselves."

As an introvert, I am in my comfort zone when I can melt into a crowd unnoticed. However, the rank system in the military has nudged me to move out of my comfort zone and to take a leadership role when required. I quickly realized that the officer rank I occupied, and its status, protects me from being ignored or looked down upon. I remember, in my first assignment, some enlisted soldiers were being too casual with me and telling me about women they met at bars while they were assigned in Korea. I felt that they were identifying me with the women they met at bars during their assignment and not as their chaplain. I had to learn to change the conversation discreetly without creating an awkward situation.

The majority of Army chaplains start as a battalion chaplain, where she or he is responsible for providing religious support to soldiers who have been assigned to the battalion and their families. The size of a battalion varies, as small as a few hundred or as large as over a thousand soldiers. A battalion chaplain has direct supervision over a chaplain assistant: a soldier who functions as the assistant at the home base and as the body guard in war since chaplains do not carry a weapon. Chaplains promoted to the rank of major are assigned as brigade chaplains. A brigade is an echelon above battalion and is comprised of few battalions. A brigade chaplain is responsible for one's own assistant as well as battalion chaplains and chaplain assistants who are also members of the same brigade. A select few are promoted to the rank of lieutenant colonel; they assume the position of division chaplain. A division chaplain is responsible for all chaplains and chaplain assistants assigned to that division.

In my first assignment as a battalion chaplain, I had to work with three different assistants. The first was a war veteran and knew his job but was in transition to his next assignment. The second assistant had a drinking problem, and his life before joining the Army was rough. He told me about his previous life in a gang. At first, I assumed that he was sharing his past with me to be more open. I realized later, however, his intention was to scare me with his stories. What he did not know about me was that I, too, interacted with a few Korean gangs in Flushing, New York, where I worked as a youth director for YWCA. The third assistant was of a good and caring heart but was naïve and financially irresponsible. As I look back, my struggles with three assistants were in large part due to my unrealistic expectations of them. I expected them to have my same work ethic and a similar level of integrity. Rather than accepting them for who they were and then helping them to grow, I expected them to be more disciplined and mature than they were at the time. I struggled to make them more responsible and accountable. And along the way I gained the label of "worst chaplain" among chaplain assistants. Looking back, and even now, I sometimes wonder, if I were a white male chaplain, would I have struggled as much as I did as a battalion chaplain?

Challenges as a leader in the military also surfaced during my deployment to Iraq as the brigade chaplain. I was deployed with four battalion chaplains and their assistants from the same base and later on, two additional battalion chaplains came under the brigade during the deployment. Two were brand new chaplains who came fresh out of basic training, and they created more problems for me than the other four chaplains combined. Not only were they passive aggressive and defiant, but they were also divisive. I recall receiving a call from a male chaplain's supervisor during the deployment. The supervisor was the executive officer of a battalion, as was I. Prior to the phone call, he questioned everything I asked of his battalion chaplains and demanded that I offer the direct clauses from Army regulations to justify my action. I obliged his demand many times in the hope of educating him, until the day when he called me and accused me of not communicating effectively with his battalion chaplain. It seemed that his battalion chaplain had been complaining about me to his direct supervisor. I tried to explain to him what I expected of him and other battalion chaplains, but his condescending tone of voice and attitude irritated me so much that I found myself screaming at him. I told him to train his battalion chaplain himself and hung up on him. Afterward, I noticed the change in his attitude toward me, even though his battalion chaplain remained a source of many headaches for me. In situations like these I had to prove myself to be worthy of my position. And this trend of needing to prove myself worthy of leadership roles persisted every time I was given a new assignment. At times, I rationalize for others, reminding myself that it is not common to see and deal with an Asian American woman in the role of military chaplain.

In spite of many heartaches and headaches the Army chaplaincy has caused me, I would not wish to exchange my military experience for any other type of ministry; it forced me to grow spiritually, mentally, and physically. One privilege of Army chaplaincy is to listen to the life stories of many soldiers— both good and bad. Through counseling, many soldiers shared their personal struggles and invited me into their world. I have met many soldiers who I admired for their survival skills, shown through horrendous life struggles. Some had survived incest and others overcame homelessness. Many of them were coming from dysfunctional family dynamics and trying to break the

cycle of inter-generational curses. In my service, I have learned the importance of listening to people, not only to understand them but to learn from
them. I have learned that a wise leader listens and learns from those s/he leads
to maximize their God-given potentials. In listening, I have received much
inspiration from their struggles and triumphs. For that, I am thankful to God,
who "tricked" me to enter into military ministry.

8

Phronēsis, the Other Wisdom Sister

JIN YOUNG CHOI

Since Asian and Asian American women are diverse in their individual and collective identities and experiences, it is difficult to generalize wisdom leadership as the one model of ministry for all women.[1] One may ask if "wisdom" can represent all of the experiences of Asian and Asian American women leaders. If it is wisdom that primarily characterizes Asian and Asian American women's leadership, then we should rearticulate and contextualize wisdom of these women and the practice of wisdom leadership in societal, cultural, and ecclesial structures. In developing Asian and Asian American women's wisdom leadership in its pluriform, then, it is necessary to start from shared experiences of Asian and Asian American women.

Asian and Asian American women in church have been multiply silenced under the influence of Asian cultural traditions and political histories, as well as of Euro-American Christianity. For Asian women, silence may have been enforced not only by political oppression under colonial rules and during civil wars but also by East Asian cultures that regard reticence as virtue. While assimilating to the dominant culture, many Asian immigrants in the United States still hold or inherit the traditional values and oppressive practices of women in their communities. Racial discrimination against, and language imposition on, Asian Americans can further silence women. Moreover, andro-logocentric Western culture and Western Christianity have suppressed the voices of women—including both Asian and Asian American—by exploiting such teachings as "women should be silent in the churches" (1 Cor. 14:34–36).[2] Despite the fact that Asian and Asian American women in church are heterogeneous, the majority of these women encounter silencing forces to varying degrees regardless of their geographical locations and generations.

Problematizing Asian and Asian American silence as reinforced by gender stereotypes, cultural norms, and racial discrimination, women need to speak in their own voices to struggle against those oppressions. In this sense, wisdom leadership may be a model of leadership for Asian and Asian American women. While this wisdom leadership stands against the model of kyriarchal and andro-logocentric leadership, it also critiques the Western feminist appropriation of wisdom, which highlights "speaking out" and ignores different types of knowing and speaking.[3]

Thus, I shall begin by examining the concept and construction of *sophia* as wisdom in the feminist theological discourse embedded in Western culture. And I will argue for another conceptualization of wisdom, *phronēsis*—embodied wisdom—by drawing on the Gospel of Mark and Asian American women's writings. In particular, I will focus on the topic of silence, which is not necessarily opposite to speech, to highlight listening as a vital asset for wisdom leaders, as well as the embodied aspect of women's knowing. Finally, these discussions will lead to understanding some important aspects of Asian and Asian American women's leadership.

CONTEXTUALIZING SOPHIA IN WESTERN CULTURE

Western feminist biblical scholarship has explored *sophia* as the personification of the feminine deity, the identification of Jesus, or the ideal characteristic of women in the Bible. Considering that biblical texts were written by males and have been interpreted predominantly by males, the exaltation of *sophia* as either a female divinity or a feminine ideal is a way of refuting the androcentric text and interpretation and may function to enhance the status of women in church.

However, from another feminist perspective, some issues can be raised in the uncritical celebration of *sophia*. First, the exalting of the feminine presence of divinity or wise female characters actually reinforces the patriarchal order and androcentrism embedded in the biblical text and interpretation. While *Sophia*'s feminine deity can be praised, it is the male God who created her before all things and knows her because she is his creation (Prov. 8:22; Sir. 1:8).[4] *Sophia* is a derivative and mediator of God (Wis. 7:25; 8:4). She is subject to and subjected by God. Although feminist theologians capitalize the term *Sophia*, the Greek text does not do so even when *sophia* is personified (Prov. 8:12). In contrast, the different masculine names of God are capitalized in the text.[5] Therefore, despite her divine character and power, to just claim the presence of a feminine deity in the Bible is to leave the structures of androcentric language, history, and theology—under which the feminine is derived from and dependent on the masculine—intact.[6]

Second, Anglo-European feminist interpretation constructs the goddess *Sophia* in light of Western logocentric tradition and culture, where the *telos* (end or goal) of *sophia* is the truth. Feminist theologians highlight *Sophia* as speaking aloud and proclaiming the truth. While some texts describe wisdom as a female figure or depict wise women speaking in public (2 Sam. 20:22; Jud. 11:20; cf. Wis. 10:21), feminist interpretation overly stresses the oratorical ability of female wisdom. Such an interpretation assumes that wisdom's primary characteristic is verbal. *Sophia* and women who have wisdom may "gain success through rhetorical means. Wise in tongue, their speech is adept and persuasive."[7] This exceptional female figure, *Sophia*, crosses over to the man's domain of rhetoric so that she interacts with men and even becomes at times the lover of men and kings.[8] She is identified with the Word (*logos*) that is incarnated in Jesus (John 1:1).[9] Unlike the fully embodied Jesus, however, *Sophia* is not historicized nor embodied. While *Sophia* is omniscient and omnipresent (Prov. 8:5, 8), she is not incarnate.

Third, Western feminist representation of *Sophia* essentializes the experience of particular women. Due to the compounded difficulty experienced by women who must break silence to liberate themselves, verbal assertiveness of Western feminists may not be a viable option for knowing and speaking for all women. When *sophia* is personified and deified in Jewish Wisdom Literature and early Christian traditions, it refers to God's "saving activity" rather than pointing to a feminine deity.[10] *Sophia* is primarily a type of knowing or knowledge. As Wisdom Literature lists and uses different words that parallel *sophia*-wisdom, there are various kinds of knowing such as prudence, discernment, understanding, perception, and heart, which are also all feminine nouns in the Greek text. However, Western feminists project their ideal of the woman by promoting wisdom as the goddess *Sophia* who dominates and proclaims the truth.

THE PRESENCE OF ANOTHER WISDOM, PHRONĒSIS

Sophia has been at the core of feminist advocacy. However, Western male and female translators, interpreters, and theologians have constructed *Sophia* as the extraordinary female character, and by doing so they removed other female figures or feminine attributes in the text. Just as Asian and Asian American women are diverse, so too is wisdom; wisdom has many names and many faces. Wisdom can be even silent or invisible. Just as Western feminist scholars rediscovered *Sophia* as the feminine deity and constructed her status in their own context, I will attend to *phronēsis* in order to recognize the wisdom that Asian and Asian American women have already embodied.

In addition to biblical books classified as Wisdom Literature such as the Book of Proverbs and Ecclesiastes, some feminist scholars use Baruch to show that *Sophia* is not secondary or derivative.[11] However, in many places the Greek word that is translated as wisdom (NRSV) is not *sophia* but is *phronēsis*. In Baruch 3, other feminine nouns are also used to indicate knowledge and wisdom.

> [9] Hear the commandments of life, O Israel;
>   give ear, and learn wisdom (*phronēsis*)!
> [12] You have forsaken the fountain of wisdom (*sophia*).
> [14] Learn where there is wisdom (*phronēsis*),
>   where there is strength,
>   where there is understanding (*synesis*),
> [23] The descendants of Hagar
>   . . . .
>   have not learned the way to wisdom (*sophia*),
> [27] God did not . . . give them the way to knowledge (*epistēmē*);
> [28] so they perished because they had no wisdom (*phronēsis*).

When the third person feminine "she" is used in the text, feminist interpreters assume that she must be *Sophia*. An example of this construction of *Sophia* at the expense of other feminine or female presences, including *phronēsis*, is seen in the translation of Wisdom 8 in *Wisdom's Feast*.

> [5] If in this life wealth be a desirable possession,
>   what is more wealthy than Wisdom (*sophia*) whose work is everywhere?
> [6] Or if it be the intellect (*phronēsis*) that is at work
>   where is there a greater than Wisdom [she] designer of all?

The word Wisdom in verse 6 does not appear in the original text. Moreover, the closest antecedent to this "she" is not *sophia* but *phronēsis*.

Here are a few other examples from Proverbs (NRSV) that support my argument.[12]

> 3:19 The LORD by wisdom (*sophia*) founded the earth;
>   by understanding (*phronēsis*) he established the heavens.
> 7:4 Say to wisdom (*sophia*), "You are my sister,"
>   and call insight (*phronēsis*) your intimate friend [or your nearest kinswoman].
> 8:1 Does not wisdom (*sophia*) call,
>   and does not understanding (*phronēsis*) raise her voice?

When the Hebrew Bible was translated into Greek, the translators and the readers probably knew Aristotle's differentiation between *phronēsis* as practical knowledge as presented in administrative ability and *sophia* as objective or theoretical knowledge.[13] Contrary to *sophia*, *phronēsis* does not presuppose existence of *the* truth somewhere out there but embodies a qualified truth. *Phronēsis* resists a singular formulation of wisdom. *Phronēsis* is knowledge in action or knowing what to do in a particular situation. Thus, phronetic knowing requires one to discern what the concrete situation is, which in turn, then, guides her to act. It is a type of wisdom Asian and Asian American women often experience when they act with moral consciousness to engage in tradition and care for the community.[14] I am not arguing for replacing the feminine abstraction of *sophia* with *phronēsis*. Rather, I am focusing on the embodied knowing that sheds light on the significance of wisdom leadership.

EMBODIED WISDOM OF WOMEN IN THE GOSPEL OF MARK

The Gospel of Mark does not use the words *sophia* or *phronēsis* or depict women as speaking their own voices.[15] Since Mark may simply be reiterating the cultural norms of ancient patriarchal society and the logic of imperial politics, it is not surprising to read individual and collective silences of women throughout the Gospel, except in the story of the Syrophoenician woman in Mark 7.[16] However, even in the general silence, women's agency in knowing and embodying truths in this oppressive situation can be observed.

One example is the hemorrhaging woman whose body knows. Having been exploited by the dominant system represented by many physicians, she discerns Jesus' power to heal her body and approaches him despite the restrictions of gender and cultural impurity (5:27). Still, she speaks in her mind: "If I but touch his clothes, I will be made well" (v. 28). She touches Jesus' clothes. Immediately her bleeding stops, and she "knows" in her body that she is healed of her disease (vv. 29–30). Only after being healed as the result of her touching of Jesus is she allowed to speak. In spite of the silence imposed when Mark erases her voice by only reporting that she tells Jesus "the whole truth" (v. 33), she knows that her action, though silent, will bring wholeness. Hearing the whole truth, Jesus repeats the words she has spoken in her mind but changes the voice from passive to active: "Daughter, your faith has made you well; go in peace, and be healed of your disease" (v. 34). According to Jesus, she has made herself well. It is she who achieves her wholeness. In short, while being multiply silenced, this woman knows what action should be taken under the constrained circumstances, and she practices agency in healing her body. Such knowing in action could be called *phronēsis*.

There are other women in Mark who know what Jesus' ministry truly means, while the male disciples appear to misunderstand. Jesus asks them, "Do you not yet perceive or understand?" (8:17). This question has been often interpreted in terms of christological knowledge. However, women in Mark demonstrate their knowing in their bodies, rather than as rational knowledge. Shortly after being healed by Jesus, Peter's mother-in-law quietly serves Jesus and his disciples. Surely, she is unnamed, silenced, and domesticated. Yet her gesture of attending (*diakonein*) embodies Jesus' life-giving practice, which eventually leads him to the cross (1:31).[17] The woman who anoints Jesus also anticipates Jesus' death and burial as if she knows what would happen to Jesus (14:3–9).

Among many silenced women, the women in Mark 16 may be viewed as most problematic. There are some female disciples who have followed Jesus from Galilee and watched Jesus' dying on the cross from afar, and the Gospel ends with the story of the women disciples' fear and silence at the empty tomb. Although the later editor adds that Mary Magdalene finally proclaims Jesus' resurrection to the disciples (16:9), the women's silence in the original ending still speaks in that it attends to Jesus' death as a life-giving event. Their silence cries out, asking where Jesus is and where God is in the midst of hardship in life. These women are with Jesus even when he is absent.

Whether Mark intended it or not, the women's silence and tacit actions powerfully display their embodied understanding of Jesus' life-giving ministry. Asian and Asian American women are especially able to understand such a way of knowing and speaking in and through silence because they have also experienced silencing both in the imperial-colonial or postcolonial contexts and in the patriarchal society.

ASIAN AMERICAN WOMEN'S SILENCE AND WISDOM

In her book *Articulate Silences*, King-Kok Cheung, a Chinese American literary critic, argues that while the monolithic Western viewpoint of language regards silence as absence, silence can speak many tongues and should be articulated and heard. She explores silence represented in fiction by three second-generation Asian American women and contends that silence is not merely a limitation brought about by social suppression but a "versatile strategy in its own right."[18] A brief discussion of what Cheung calls "enabling silences" will provide some insights into the embodied aspect of silence for discussing Asian and Asian American women's wisdom leadership.

Cheung notes that Asian American women writers, like Hisaye Yamamoto, often describe the female protagonists in the relationship between mothers and daughters, who are confined in silence stemming from patriarchy. In "The Legend of Miss Sasagawara," Yamamoto illustrates the silence pressed upon the female character, Sasagawara, by her father, the community, and the larger American society in the context of the Japanese American internment camp.[19] The protagonist appears to be both silent and mad at the same time, but in actuality she is speaking to people in a different way by using voiceless gestures and postures. It is also the author who speaks through the protagonist's silence, narrating social commentaries on the Asian American women's silence that is caused by patriarchal and racial oppression. Cheung calls this kind of complex silence "rhetorical silence."

Yamamoto is not alone in depicting women's silence as a different way of speaking. Although Joy Kogawa denounces forced silence and invisibility, both the theme and style in her work *Obasan* exhibit a nonverbal mode of understanding that is characterized by attendance and empathy.[20] Kogawa presents the narrator, Naomi, a Canadian Japanese. During forced evacuations in Canada, the first-generation Japanese *issei*, like Naomi's father, uncle, and aunt (*obasan*), survived through protective and sober silence. Naomi's mother was disfigured in Nagasaki due to the aftermath of atomic bombs, and this secret is kept in the silence of Naomi's uncle and *obasan* to protect her.

Naomi remembers her mother who was capable of responding to her need without a word—but with the "eyes that protect, shielding what is hidden most deeply in the heart of the child."[21] Even the word "heart" is not sufficient enough to describe this calm understanding of the child's "small stirrings underfoot and in the shadows": "Physically, the sensation is not in the region of heart, but in the belly."[22]

Kogawa highlights this embodied knowing in "attentive silence," embedded in the matrilineal tradition. Conjuring up the presence of her young mother in Nagasaki, Naomi speaks,

"Gentle Mother, we were lost together in our silences. . . ."[23]
"Mother. I am listening. Assist me to hear you."[24]
She then hears "the sigh of . . . remembered breath, a wordless word."[25]
Silence, paradoxically, strengthens the bonds between mother and daughter.

Interestingly, all the other women writers that Cheung discusses in her book connect the silence of the female protagonists to their matrilineal heritage in their fiction. In Kingston's autobiographical work, *The Woman Warrior*, for the young Maxine "silence had to do with being a Chinese girl."[26]

So she represses her Chineseness, trying instead to adopt Americanness, as is exposed when she harasses the other silent Chinese girl at school. She also despises her mother for telling stories in which Maxine is not able to distinguish between what is true and what is made up. However, while the young Maxine refuses to listen to her mother and is silent about her mother's story, the adult Maxine, as the author, has been listening carefully all the time so that the reader can also listen to her mother. Through this "provocative silence," the adult Maxine continues to tell her mother her own talk-story.[27]

These Asian American women writers not only reflect their experiences but also reconfigure situated realities by making the silent female characters speak in their own ways and also by speaking through their silences. Cheung argues for articulating these enabling silences. Indebted to her argument, I have highlighted the embodied silence that listens, as well as the strong affective bond of daughters and mothers who speak in their silence.

Silence is not absence of speech; rather, it is a different kind of speech. Silence is not merely verbal restraint, an impairment deriving from social restriction. Silence listens. Listening is an integral part of speaking. Silence can be a figure of speech signifying tacit understanding. In silence the body speaks. Such embodied silence can resist silencing and speak truths. In this context, what is needed is to listen to silence and attend to what the body speaks.

Attending to the ways in which women speak in silence, I would like to emphasize three points that connect embodied silence to Asian and Asian American women's wisdom leadership: (1) constructing knowledge based on multiple ways of knowing and embodying; (2) listening to what the body speaks; and (3) honoring wisdom embodied in the matrilineal tradition. In this way I am arguing for enabled silences that can serve as an alternative form of wisdom leadership.

ASIAN AND ASIAN AMERICAN WOMEN'S
PHRONĒSIS LEADERSHIP

I propose *phronēsis* as a type of wisdom that Asian and Asian American women can embody as a model of leadership. First, *phronēsis* wisdom strives to produce knowledge and discourse based in Asian and Asian women's experiences. *Phronēsis* is an alternative to *sophia*-centered wisdom and a critique of the logocentric tendency of *sophia* discourse. As I have argued, *sophia* is not the only type of wisdom; wisdom has different names, faces, and voices. *Phronēsis* is embodied wisdom—a way of knowing and a voice that has been suppressed by both patriarchy and Western feminism. While Western feminism also discusses the woman's body as a source of wisdom, in many cases the discourse focuses on individualized sexuality or the wellbeing of the body. The history and experiences of colonization and enslavement distinguished many Asian and Asian American women's perception of the body from the discourse of Western feminism.

According to Kwok Pui-lan, it is the body that remembers and transmits knowledge and truth through generations by speaking "a language of hunger, beating, and rape, as well as resistance, survival, and healing."[28] This language displays embodied truths that official history has obliterated. Thus, affirming the different voices and experiences of women, Asian and Asian American women leaders are constructing their own knowledge that they pass on through their bodies. This is a corporeal and communal act of producing knowledge that demands the leaders to attend to how bodies of women speak.

Second, Asian and Asian American women leaders need to listen to the voices and cries of their own and the other's bodies. Sometimes, it is liberating to encounter *Sophia*, Woman Wisdom, telling us to "listen" (Prov. 1:8, 20–21, 23; 5:1; 8:6, 32, 34). Other times, *phronēsis* wisdom practices by stating, "I am listening." For Asian American women in both ministry and academy, language is an indispensable tool of writing, teaching, and preaching. Despite their work within the dominant language system, in addition to imposed silence, breaking silence is often a burden for Asian and Asian American women. In this context, Asian and Asian American women leaders need to attend to what women's bodies know and how and what they speak.

Last, *phronēsis*-wisdom points to the importance of the matrilineal tradition in developing its leadership. We remember our mothers. Some Asian and Asian American women have mothers like *Sophia* who have spoken for their daughters and struggled to build a more just world in which their daughters take their rightful place. We also have mothers who had to sacrifice themselves in silence in order to make their daughters *Sophias*. And more importantly, our mothers also embodied *phronēsis*-wisdom, in order for their daughters to be their own persons. Like the young Maxine, we might have once disparaged our mothers, their stories, and their struggles, but we are connected with their bodies and retell their stories. As Jesus restored the bleeding woman both as a daughter and as a mother, we can also regain the wholeness of our beings and of the world because we know in our bodies.

Acknowledgment

In closing, I would like to honor the mothers of PANAAWTM, who have passed down living knowledge and embodied wisdom. Asian and Asian American women are connected in remembering our shared maternal heritage and embodying their wisdom through different types of silences and stories. The second and subsequent generations of Asian and Asian American women leaders wish to bring our embodied knowledge and discursive practice to inform and transform the places where we belong and where we do not belong. And we envision a global-scale solidarity with other women and men whose vulnerable bodies are, paradoxically, a sign of the faithful community and a source of liberation.

9

Foolishness of Wisdom

UNZU LEE

LEADERS THROUGH A CHILD'S EYES

Based on observations of my social surroundings, I knew what leadership was even as a child. In my world, I saw that leaders were few and followers were many. Leaders had power and the rest did not. My paternal grandmother, a devout Christian, offered a prayer daily for us saying, "Let all our children become only the head and not the tail." I knew she wanted all of us to become the kind of people who could not be trampled on by those in power. Yet, growing up in a divided country that was ravaged by war, it was very clear to me that only a small number of people seemed to have power, and that power was inevitably unstable and dangerous.

For this reason, I was suspicious of "leaders" from early on, including leaders in school, such as class presidents. To my horror, however, I was "made" class president when I entered junior high school because I was one of the seven students who scored the highest in the entrance examination. As the class president, I had to carry out duties that included shouting orders such as "Attention!" when a teacher entered the room. I hated ordering people around, and I was mortified by the experience. I begged my mother to plead with my homeroom teacher to select another student for the position. She did, and my illustrious path to leadership came to a quick end.

My discomfort in occupying a leadership position should not be interpreted as shying away from visibility or popularity. As a child, I liked to sing and dance in front of an audience and very much enjoyed the accolades I received. I also cared much about becoming someone that mattered, especially for the disenfranchised. In order to become this "somebody," I tried to excel in studies on the one hand and to make friends with those who ranked last in the class on the other hand. It mattered to me that my classmates who were treated like nobodies considered me their friend. I am not sure how genuine my motives were, but I was quite successful at winning their friendship. At every Christmas, for example, I was the only one among the class "elites" who received cards from them, and this meant a great deal to me.

My distrust of power was deeply ingrained in me even in the context of family. I grew up in a family where my mother sought invisibility and my father sought high visibility. Since my father was very much absent in my childhood, I strongly identified with my mother, especially as the firstborn. My mother, at the age of fifteen, made up her mind to become a medical doctor and to work with the poor; she was inspired to do so after reading books by Toyohiko Kawaga (1888–1960). He was a Japanese Christian social reformer who lived his life among the poor and worked tirelessly to transform the social order that bred inequality and injustice. My mother became a medical doctor, but her life took many unexpected turns when the Korean War erupted. The war made it impossible for her to practice her dream. Still, that flame kindled by Kagawa at a young age never went out, and my mother instilled in her children a life philosophy of transforming social orders by working against injustice.

STRIVING TO BE SOMEBODY IN A FOREIGN LAND

When I turned fourteen, my family boarded a Dutch ship for Brazil along with fifty-two other Korean families. Some described us at the time as the chosen few bound for the promised land. During the journey that took fifty-five days, I spent a lot of time daydreaming about my life in this promised land. Much to my dismay, however, I found myself sitting in a classroom with a group of kids who were too young to even hold a pencil. Not knowing any Portuguese, I had been placed in the first grade! Feeling totally humiliated by my new station in life, I strove mightily to get to the grade level commensurate with my age. In less than three years after arriving in Brazil, I boarded a flight bound for Los Angeles, where people spoke English.

Looking back, these experiences of repeated uprooting probably seriously compromised my development as a person. Every time I was thrust into a new culture with a new language, I felt infantilized and turned into a nobody. It is no wonder that I did not know what I was good at until much later in life. To say the least, I certainly did not have a promising trajectory to become a "leader" in any shape or form. Yet there was saving grace. Even in the midst of all these changes, there was one thing that remained constant in my life—my faith community.

My family's immigration to Brazil was facilitated by the Catholic Church in Korea. Of the fifty-three families that traveled together to Brazil, forty-three were Catholic, and the rest, including my family, were Protestant. Every Sunday of our voyage, the Catholics gathered for mass with the priest and the Protestants worshiped under lay leadership. The same trend continued when we settled on a vast tract of land that was supposed to become our collective farm. After worship and a fellowship meal, we Protestants stayed together to learn Portuguese from Protestant Brazilians who drove from Ponta Grossa, a city an hour away, to come and teach us. In their presence, I felt welcomed in a strange land; I realized that I belonged to a much larger faith community that cuts across languages and cultures. This was my weekly, albeit temporary, experience of haven.

As an immigrant in the United States, the Korean ethnic church was also a haven, the place where I could be somebody. In the church, I found my voice and a supportive community where I could learn, play, and exercise some leadership. Moreover, the church helped me make sense of my life. At the Korean ethnic church that I attended from 1973 to 1979, I learned about Dietrich Bonhoeffer, the Trail of Tears, the civil rights movement, the divided Korea, and more. Learning about these people and history from a faith perspective helped me to understand my own social location and to gain some sense of who I was and who I wanted to be. I left Los Angeles in 1985 for seminary training, hoping that theological education would further guide me to become that somebody.

WISDOM AND LEADERSHIP

In seminary and beyond, I wrestled with teachings that I received from my faith tradition. In my attempt to become somebody, the teachings I relied on most were difficult and rather contradictory. For example, I was told, "to gain life, one has to die"; "the first will become the last"; and "a good follower of Jesus is to be a servant of all." I also learned that Jesus, the exemplar who per-fectly embodied all these teachings, was God with infinite power; yet, Jesus emptied himself and became a sacrifice for humanity. I wondered about how one could be somebody by serving others, especially when it seemed to be a human condition that people with power exploit those without power.

Growing up in this kind of faith tradition, with its deeply embedded servant theology, I often felt conflicted by what seemed to be a paradoxi-cal teaching. It is not surprising, then, that the very first paper I wrote in seminary was a reflection on the foolishness of God's wisdom as explicated in 1 Corinthians. The author of 1 Corinthians wrote that, Jesus, the Christ, was "the power of God and the wisdom of God" and that "God's foolishness is wiser than human wisdom, and God's weakness is stronger than human strength. . . . But God chose what is foolish in the world to shame the wise; God chose what is weak in the world to shame the strong" (1 Cor. 1:24b–25, 27). I contemplated on this paradox of becoming a fool in order to become wise as I considered the idea of becoming a leader in the context of ministry. How could I apply these words in my life and ministry? Is the risk of becoming a fool for God's wisdom to prevail worth taking? What might that risk look like? Though I neither fully understood this paradoxical teaching nor did I think I could really become like Jesus, these words had tremendous power over me; for I intuited that the wisdom that guided Jesus' life journey had the ultimate saving grace and the strength that I needed in order to become that somebody. Jesus, however, was too perfect, and I needed someone more like me. Then I heard the following story about my grandmother from my mother.

Soon after the Korean War started, Seoul was under siege by the people's army of the Democratic People's Republic of Korea (DPRK). To strengthen their own army, DPRK soldiers searched every household and conscripted all young men they saw into their army. My uncle, her eldest son, who was sixteen at the time, was a perfect candidate. Keenly aware of impending danger, my grandmother decided to take control of the situation. Instead of waiting for them to come and draft my uncle, my grandmother hid him and then went to the army headquarters set up in her neighborhood. Wailing, she said to them, "My son is missing! I don't know what's happened to him. Please help me find him. I cannot live a day without my son!" Feeling very sympathetic to my grandmother, the person in charge said, "Grandma, I am so sorry to hear that your son is missing. Don't worry. We'll do our best to find him. You will soon have your son back." And the army officers took very good care of my grandmother's family, without ever ransacking the house to look for any men. When Seoul was recaptured by the South Korean army and the U.N. troops later on, my mother's family, including my uncle, fled Seoul and sought refuge in the southern region until the armistice treaty was signed on July 27, 1953.

My grandmother had no formal education and held no leadership position of any sort. How did she know what to do in such a challenging situation riddled with so many unknowns? How did she exercise such decisive leadership when the situation called for it? What was the source of her leadership? I would say that it was her wisdom. Her wisdom gave her courage to take a risk by acting like a fool when faced with imminent danger. My grandmother's action reminds me of the serpent song written by my friend, a feminist composer:

> In the places that reek of impossibility
> The Serpent of Life coils
> She crawls upon the swollen stone
> crawls upon the swollen stone
> crawls upon the swollen stone
> And loosens her only garment[1]

My grandmother lived an invisible life of serving others. But when she found herself in a place that reeked of impossibility, she crawled upon the swollen stone, loosened her only garment, and in total vulnerability enacted her wisdom with such courage. Indeed, she exercised vital leadership by enacting her wisdom—by becoming a fool and risking her own life.

There are many biblical passages that point to precisely this type of wise leadership. One in particular is the story of Exodus. The Exodus story is inundated with the names of courageous women who outwitted the Pharaoh. They are Shiphrah and Puah, Jochebed, Miriam, and the Egyptian princess. Each of them took courageous actions in defiance of the king's verdict to kill Hebrew baby boys, and together, they set the salvation history in motion. Each one is a wise woman who enacts her wisdom when she is called to lead in the moment. My grandmother belongs to the ranks of these extremely wise women who exercised their leadership by drawing on their foolish wisdom.

MY LEADERSHIP IN CONTEXT

It is important to point out that my grandmother and the women in the Exodus story, except for the princess, did not hold any position of authority. Yet they each and together exercised their agency, becoming wise fools. Their stories teach us that each of us has power and a God-given authority to determine what to do with that power to exercise leadership, regardless of our station in life.

During my tenure at the national offices of the Presbyterian Church (U.S.A.), I did not rise to the top level of leadership positions; hence, one can say that I had limited power. However, it did not stop me from exercising leadership when I felt called to do so because I fundamentally believed that my authority and power came from God, who dwells in me as Wisdom. I once made it known at a staff meeting with the newly elected CEO of the agency. In the course of discussion, I said, "Ultimately, I am accountable to God and myself." Immediately, the new CEO turned to me and said, "No.

You are wrong. You are accountable to the board of this agency." That was the power structure in which I worked, and the following episode illustrates how my perspective on power and leadership allowed me to exercise freedom even within such a power structure.

This particular episode occurred when I served as coordinator for women's advocacy in the Presbyterian Church (U.S.A.) from 1994 to 2000. My position had two interrelated yet different aspects: programs and policy. This latter aspect involved serving the Advocacy Committee for Women's Concerns (ACWC), the church's institutional mechanism created in 1993 to address issues of sexism and to promote gender justice in the church and society. Since my tenure with this position started in January 1994, I was with the committee from the very beginning.

ACWC was a General Assembly committee with direct access to the General Assembly, the highest governing body in the institutional church. ACWC introduced resolutions to General Assembly, and it provided what is called "advice and counsel" memoranda (somewhat like legal briefs) to commissioners on business matters with a particular significance to women. This committee had a lot of institutional power invested in it. Yet its budget was pitiful. The budget could not support the work assigned to it, and the committee struggled year after year for lack of financial resources. What surprised me, however, was that none of the ACWC members ever questioned the rationale for the budget; instead, everyone's focus was on cutting the committee's spending. Halfway into my fourth year of working with ACWC, I knew that we were going to go over the budget if the committee did all that it planned to do at the General Assembly, which usually took place in June, the midpoint of the fiscal year. As staff, it was my responsibility to advise the committee on its financial status and help the committee stay within the budget. This time, however, I chose not to bring it to the committee's attention because I intuited that the only way to bring the board's attention to the injustice of this situation was to allow it to happen, and it happened. The budget sheet I received in August showed that ACWC was already in the red. Even though it was anticipated, I was badly shaken, but I knew that this crisis was also an opportunity. After a series of events, ACWC was successful in drawing the board's attention, and the chair of the committee and I, its staff, were finally invited to sit at the table with the board. In the end, the board was persuaded that the current budget could not support the committee's work and decided to almost double ACWC's budget as well as the budget of the other two similar committees. This is one experience I treasure because it proved to me that it is possible to negotiate patriarchy for a positive outcome by becoming a wise fool.

As a staff person at the national level, I often was asked to provide leadership at church functions. I preached, delivered keynotes, and led workshops as a leader. I also worked with various groups made up of church volunteers, people appointed or elected to represent their constituency. When working with these groups, I made sure the decision-making power belonged to the entire group and did my best to support the group to live out its purpose. As a national staff member, my location determined my role and function in relation to these groups. I was not a member of any group, and I was there to be faithful to the group process. What I learned from exercising leadership in such a location was that serving as a staff to the group process is like learning to dance. At times, I functioned as a choreographer, back-up stage person, dance trainer, cheerer, promoter, and dancer. Mostly, I moved in and out of dances to encourage those not being given enough space to dance. Sometimes I helped others to dance collaboratively to fulfill the purpose of the group. The key to leading groups from my particular location was to cultivate the wisdom and to know when and how to enter various dance processes.

DRAWING ON CULTURAL WELLS OF WISDOM TO LEAD

For a number of years, I worked as staff to Presbyterian Women (PW), a nationally organized volunteer organization of women in the Presbyterian Church (U.S.A.). PW elects a new Moderator every three years. Several years ago, upon learning the name of the one who was nominated for the moderator for the next triennium, a Korean American member of the board said to me, "I guess Americans do not look for the virtue of *deok* in a leader." Her comment has stayed with me.

This term pronounced as *deok* in Korean is a very complex, multivalent concept that probably originated with Taoism and was later incorporated as one of the core concepts of Confucian philosophy. One of many possible understandings of the term is:

> The power or virtue that a Taoist practitioner attains, as they align themselves with the rhythms of the Tao, and in so doing, perfects their character. [It] refers to a code of conduct or way of life characterized by moral integrity, honor, kindness, graciousness, and benevolence. It also refers to the fruits of these actions: the blessings (e.g. of power and wisdom) and good fortune that manifest when our personal intentions or life-purpose are in alignment with the "will of heaven," i.e. the Tao.[2]

This definition is aligned with the way in which I came to understand the term while growing up in Korea. The term, to me, means that a measure of one's maturity is found in an exemplary person, and she is not self-interested but is a blessing to others. The power of *deok* is, for me, in its affect. The term evokes in me a feeling of warmth, gentleness, and intimacy. A woman with *deok* has a huge heart, is extremely wise and therefore dependable. She has "the inner moral power through which a person may positively influence others" and can earn the support of others.[3] The great Taoist teacher Lao-tze likened such leadership to water that is "soft and gentle, but also persistent and powerful."[4] My efforts of self-cultivation, self-examination, and self-regulation probably have been my attempts at attaining *deok* with the hope of becoming a good, mature person with authenticity and integrity. In the East Asian perspective, then, becoming a mature person is integral to leadership development. Looking back and knowing what I know now, I would like to share a few lessons of leadership that may be of interest to other Pacific Asian and North American Asian women leaders in the context of ministry.

POWER OF STRUCTURE

Some scholars argue that women tend to be more collaborative and good at horizontal relationships with colleagues. I used to believe this, but I believe it less so now. Institutions are not innocuous. Rather, they are living organisms with their own logic and culture (usually patriarchy). Although women historically have been structural outsiders, I have witnessed many women being changed by the patriarchal system once they become structural insiders. We should not be naive about the long history of the patriarchy's persistence and its influence on everyday life. To borrow an ordained woman's concern in the church context, for example: "Will the institutional church be transformed by new winds of the spirit blowing, or am I slowly being co-opted into an institutional maintenance supporter?"[5]

POWER OF SELF-EXAMINATION

My strongly felt suspicion about all people in positions of power, and my subsequent and relentless self-regulation and self-examination, may have prevented me from dreaming big dreams. While my suspicion and uneasiness of power have protected me from forces of institutional corruption and helped me to stay more true to myself, I wonder if such unfounded resistance to all leadership may be a shared experience among many Pacific Asian and Asian

North American women. And if so, how might have this critical look at leadership hindered us to rise up to leadership positions in the church and society?

POWER OF WISE DISCERNMENT

A study has shown that "effective women are not superwomen who hold themselves to the highest standards for all of the role-related tasks of being wives and mothers," for example, but rather they "adopt different internal and external strategies to redefine their roles."[6] This is very true to my own experience of leadership. Although I am quite a principle-oriented person, I have learned that different circumstances require different styles and types of leadership. For example, some contexts do not allow time or place for collaboration and may demand quick and decisive leadership. Some other contexts may require all stakeholders be involved in the time-consuming discernment process to reach an agreeable decision. How do we know what type of leadership is called for which contexts? I believe that our lived experience is the best teacher of such wisdom and that we can attain it if we pay attention and consciously reflect on our life lessons.

POWER OF ENACTING WISDOM

And last, I agree with Elizabeth Smythe and Andrew Norton, who ask that we think of leadership as a verb, since "to lead is to always be in play, enacting the wisdom of leadership."[7] They also assert, "Leadership that enables individuals to play with wisdom, foresight and sound judgment can only be learnt through experience" and that "strong leadership requires wisdom that is enacted in the moment."[8] Based on this definition, my grandmother certainly exercised strong leadership. Her story, I believe, has much to teach those of us who live in a culture that asks experts to train us with mechanics and "know how" of leadership.

We are living in the ever-globalizing, digital age. Changes are taking place much faster than ever before. This is especially true for Pacific Asian and Asian North American women in ministry who must traverse so many different worlds; we are often compartmentalized and organized by labels such as race, ethnicity, theological orientation, language, gender, and sexual orientation, to name just a few. We cannot become good leaders simply by having a five-year strategic plan with the resources to implement it. Recognizing our hybridity and complexity as our greatest assets will help us become great leaders and wise fools. May we all be blessed with wisdom that empowers us to enact leadership.

Three Tales of Wisdom

Leadership of PANAAWTM

KEUN-JOO CHRISTINE PAE

INTRODUCTION

A few weeks before I first attended the annual meeting of Pacific, Asian, and North American Asian Women in Theology and Ministry (PANAAWTM), I had a short conversation with my professor, a well-known feminist theologian. As an international student from Korea studying theology and ethics in English at a prestigious divinity school in New England, I struggled with feelings of uprootedness and marginalization. I desperately sought someone in the faculty who might empathize with me, encouraging me to respect my own voice. She was sympathetic but not empathetic. In her eyes, I was too foreign to study mainstream feminist theology, which is spoken with heavy German and French accents. I knew I had the potential to be a great feminist theologian, but when I shared my desire to be an academic and to teach "Asian" feminist theologies and ethics in solidarity with postcolonial liberationist movements, she responded, "It must be difficult for you to pursue that dream because you do not have Asian feminist role models in the religious academe."

I still wonder whether or not she had heard the rich voices of Asian and Asian American feminist theologians, or if she considered our voices theologically insignificant because our theologies were spoken with heavy Asian accents. Regardless, my first PANAAWTM conference in Boston in 2002 immediately proved her perception wrong. To be a feminist ethicist, I did not need to speak like Luce Irigaray or Julia Kristeva. The Asian and Asian American feminist theological voices presented at the conference were vibrant and liberating. Since then, PANAAWTM has been my home away from home—I have felt grounded wherever I go because I know that there are women who understand my voice as it has grown out of intellectual, spiritual, and physical struggles.

This essay is written from my thirteen-year-journey with PANAAWTM. Reflecting on the wisdom-leadership that PANAAWTM mentors and colleagues have practiced, I interweave the tales of PANAAWTM which challenge the conventional ideas of "wisdom" and "leadership."[1] These tales will also contemplate the future of the wisdom-leadership model suggested by PANAAWTM.

In order to patch the tales of the oldest grassroots organization of Asian and Pacific American women in the theological field, my essay takes Kwok Pui-lan's postcolonial feminist imagination as a tool in interweaving stories. Kwok, one of the founding members of PANAAWTM, submits the image of the storyteller who "selects pieces, fragments, and legends from her cultural and historical memory to weave together tales that are passed from generation to generation."[2] As a second generation PANAAWTM member, I "refashion and retell" the tales of this organization with "new materials added to face new circumstances and to reinvent the identity of a people."[3] Therefore, this essay is "my" and "our" stories inspired by the past, present, and future members of PANAAWTM. These tales, however, are not meant to represent the entire body of PANAAWTM. Rather, they are a contemplation on how PANAAWTM, as a "diasporic community," has consciously and wisely negotiated with the multiple boundaries of race, class, gender, religious identity, citizenship, and so forth. By crossing multiple boundaries and negotiating existing power structures in the church and the theological academe, PANAAWTM sisters generated wisdom in their concrete contexts.

Telling the wisdom tales of PANAAWTM is threefold. The first tale frames "the power of imagination" that must be fostered in a historically concrete context. Introducing Kwok's postcolonial imagination (historical, dialogical, and diasporic imagination), the first tale challenges the concept of "wisdom" and "leadership" in search for the sources of PANAAWTM wisdom.

In light of Kwok's historical imagination lined with dialogical and diasporic imagination, the second tale is a composition of the PANAAWTM sisters' memories of and hopes for PANAAWTM. The twelve sisters whom I interviewed for this essay will help understand the survival wisdom and open-ended legacy of a diasporic community that they want to hand down to new generations.

The last tale is imagining the future of wisdom-leadership of PANAAWTM. After listening to twelve sisters' stories, I will map out the future of wisdom-leadership grown out of the PANAAWTM context which can be shared in larger society.

THE FIRST TALE: IMAGINING WISDOM LEADERSHIP

Before contemplating wisdom-leadership in the PANAAWTM context, we need to critically examine the language of wisdom as influenced by religion and culture. What do we mean by wisdom? How are we using and co-opting "wisdom"? These critical questions are especially important for Asian Americans, because unexamined use of wisdom can unintentionally (or intentionally) leads to a commodified, Orientalized, or essentialized feminine notion of wisdom as a modern day alternative to the top-down leadership model.

In *Virtual Orientalism*, Jane Iwamura offers an important critique to the American perception of the "Orientalized" wisdom. Hollywood's portrayal of "the Oriental monk" became the representative image of Asian spiritual and religious traditions of wisdom. This "Oriental Monk" and his wisdom were perceived as saving the West from "capitalist greed, brutal force, totalitarian rule, and spiritless technology."[4] The Oriental monk, who had a penchant for aphorisms, was considered to be offering a new leadership model to the West.[5] Although wisdom can be easily tied with religious teachings and practices, Iwamura's analysis suggests that if we conventionally use the terms "wisdom" and "leadership" together without critically thinking of them in a historically specific context, we may participate in Orientalizing wisdom-leadership. Since these two concepts can imply multiple meanings and interpretations, it is not easy to define or imagine wisdom-leadership as one concept. Nonetheless, it would be safe to say that wisdom-leadership should be considered in the concrete and particular context in order not to fall into the perception of Orientalized wisdom, or as an alternative to the so-called Western models of masculine leadership marked with aggression, assertiveness, discernment, forcefulness, and top-down decision making.

Taking PANAAWTM as a historically tangible ground for us to critically analyze and concretely imagine wisdom-leadership, I tentatively define wisdom-leadership as leaders' abilities to respond to their ever-changing social environments. In light of this definition, the imagination of wisdom-leadership is important, for as Kwok says, without the power of imagination, "we cannot envision a different past, present, and future."[6] How, then, can we imagine wisdom-leadership that is historically concrete and powerful enough to suggest the future direction of leadership in an organization like PANAAWTM? Kwok presents three critical movements of postcolonial imagination: historical imagination, dialogical imagination, and diasporic imagination. While imagination is an important epistemological tool for Asian women in knowing, understanding, and interpreting the world around us and for steering us away from Eurocentric knowing or romanticizing our inheritance, all three critical movements must be grounded in the concrete context.[7] In other words, although we "imagine" what we have not experienced, our imagination should be concretely grounded in relations with others and their stories in the past, present, and future.

If historical imagination aims to reconstitute the past and to release the past so that the present is livable, dialogical imagination opens the multiple spaces or contact zones where different cultures meet, clash, collaborate, colonize, resist, and experience tensions and fractures.[8] Often remembering and resisting multiple layers of oppression such as colonialism, patriarchy, racism, and gender-based violence, Asian women's bodies generate wisdom as a source of survival from these forms of oppression.

Diasporic imagination consistently challenges the center and the periphery by focusing on the traces of the diasporic subjects that cross multiple borders and boundaries. "A diasporic consciousness" enables us to find similarities and differences in both familiar territories and unexpected corners, just as we, Asian Pacific American women (APA women), see ourselves in the diasporic narratives of enslaved black women and in those of Native American women.[9]

The three movements of feminist postcolonial imagination may open a familiar and unexpected door to wisdom. If so, what kind of water of wisdom can we drink from the familiar and unexpected well of PANAAWTM?

SECOND TALE: WISDOM-LEADERSHIP IN THE PANAAWTM CONTEXT

As Kwok insightfully points out, "memory is a powerful tool in resisting institutionally sanctioned forgetfulness."[10] While the mainstream Christian theology forgets and often erases the presence of the colonized bodies of Asian and Pacific women in history, PANAAWTM made a collective effort to intentionally remember the bodily experiences of these women. Historical imagination of the concrete is a form of feminist activism that allows PAN-AAWTM to holistically remember the past, present, and future. Therefore, our hope is more practical and not so disillusioned; the trust among us is born of necessity and well-worn wisdom. In light of historical imagination, the following section shows how PANAAWTM sisters remember and reconstitute past wisdom-leadership so that the present is livable and the future holds a concrete hope. At the same time, the reader will find that historical imagination in the PANAAWTM context is naturally accompanied with dialogical and diasporic imaginations.

Wisdom-Leadership as Servant Leadership

"After Letty had visited churches in Japan and Korea, she decided to offer a physical space for Asian women who study theology or are in ministry so these women would continue to do feminist theology when they went back to their home countries," said Shannon Clarkson. On a chilly day in October 1984, thirteen Asian women sat together in the living room of Letty Russell and Shannon Clarkson's lake house at Guilford, Connecticut. Sharing their experiences at graduate schools and churches, these women agreed on the necessity to build up a supportive community for Asian feminist theologians and ministers. This small house gathering was the beginning of Asian Women Theologians (AWT), the only theological organization for Asian women of its kind at that time.[11]

Letty and Shannon wanted to exercise "servant leadership" for the birth of AWT. Shannon said,

> We simply wanted to offer a space for Asian feminist theologians. There were not many any sort of feminist theologians in the 80s. So, we had to start. Letty and I used our network to collect the seed money for AWT. She wrote grant applications and I was a treasurer and bookkeeper. Basically, we took care of logistics for AWT and early PANAAWTM conferences rather than supervising or directing the organization. Letty saw herself as a servant for AWT.

Letty and her Asian female students at Yale Divinity School would cook for the participants in the AWT East Coast conference. She would also pick up trash and clean up the meeting rooms as well. The long-term members of PANAAWTM still share loving memories of Letty and Shannon, who fostered the organization and let it flourish without them when its members were ready to take full responsibility of it.

In light of Kwok's historical imagination, "servant leadership" is not simply PANAAWTM's past model of leadership, but also a model lived through the history of the organization. Hebrew Bible scholar Seung Ai Yang, who was recruited and has served on the PANAAWTM board since 1998, remembered, "The long-term members who are serving on the board now joined PANAAWTM as doctoral students or junior faculty and are now seasoned scholars in our respective academic disciplines. We have always understood our work as service for the Asian Pacific American feminist community and academic guild." These members have been committed to educating next

generation APA feminist theologians, when Eurocentric institutions under-
value or essentialize their Asian feminist students' Asian perspectives or
research topics.

Servant leadership takes various forms. Jin Young Choi, an emerging New
Testament scholar, understood her role in serving newcomers. For a while,
Choi saw herself as a peripheral member, although she had steadily attended
PANAAWTM annual meetings for almost a decade. Instead of feeling marginalized, Choi exercised her leadership in the periphery—according to her
definition. She recruited new members, listened to self-defined peripheral
members, and encouraged them to take advantage of PANAAWTM. In her
usual soft and considerate voice, she said:

> There is a perceived leadership group at PANAAWTM that usually
> includes long-term members and accomplished scholars. Newcomers
> and student members may feel a distance from them. At the lunch
> and dinner tables, I talked to them and listened to their complaints
> because they felt more comfortable talking with me than with the
> senior faculty. I encouraged them to continue to attend the PAN-
> AAWTM annual meeting just as I had kept coming. At the margin of
> PANAAWTM, I exercised my own leadership, serving the members
> who may not feel fully included in the annual meeting."

Choi's reflection on her servant leadership further opens another door
to wisdom-leadership, which I define as "community building" based upon
friendship.

Wisdom-Leadership as Community Building
Based on Friendship

At the Asian North American Theological Educators Conference in October 2014, Choi, speaking from a New Testament feminist perspective, suggested the image of wisdom that belongs to the community, specifically one's
embodied wisdom being the product of her relationships and experiences
with the community.[12] This sort of wisdom, from my perspective, is dialogical between individuals and the community; it is based on communal sharing
rather than privatized knowledge. In order to make wisdom communally ben-
eficial, healthy community building is essential.

My interviewees remember the sense of community and belonging, as
they have been more deeply involved in the organization. Their first PAN-
AAWTM meetings were usually colored with surprises and wonders. Su Yon
Pak says that her first PANAAWTM annual meeting was a life-changing
experience. At the 1985 Asian Women Theologians meeting at Stony Point,

New York, Pak, an MA student at that time, encountered professional Asian women around her mother's age. These women challenged the dominant images of the first generation Korean American women who were perceived to have a lack of communication skills in English and had leadership roles in largely domestic and women-only spaces. The Stony Point meeting inspired Pak to read and study feminist theology, although her school did not offer any courses related to the topic. Recalling her first love with AWT (Asian Women Theologians, former PANAAWTM), "I still remember the ritual at the 1985 meeting. All of us were standing in a circle, and taking off our shoes. Through the different style of ritual that I had not experienced before, I could see an alternative vision for community." Pak called PANAAWTM "home away from home." "Home away from home" was an expression often shared by the interviewees. Most of us experienced moments of epiphany at the PANAAWTM meetings as if our true selves were finally revealed to us and we were home.

The founding members of PANAAWTM dedicated themselves to creating a safe and liberative community for APA women. The building of strong community requires honest dialogue among members. Kwok said,

> At the first AWT conference at Stony Point, we learned that Asian women were not good at understanding Asian American women's experiences of immigration, classism, and racism in the United States. We had to honestly talk to one another so everyone in the conference felt included and understood. Then, we officially adopted a new name, Asian and Asian American Women Theologians [AAAWT], at the 1986 conference.

Ten years later, the name of Pacific, Asian, and North American Asian Women in Ministry and Theology would be officially adopted in order to reflect the diversity of members in terms of culture, ethnicity, citizenship, geographic location, and vocation. Those who participated in the PANAAWTM in the mid-1980s remember how rigorously they engaged in dialogue with one another. This dialogue revealed the multiplicities and complexities of Asian diaspora and the richness and fluidity of APA feminist theology. In light of dialogical imagination, PANAAWTM created the contact zone and offered multiple spaces between Asian and Asian American women where they could see more clearly how their identities were differently affected by European colonialism. At the same time, as Kwok's diasporic imagination submits, a PANAAWTM sister could also see herself in others' different and simultaneously familiar stories. The founding mothers of PANAAWTM accumulated wisdom through their experiences to initiate and sustain honest and sometimes tense dialogue among diverse women.

The second important leadership skill for sustaining community is to build up friendship. Most interviewees who joined the board as early as the 1980s named friendship as the number one reason they were loyal to PANAAWTM for many years. Gently smiling, Kwok said that friendship among senior members encouraged them to spend time and energy for PANAAWTM. Thanks to this rare friendship, senior members could accomplish a lot when PANAAWTM was nascent. Senior members on the board used to spend time together discussing challenging issues for PANAAWTM, conferencing for the first book project *Off the Menu*, having social time at the American Academy of Religion meetings, and making important organizational decisions based on mutual consent. The senior members whom I interviewed wished for future generations to form the friendships that they have cultivated. Friendship can be intergenerational and dialogical.

Friendship requires an alternative understanding of power relations. If human differences such as age, ethnicity, marital status, vocation, nationality, and sexual orientation among women were considered the distinctive characteristics of PANAAWTM, it would be important to reimagine power relations among these diverse members. Navigating power relations is one aspect of wisdom-leadership to which I now turn.

Wisdom-Leadership as "Taking Power and Making Power"

With her usual sparkling eyes, Nami Kim defined wisdom-leadership in the PANAAWTM context:

> Regardless of how little power I have, leadership means how to use my power. Serving on the steering committee of PANAAWTM, I have learned how to exercise power, distribute power, and respect others' differences. Because my power is confirmed by community, it requires greater responsibility of me. This is why I have to exercise my power carefully and wisely.

She further added that the impact of PANAAWTM on her life was to seek activism in scholarship. Kim's words resonate with a community-based organization for young women of color, Sista II Sista's understanding of power. Sista II Sista, according to Andrea Smith, relies on the dual strategy of "taking power" and "making power":

> [I]t is necessary to engage in oppositional politics to corporate and state power by taking power. Yet if we only engage in the politics of taking power, we will have a tendency to replicate the hierarchical structures in our movements. So it is also important to "make power"

by creating those structures within our organizations, movements, and communities that model the world we are trying to create.[13]

As a grassroots organization like Sista II Sista, PANAAWTM has engaged in oppositional politics to mainstream theology marked by so-called high theories, abstract thinking, doctrines, etc. PANAAWTM does not deny the importance of theory as a tool in shaping and naming our thinking. The organization also emphasizes social transformation and activism in scholarship and understands theological education and ministry to be inseparable. The practicality of theological discourse rooted in APA women's political experiences of oppression and liberation is crucial to "doing" theology. Creating a safe space for APA feminist theologians and ministers is the most important strategy for PANAAWTM to "take power." One exemplary story comes from Gale Yee. PANAAWTM encouraged Yee, who is also an active member of the Ethnic Chinese Biblical Colloquium, to be more conscious of her social location in terms of race and gender. During our conversation over breakfast, Yee confirmed, "Reading the text closely is still important in biblical scholarship. But being aware of the interpreter's social location is equally important. Without critically considering race, gender, class, and imperialism, it is impossible to do biblical scholarship."

How, then, have the members exercised making just power relations within PANAAWTM? We currently have two leadership groups within the organization: the board and the steering committee. The board includes the steering committee and the faculty advisors who mentor doctoral students and junior faculty. The board makes decisions for the running of PANAAWTM such as raising funds, recruiting new board or steering committee members, creating policies for the board members, and distributing resources. The steering committee, of which members serve on the board at large, organizes the annual conference. The committee selects the theme for the conference, names the speakers for the public panel on the first day of the annual meeting, compiles the daily programs, and works with the local conference committee.

What makes the PANAAWTM leadership model unique is "teamwork." The board does not have a chair but shares responsibilities and practices consensual decision making. A few interviewees believe that PANAAWTM board exercises a feminist praxis of shared power relations or what Jung Ha Kim calls an "organic relationship." The members organically work together by voluntarily bringing their leadership skills.

The earlier leadership model of PANAAWTM, according to Kwok's memory, was a somewhat leaderless movement. Local students used to organize annual meetings held in different locations, mostly in Boston, New York City, Atlanta, and the San Francisco bay area. Rather than having a centralized group, regional networks were committed to organizing annual conferences and small meetings in order to introduce the presence of PAN-AAWTM and its feminist theology and ministry to the local community. Now Kwok sees PANAAWTM leadership as "rotating leadership." Our leadership model is not like an ad hoc committee, which is often found among leaderless movements. We have a leadership group recognized and confirmed by the larger body of the PANAAWTM. Those who constitute this leadership group rotate their roles. For example, after the departure of Letty and Shannon from PANAAWTM, Kwok took responsibility of raising funds for the organization. Now Pak, who was trained in institutional development, plays a major role in raising funds, although everyone on the board participates in fundraising one way or another.

Perhaps shared power relations among the members were best exercised when *Off the Menu* was published in 2007. Not only the editors but also all the contributors read chapters together and offered constructive feedback to one another. Although it took longer to compile all the chapters for the book, the editors successfully created a non-hierarchical relationship among the authors by giving them back the power to edit their essays by commenting on others'.

The three aspects of PANAAWTM wisdom-leadership only serve to show how, for the last thirty years, the PANAAWTM has evolved in response to social changes surrounding the organization. The historical imagination now enables us to retell and reconstruct these stories and to formulate the stories of the future.

THIRD TALE: THE FUTURE OF WISDOM-LEADERSHIP—CHALLENGES AND OPPORTUNITIES

"What would you like to see in PANAAWTM for the next thirty years to come?" When I asked all the interviewees this question, all of them unequivocally said they wanted PANAAWTM to continue. For all of us, PANAAWTM is the only place exclusively for, with, and by Asian and Asian American women. This gendered and racialized space gives us freedom to be who we are. Borrowed from Jung Ha's expression, "PANAAWTM allows us to reveal our weaknesses and ask others for help."

As long as various layers of oppression, such as racism, sexism, colonialism, and heterosexism exist in our society, PANAAWTM should exist as a space of oppositional politics. However, we cannot simply imagine the longevity of PANAAWTM at this time. The continuation of PANAAWTM now depends on younger generations' commitment to the organization and their wisdom in dealing with future ambiguities. My third and last tale suggests the future model of wisdom-leadership as an outgrowth of the PANAAWTM context.

From Closed Friendship to Engaged Friendship: Dialogical Imagination

Friendship is an important factor to grow the organization. As I mentioned earlier, friendship among senior members enabled them to work for PAN-AAWTM out of love. Mentioning the danger of friendship, however, Kwok said that some people perceived PANAAWTM as the organization of a few notable Asian American feminist scholars. This perception may give both insiders and outsiders a false impression that PANAAWTM is a closed inner circle of APA women rather than an emancipatory space for the marginalized women in the theological field. Although friendship is important for genuine human relations based on shared power relations, the kind of friendship that will sustain a healthy community must actively engage with newcomers, truthfully recognize the differences among ourselves, and reconstruct an alternative idea of friendship. Namely, friendship does not need to be pursued among those who share similar interests or backgrounds. Rather, friendship fosters a culture that enables anyone to freely speak up with her own voice without fear and enables the community to be open enough to engage with any voice. For robust friendship, the organizational members must not turn away from tension and conflict among them. Rather, we must learn how to harmoniously work with one another in spite of our differences.

Furthermore, the healthful future of PANAAWTM depends on friendship that is intergenerational. Repeatedly telling the institutional memories of the organization may help us build up intergenerational and stronger friendships beyond our intimate circle of friends. At the same time, we must be aware that institutional memories are selective and thus are not delivering plain facts. Those who deliver institutional memories need to recognize the critiques of new voices from younger generations.

Multiplicity, Fluidity, and Engaged Diversity

Rita Nakashima Brock argues that a hermeneutics of wisdom exercised by Asian American women is finding ways to be "ethical agents of our own survival and taking responsibility for the complex voices we carry within us."[14] So empowerment comes with taking responsibility for our lives and understanding our need for others. The "complex voices" we carry require us to maintain multiple perspectives on our self-understanding, survival skills, and theological resources, so that practical wisdom enables us to contemplate life's deep ambiguities and to make responsible decisions for us and others related to us.

Although complex voices and multiple perspectives are distinctive characteristics of many politically oppositional organizations, certain voices can be heard more loudly than others. In the PANAAWTM context, for example, Koreans outnumber any other ethnic group and Protestants' voices are louder than Catholics. If one group outnumbers others, it may become difficult to listen to other groups' experiences, and the dominant group can be tempted to represent the entirety of the organization. An organization like PANAAWTM may try to recruit more underrepresented Asian women in the theological field. In order to maintain multiple perspectives by challenging hierarchical diversity in patriarchal society, however, it seems wiser to critically examine ethnic privilege in the theological field or ethnic churches' lack of social responsibility. Furthermore, critical self-reflection can be used to examine our own class and intellectual privilege so that we can continue to analyze the complex layers of privilege and oppression in our ever-changing society.

These days many religious organizations are also social justice organizations. PANAAWTM is one of them, including academic theologians alongside ministers and activists. Those who are teaching seminarians seemed content with PANAAWTM for dealing with the intersection between academically rigorous theological discourse and practical church ministry for social justice. Yet, as Pak correctly points out, PANAAWTM members often "default" to the narrow standards of success prevalent in academia. Theology as academic discourse needs the church and activism grounded in community and vice versa. A theology detached from real human context becomes void, and the church without critical theological reflection loses its spiritual strength. Wisdom that deals with life's deep ambiguities comes from lively engagement between academic theologians and minister/activists as well as harmonious leadership exercised by both groups. An organization like PANAAWTM raises challenging questions: How can we continue to promote harmonious leadership of social activism and scholarship (or a model of praxis leadership)? How can we practically challenge the ideas of "success" in the theological field? How can we respect each other's vocations and differences without condescension?

CONCLUSION

My exercise of postcolonial imagination with PANAAWTM proposed four phases of wisdom-leadership: (1) a process unfolded through relationships and interpersonal dynamics, which often result in self and communal transformation; (2) an ability to see challenges and problems with increased awareness and complexity; (3) a feminist praxis of taking power and making power; and (4) willingness to allow multiplicity, complexity, and fluidity within the organization. As PANAAWTM embarks on a new journey toward the next thirty years, its wisdom-leadership will suggest different practices in response to life's deep ambiguities.

Liturgical Interlude 2

"Ricing Community"[1]: Liturgy of Gathering

Opening Ritual for the Celebration of PANAAWTM's Thirtieth Anniversary

BOYUNG LEE

INTRODUCTION TO THE LITURGY

This liturgy, designed to celebrate the thirtieth anniversary of PANAAWTM (Pacific, Asian, and North American Asian Women in Theology and Ministry), is based on several key characteristics of Asian and Asian North American women's ways of knowing: communal, holistic, ontological, and political. As one of the core elements of Asian and Asian North American feminism is challenging both Western individualism and many Asian communal values based on patriarchy and hierarchy, it is important for Asian and Asian North American women to celebrate and affirm communal cultural values that are life giving for them. Moreover, Asian and Asian North American women's theological resources include lived experiences and narratives of women of Asian heritage beyond written works, and thus this ritual reflects liturgical "ingredients" from Asian women's lives to affirm who they are and to encourage them to be makers of a just world.

Those of you who are not descendants of Asian heritage but interested in adopting this liturgy, I encourage you to critically reflect on your community's shared values and identity first. Please feel free to adopt the format of this liturgy, but the contents may have to be filled with your community's evoked life stories.

LITURGY

Bringing Community Together

While "Kekai no Tomo" (Here, O God, Your Daughters Gather)[2] is played by the pianist, different participants bring various ingredients of the service—rice flour, salt, sugar bowl, water pitcher, nuts, raisins, and so on to the center table.

Welcome
Liturgist A

Come,
Be Fed and Nurtured,
Rest and be Renewed,
Be Challenged and Confronted
Construct and Reconstruct

Song Invocation

"Here, O God, Your Daughters Gather" (v. 1)[3]

Prayer
Liturgist

Look upon us gently our
  God,
  Light,
  Divine,
Remind us that in the evening you cradle the world.
And in the morning you are our comforter.

Thank you for this community of PANAAWTM that has been a home for
  many of us.
As we have left this home rejuvenated, and return to be embraced by its love
over the last thirty years, we are reminded that
  You are here when we go away,
  And you are waiting when we return.
  You are the presence around whom our tears can run unguarded
  And the place from which our hope arises.

Our Light, but sometimes we feel fragile.
Our language is composed of heartache or signs because we are speechless
  sometimes.
Our vision can be blurred because we do not know what the future may bring.
So in your love, O Divine, wait here with us again this time.
Be our very present help in waiting.

Calm our minds and touch our hearts.
Transform us and remind us that we are surrounded by your divine presence
and one another.

May we be mindful of your call upon each of us to be
Committed partners.

Amen

Litany of Coming Together[4]

Liturgist A invites by sharing her journey with PANAAWTM.

"What PANAAWTM has been for you . . ."

To me PANAAWTM has been an intellectual and spiritual home where I did
not have to explain who I am, what I am, and why I do what I do.

It has been a home that has kept me on track, at times confronting and
challenging me so that I do Asian feminist theology with honesty and integrity, other times putting balms on my soul wounded by white institutional
churches and academy.

> For many PANAAWTM has been a home that fed us intellectually and
> spiritually for the last thirty years.

> How is PANAAWTM feeding you?

> Silent reflection . . .

> Let us join together in the Litany of Coming Together.

Liturgist B says the following:
Making a rice cake . . .
Take five pounds of rice flour says the recipe . . .
We thank you, God, for rice flour (*lifting up the rice flour bag and pouring it into
the large mixing bowl on the table*):
This flour made from rice,
grown in the mystery of the earth,
ripened in the warmth of the sun;
ripened, then cut down at the harvest by the farmer's skill,
ground by the miller,
sold by the shop assistant,
placed in the bowl . . .
we thank you, God, for rice flour.

ALL: We thank you, God, for PANAAWTM community that is like rice flour for us, providing spiritual and intellectual staple food for our long journey!

Participants from New England, New York, and New Jersey, come forward.

Self Introduction: Participants from New England, New York, and New Jersey come forward and share:
 Your name and your current vocation and an ingredient you bring to PANAAWTM.

Communal Song Response: "Here, O God, Your Daughters Gather" (v. 2)

Litany of Coming Together

Liturgist A:
We thank you, God, for salt (*sprinkle salt on rice flour in the bowl*):
Jesus told us we were to be salt of the earth,
and we must never lose our flavor.
The salt, which adds flavor to our food,
is also antiseptic to our wounds,
reminding us of the challenge to our life
and the healing power of Jesus . . .
We thank you, God, for salt.

ALL: We thank you, God, for PANAAWTM that is like salt for us, flavoring our intellectual and spiritual life, healing our wounds . . .

Participants from California, Arizona, and other western states come forward.

Self Introduction: Participants from California, Arizona, and other western states come forward and share:
 Your Name and your current vocation and an ingredient you bring to PANAAWTM.

Communal Song Response: "Here, O God, Your Daughters Gather" (v. 3)

Litany of Coming Together

Liturgist B:
We thank you, God, for sugar (*sprinkle sugar on the bowl*):

that small amount of crystals that enables sweet flavor of rice to rise,
that creates tenderness in coarse rice flour and water mixture,
that enables rice cake soft and moist,
that reminds us of the fact that even small works we have done can enable our
*shalom, héping, pyeonghwa, heiwa, kapayapaan, shanti, perdamaian, khwām ŝngb
ŝukh, hòa bình*
for all people to be the sweetener for the troubled world . . .
we thank you, God, for sugar.

ALL: We thank you, God, for PANAAWTM. Like the tiny amount of sugar in rice cake, the vision of a small group of women gathering thirty years ago enabled the community to rise, be abundant, tasty, and bold!

Atlanta, Texas, Tennessee, North Carolina and other southern states come forward.

Self Introduction: Participants from Atlanta, Texas, Tennessee, North Carolina, and other southern states come forward and share
Your Name and your current vocation and an ingredient you bring to PANAAWTM.
Liturgist B add nuts to the bowl.

Communal Song Response: "Here, O God, Your Daughters Gather" (v. 4)

Litany of Coming Together

Liturgist A:
We thank you, God, for water (*pouring water into the bowl*):
water, without which none of us could live,
water, which forms the other elements of our bread into dough,
which, having risen, and been formed and drawn into shape by human hands,
    is baked to give us the stuff of life;
water, which cleanses and renews us,
refreshes and revives us,
the water of baptism, which commits us to our faith . . .
we thank you, God, for water . . .

ALL: We thank you, God, for PANAAWTM being fresh water for women in the wilderness of white institutions, for sending us back to the world with renewed will for life for all!

Participants from Canada and other countries come forward.

Self Introduction: Participants from Canada and other countries come forward and share:

Your Name and your current vocation and an ingredient you bring to PANAAWTM.

Liturgist adds raisins to the bowl.

Communal Song Response: "Here, O God, Your Daughters Gather" (v. 1)

Litany of Coming Together

Liturgist B:

We thank you, God, for rice cake we will bake together (*lifting up the mixing bowl*):

Rice, the basis of the food we eat.

"Rice is heaven."[5]

Rice cake for our spiritual feast,

Rice cake for needed energy in the middle of a long and hard day,

and rice cake that is broken and shared in communion with one another,

in remembrance of many dear to our hearts far and near . . .

We thank you, God, for rice cake.*

Participants from Chicago and Midwest come forward.

Self Introduction: Participants from Chicago and Midwest come forward and share:

Your Name and your current vocation and an ingredient you bring to PANAAWTM.

Communal Song Response: "Here, O God, Your Daughters Gather" (2–4)

Closing Prayer

Liturgists: Oh God who looked across the expanse of the universe and called it good, thank you for your grace in past thirty years, this moment and many more years to come for PANAAWTM.

Participants from New England, New York, and New Jersey:

As we start another thirty years with all who love and believe in the mission of PANAAWTM who figuratively and physically crossed streets, rivers,

---

* The rice cake baked with these ingredients will be brought in at the closing worship service for communion.

mountains, and oceans to be here, Holy One, we lift them and us up to you. Be with us every moment, and help us to hear each other to learn and grow together.

Participants from California, Arizona, and other western states:
As we remember journeys that we made together, we are also reminded that our spiritual landscape has mountains and valleys too. Rainbows and oceans depth. Deserts of hot and cold, and now and again there are barren emotional terrains with lack of feeling or fear, sometimes. In each place, thank you for your presence. Thank you for your promise to be with us through thick and thin, now and evermore. Thank you for your keen eyesight and vision. Know that we revel in your invitation to be reborn each day.

Participants from Georgia, Texas, Tennessee, North Carolina, and other southern states:
As we continue our journey as a community, O God, give us patience to slow the pace; to rest and relax, and to engage one another in new ideas and pursuits. Help us to see that of you in one another and, instead of imagining ourselves to be in it alone, to instead see in one another, and in your life-giving presence, hope and rejuvenation for our individual lives, PANAAWTM, and the world.

Participants from Canada and other countries:
O Holy One, where there is brokenness in our hearts, spirits, relationships, families, neighborhoods, and nations, take those pieces and keep them near your heart. Where there is hurt or hardship, be our strength. Give us assurance that in all things you are with us in this world and in the coming world that we are co-creating with you.

Participants from Chicago and Midwest:
As we make our rice cake together for our soulful journeys for the next thirty years, as Thich Nhat Hanh said, in this food, let us see clearly the presence of the universe supporting our existence. Give food to those who hunger, and hunger for justice to us who have food.

ALL: In our fellowship throughout the conference we also remember our spiritual and intellectual ancestors (particularly the vision and dreams of Letty Russell and our founding members and their visions for PANAAWTM), friends, partners, and loved ones who made our journey this far possible. Unite us with them wherever they are, creating a community around the table for fellowship.

We pray all these in your holy and many names.
Amen!

PART 3

Inciting Wisdom

11

Becoming Wisdom Woman and Strange Woman

*Asian and Asian American Women's Leadership
in Coping with Stereotypes*

MIN-AH CHO

> The Strange Woman is a *mise en abyme*: with her wise sister and her
> sometimes unholy God, she is a mirror of language itself. From her
> lips we hear the trickster's riddles. In her house of mirrors we see the
> infinite regression of boundaries written on priestly bodies, a regres-
> sion built into the canonical myth of identity.
> —Claudia V. Camp, *Wise, Strange, and Holy*[1]

I am a female Korean theologian who teaches at a Catholic women's college in Minnesota. While I truly enjoy working with my students, I experience challenges that are particular to Asian and Asian American women who
teach at a predominantly white institution. Stereotypes and biases based on
my ethnicity and culture follow me into the classroom and interfere with my
teaching and interactions with students. I often ponder how my Asian identity
shapes my teaching and students' learning and how I can transform the challenges into a teaching opportunity while navigating the conflicting needs of
empowering both the students and myself.

This chapter portrays my struggles and hopes in building leadership as I
teach young American women.[2] As a Korean woman faculty member, leadership development involves facing Asian stereotypes and enhancing my ability
to observe the multilayered power dynamics that surround me. My experience
illuminates how stereotypes create expected and unexpected obstacles *as well
as* opportunities for Asian American women in leading a faith community. For
the purposes of this chapter, I specifically share my examples and discussions
in the classroom context, as I consider my teaching to be my main leadership
role. Nonetheless, I hope to extend my discussion to a broader context, since

the challenges I experience in the classroom can be shared with many Asian American women leaders in theology and ministry.

The wisdom leadership I propose highlights the ability to create a reflective community in which the leaders and their members share and discern their often contradictory and conflicting experiences. In order to describe such a wisdom leadership, I draw inspiration from the wisdom literatures of the Hebrew Bible, particularly from the paradoxical relationship between "Wisdom" and "Strangeness" in the book of Proverbs. The social context revealed in the labeling of Wisdom and Strangeness is instrumental in describing the ways stereotypes affect Asian American women's leadership and also in discerning how to cope and transform them into opportunities. Through this paradoxical reading, I invite Asian American women leaders to speak through and with myriad images perceived both by themselves and by others, to observe their historical and social complexity through those images, and to disclose the discrepancy among those images. This chapter highlights the multiplicity of stereotypes. As if seeing oneself through *mise en abyme*, the stereotypes could lead Asian American women to regress into perceptions of themselves imposed by others.[3] Yet, once we are able to identify the discrepancy among those images, we can reveal the frame of the mirror, in other words, the social structure that reinforces the stereotypes. We can further utilize the stereotypes as a counter-hegemonic tool through which we challenge the members of our community to reflect on their own location within the community and the larger society.

This chapter discusses how we can make the stereotypes useful for our leadership, if we cannot avoid them. The question I pose as I seek wisdom leadership is, therefore, not "What is wisdom?" as much as "What is wisdom in strangeness?" and "What is strangeness in wisdom?" Strategic use of the stereotypes will help us attend to contradiction and ambiguity woven into our community life and offer us clues for advancing our understanding of Christian leadership practice.

STICKY STEREOTYPES: ASIAN "WISDOM WOMAN" OR "STRANGE WOMAN"

The nine introductory chapters of the book of Proverbs in the Hebrew Bible present the personifications of wisdom and strangeness, each of whom are called "Wisdom Woman" (*hokmot*) and "Strange Woman" (*'ishshah zaraj/ ishshah nokriyyah*). The two are depicted as contesting opposites. The Wisdom Woman represents everything valuable, desirable, and profitable such as creation, love, life, truth, and social order. She is "correct" and "acceptable" to marry and love faithfully (4:6; 5:15–19; 7:4; 8:17). On the contrary, the Strange Woman represents everything harmful and detrimental—death, falsehood, social disruption, and folly.[4] She is a foreign woman of dangerous charm (7:10–20) to be avoided and shunned.[5]

Proverbs' descriptions of the Wisdom Woman and the Strange Woman parallel the contradictory stereotypes about Asian women that I must negotiate as I teach at a midwestern college in America. I can be seen either as a woman of wisdom—kind, spiritual, conforming, humble, submissive, nurturing and resourceful, particularly in "Asian" cultures and religions—or as a foreign woman—awkward, odd, clumsy, deficient, and even perilous.[6]

No matter how hard I try to debunk them, these stereotypes have routinely affected my teaching, my research, my self-assessment, and my interaction with others. When I first entered the U.S. job market six years ago, I was overwhelmed by the demand to prove my "Asianness." My appearance and Korean accent were not exactly the "Asianness" that the majority of interviewers were looking to hire. They expected me to have the traits of an Asian "Wisdom Woman," to be likable, acceptable, and useful for their department. I was supposed to be "attractively" different so that I could fit in their department's need for "diversity" without challenging the status quo. They sought to draw Asian "wisdom" from my research as well. Although my main research area was women's mysticism from Medieval Europe in dialogue with contemporary Christian spirituality for marginalized groups, interviewers were interested in knowing my capacity to teach "Asian spirituality" such as Buddhism, Taoism, and Confucianism. I learned from my colleagues that many institutions commonly adopt this "buy one, get one free" strategy when they hire scholars of color.[7] Meanwhile, the hiring status of Asian American women faculty in higher education still languishes.[8]

Such struggles continue to influence my teaching. Along with graduate courses and upper-level spirituality courses, I teach an introductory theology course called "Theological Questions." This course is designed for students who are new to the field of theology and for students who need to complete their theology requirement for graduation.[9] Typically, 70 percent of the students in a theological questions class are of European descent, and the rest are a mixture of African, Asian, Latina, and Native American students. Students enroll in this course with varied amounts of fear, dread, skepticism, and excitement. Many of them are often defensive about their theological views or lack thereof. As one can imagine, it is quite a challenge to teach such a diverse group of students.

Not surprisingly, along with my Asian appearance and my Korean accent, Asian stereotypes exert influence upon students' learning. Stereotypical assumptions based on my "otherness" are not always an obstacle to my teaching. Admittedly, the Asian "Wisdom Woman" stereotype helps me to have more positive interactions with a great number of students. They deem my teaching style to be approachable and my class to be refreshing and different. Many of these students have experienced hurtful and unpleasant encounters with the Western, imperialistic aspects of Christianity, so my "otherness" seems to be subversive enough to rebut their negative assumptions about Christian theology. For the students of color, in particular, I sense that I fit their need for a mentor or role model, one who understands their own "otherness," as there are a limited number of women of color faculty members on campus.

However, some students constantly seem to feel uncomfortable with my "otherness" and discount my credibility as a professor. They find it hard to get over the "Strange Woman" stereotype. Layered presumptions based on both overt and covert forms of racism and sexism interplay in the cases of these students' reactions to my teaching. Below are my reflections on some of the instances when these stereotypes hinder students' learning.

"You don't look like a theologian"

Theology as a discipline has historically been dominated by white male scholars. Therefore, some students find my view, even the readings I select for class, to be odd, insignificant, or irrelevant. Several students wrote their entire papers referring to themselves as "We Catholics," as if they did not consider my view to be part of Catholicism. More than a few students have asked me about the credibility of my textbook selections and whether they are approved by the Church, which is often synonymous with priests and male theologians. These students regard my Asian female "otherness" as deficient and in need of white male guidance.[10] My experience with these students resonate with the observation Juanita Johnson-Bailey and Ronald M. Cervero offer in their essay "Power Dynamics in Teaching and Learning Practices" that the abilities and knowledge of teachers of color are questioned more, in spite of their academic rank, gender, or personal teaching style.[11] Students consider Asian women to be marginal in the church and society and therefore see them as a blockade that confuses, dribbles, distorts, or even delegitimizes information.

"I feel more challenged when I take male professors' classes"

Internalized sexism is another challenge in the classroom.[12] Whether intentional or not, the cumulative effects of sexism are pervasive even at a women's college. They impact the way students feel about themselves, perform in class, process new information, negotiate their interaction with faculty members and peers, and make choices about their lives.[13] A surprising number of students show resistance toward feminist theological ideas and uphold the current church systems as "natural" and "merit based." They often ignore the church systems of privilege and oppression, and even express negative feelings about feminist theological ideas as they internalize the patriarchal beliefs of Christianity. For example, some Catholic students expressed strong discomfort when we discussed women's full participation in the Church. Students who felt that their own belief was under attack became angry and critical of my teaching and the course material. They often lapsed into silence or refused to participate in class discussions.[14] Sometimes internalized sexism manifests in their willingness to comply with male professors and, conversely, in their ambivalence toward female professors. I have seen the same students perform well in male professors' classes but do poorly in female professors' classes by turning in assignments late, skipping classes, or engaging less in class activities.

"I know that non-native English speakers don't like speaking with English native speakers"

Just like many other English second language speakers, Asian women theology professors whose native tongues are not English face extra challenges in teaching due to their accent. Once while teaching a class, I became distracted by a third-generation immigrant student who kept chatting and giggling with her peers. When I attempted to turn her attention to class, she resisted cooperating, saying, "Even if you're doing fine, I just personally feel uncomfortable talking with bilingual people. My grandmother has a strong accent. I saw her feeling very challenged when she had to have a conversation with English native speakers, even with me. Whenever I talk with a bilingual person with an accent, it reminds me of my grandmother."

Among the multiple issues this case reveals, internalized racism especially in regard with one's language is noteworthy.[15] The psychic costs of internalized racism can lead to feelings of "self-doubt, disgust, and disrespect for one's race and/or oneself."[16] The student inculcated the racist comments toward her grandmother as if she herself was mistreated, and she projected her fears and anxiety onto me in class. In their research on the perceptions and attitudes of students toward non-native English-speaking professors, scholars Donald L. Rubin and Kim Smith noted that students accept or reject the messages of non-native speakers based on their bias against the speakers' group membership rather than on equitable measures like speakers' competence or academic background.[17] Language can, therefore, be a constant source of struggle and frustration for non-native English-speaking Asian teachers, especially when students consider them to be culturally flawed and incompetent.

COPING WITH STEREOTYPES AND DEVELOPING LEADERSHIP

Stereotypes also present challenges in my attempt to adapt and develop an appropriate leadership style in class. For instance, the widely accepted woman leadership model—best exemplified by Sheryl Sandberg's leadership book *Lean In: Women, Work, and Will to Lead*—does not work in my case for many reasons. Sandberg's model includes qualities like independence, assertiveness, self-confidence, and instrumental competence, based on the reasoning that "women are hindered by barriers that exist within themselves," such as a lack of confidence, misplaced insecurity, passivity and an unwillingness to own their ambition.[18]

While this model, which emerged from so called "corporate feminism," seems useful to challenge male-dominant positional leadership norms, it relies heavily on a high-level definition of agency and individual competency to describe leadership and, accordingly, overlooks systematic discrimination that limits underprivileged women from developing leadership in the first place.[19] In their book *Through the Labyrinth*, Alice H. Eagly and Linda Carli discuss how this leadership model excludes women who have never experienced the privilege of developing a strong agency due to their culture, particularly women from poor and marginalized groups.[20] What makes leadership stronger for any given woman high on the institutional ladder might make life harder for women struggling near the bottom rungs. By ignoring the systematic flaws and cultural barriers that keep women of color from empowering themselves, this model inadvertently perpetuates and benefits from sexist and racist ideologies.[21]

My experience suggests additional challenges for Asian women attempting to apply this agency-based model in the classroom. I have noticed that when professors are from marginalized or underprivileged groups, students often cannot separate the professor's status and position from the larger societal and political context, thus taking her authority as a threat to their culture.[22] This particularly happens when I introduce students to new and uncomfortable ways of thinking.[23] They see me as a "Strange Woman" who has no respect for their beliefs or threatens their culture with "yellow peril."[24] As such, students often employ self-defense mechanisms to protect their beliefs or simply disregard my teaching as a random opinion from a foreign culture.

An even more painful reality, I have learned, is just how challenging it is for women faculty of color to apply a leadership model encouraged by liberatory feminist pedagogy.[25] In their essay "Women of Color in the Academy: Where's Our Authority?" Juanita Johnson-Bailey and Ming-Yeh Lee argue that while liberatory feminist pedagogy has powerfully transformed teaching and learning by empowering students and encouraging nonauthoritative and collaborative styles, "the combination of feminist pedagogy and women of color can make for a dangerous liaison."[26] I emphatically resonate with their arguments in that, for Asian American women professors, liberatory feminist pedagogical approaches could have an adverse effect, because the power dynamic they experience in class is often very different from that of white women professors.

For example, in my first semester of teaching, I was committed to practicing the approaches suggested by liberatory feminist pedagogy. Adopting bell hooks's "engaged pedagogy," I sought to dismantle the hierarchy between teacher and students to help create a collaborative learning environment where my students and myself share the authority and mutually grow.[27] However, because of the Asian "Wisdom Woman" stereotypes, this approach often had an inimical consequence. In a classroom where the traditional hierarchy between teacher and students has always existed, I realized that students interpret the Asian "Wisdom Woman" teacher's endeavor to create a democratic teaching environment as an invitation to take over her authority.[28] When the nonauthoritative and collaborative leadership model is adopted by an Asian American women leader, I found that it magnifies the Asian "Wisdom Woman" stereotypes rather than challenging the teacher-student hierarchy. Asian American women theology educators, therefore, are forced to battle with stereotypes that aggregate what bell hooks and other liberatory feminist educators already describe as "dilemmas of the feminist classroom."[29]

These peculiar challenges of applying both the agency-based women leadership model and liberatory feminist pedagogy are informed by my marginality as an Asian woman in a predominantly white institution. Likewise, feminist pedagogy ought to be more accountable to the unique forms of racial discrimination experienced by Asian American women in teaching and leadership. As education and leadership scholar Penny A. Pasque argues, it is critical for liberatory feminist pedagogy to recognize historically and culturally distinctive feminist perspectives, focusing on a "specific race, geographic region, and/or shared language."[30]

Nevertheless, Asian American women's struggle with liberatory feminist pedagogy does not necessarily mean that we have to abandon it. Despite the challenges—or more precisely because of the challenges—I embrace liberatory feminist pedagogy as my practice since I still view it as the best way of shaping an inclusive and egalitarian classroom environment. I also believe it is important for Asian American women, particularly those in theology and ministry, to locate ourselves within the discourse of conventional liberatory feminist pedagogy.

Along with fellow women leaders of color, the presence of Asian American women in leadership challenges prevalent racial, sexual, and class dominance and reveals deep divisions in what different women would encounter when they adopt a leadership role. The investigation of the experience of Asian American women leaders will lead to new knowledge, or as Kathleen Weiler describes, a knowledge that both "acknowledges differences and points to the need for an integrated analysis and practice based upon the fact that the major systems of oppression are interlocking."[31] As such, Asian American women leadership can further enrich the discussion of liberatory feminist pedagogy and help fellow women leaders of color resist the tendency of the church to homogenize, control, and censor "otherness."

How then can we turn our experiences into new knowledge and make both systems of education and the church more inclusive while still navigating contradictions? I suggest that Asian stereotypes can be a resource of knowledge to indicate the social, cultural, and historical location of Asian American women leaders as well as a useful tool to invite the members of our community into a process of consciousness-raising. By introducing a postcolonial reading of Proverbs, the following section will explore this possibility.

MISE EN ABYME: A POSTCOLONIAL READING OF WISDOM WOMAN AND STRANGE WOMAN

The need to position ourselves in relation to our own historical and cultural contexts offers an important opportunity for carefully examining the stereotypes of Asian women. Stereotyping commands the colonial master's attention of their subjects and reinforces their views as factual and consistent with the entire population. As the members of our community adopt Asian women stereotypes, they subconsciously internalize the colonial master's gaze of Asian women and project it upon us through their knowledge, beliefs, and expectations.

Stereotypes, however, generate a multitude of possibilities. While they interfere with the ability of Asian American women leaders to build healthy relationships within their own community, they could also provide us with an opportunity to invite our members into an awareness-raising process about racism and sexism. Stereotypes typically make the cognitive structures of the colonizer visible, thus revealing the complexity of social, cultural, and historical locations where Asian American women leaders intersect with their members.

In this respect, I find the descriptions of the Wisdom Woman and the Strange Woman in Proverbs 1–9 particularly conducive because they showcase a biblical way to observe a reality filled with biases and contradictions beyond the frame of binary thinking. Many feminist biblical scholars have suggested that the pair of Wisdom Woman and Strange Woman is the "projection of womanhood invented by men" in the postexilic Judah.[32] While the feminist critique against the dichotomy helps us to see the *kyriarchal* force in stereotyping women into the dominant social frame,[33] a postcolonial reading of Proverbs, particularly offered by Hebrew Bible scholar Gale A. Yee, advises us to cope with the dichotomous stereotypes by looking at the broader context.

In her book *Poor Banished Children of Eve*, Yee locates the biblical text of Wisdom Woman and Strange Woman into the context of Asian American women by illuminating what it means for the Israelites to be "wise" or "strange."[34] Yee notes that Persian imperialistic politics, the political setting of this literature, sought to create "a highly stratified society" in which the small community of compliant elites profited. Thus, if the Israelites returning from the exile were to secure land and a means of production, they were unlikely to marry "foreign" or "strange" women but rather women of "the native population."

Contrary to traditional interpretations, Yee's analysis illustrates how the Strange Woman was not necessarily recognized as evil. Instead, the Strange Woman's value or quality did not fit within the standards of the community. She was simply one who was "not our kind," or "any woman who transgresses the values and socioeconomic norms defined by the shifting standards of the society."[35] Supporting Yee's reading of Proverbs, Claudia V. Camp also suggests that the dichotomy of Wisdom Woman and Strange Woman does not permeate ethical values but rather reveals the use of a "powerful rhetoric of Othering" during the postexilic period. The social and cultural contexts of the period necessitated the need of defining "others" and controlling "us."[36]

Both Yee's and Camp's readings of Proverbs 1–9 describe the social and cultural nuances in the post-exilic Israel and explain how the social elite created the binary oppositions of "us" and "them," thus naming native women as "Wisdom Woman" and foreign women as "Strange Woman." Furthermore, their readings warn us of the tendency to separate the Wisdom Woman and the Strange Woman, which reinforces the dualistic frame of the positive and the negative as constructed by the dominant group.

It is noteworthy that in Proverbs, the Strange Woman exists within the boundaries of society despite her foreignness. Hence, the seemingly negative

Strange Woman performs a paradoxically positive role by representing how the Israelites try to integrate disorder, deviance, and inconsistency into their daily lives. Without an appreciation for the strange, a society is unable to recognize its own boundaries. As such, the Wisdom Woman and the Strange Woman mirror each other as images reproduced by *mise en abyme*. They both infinitely regress into mirrors imposed by the norms of society.

Once we look at the broader context of the book, the "wisdom" manifested in Proverbs is more than a human characteristic to cultivate. It is, rather, the mysterious ability to see opportunity in contradictions and ambiguities. To the mind of the wisdom authors, life is not a simple set of truths to be followed flawlessly but "a continual encounter with conflicting truths, each making competing claims upon the seeker."[37] The wisdom literature recognizes and appreciates the conflicting realities and avoids fixed answers to human problems. Instead of avoiding the contradictions, wisdom literature invites us to discern the complexity of social contexts. It urges us to ask what "strangeness" the Wisdom Woman elicits from her compliant manner and what "wisdom" the Strange Woman alludes to through her spiteful riddles. And, eventually, it compels us to point toward the social contexts and surrounding ideologies that reproduce the infinite regression of the images of both women.

WISDOM LEADERSHIP: THE LEADERSHIP TO CREATE A REFLECTIVE COMMUNITY

The wisdom leadership I would like to suggest hinges on the insights we gain from a postcolonial reading of wisdom literature. If wisdom is not a certain virtue to bring out, but a capacity to think through and utilize the contradictions and ambiguity, I propose that wisdom leadership serves as a means to create a reflective community in which the leaders and their members are drawn into a collective inquiry that slowly unfolds layers of ambiguous, contradictory, and conflicting experiences among members. I define a reflective community in this context as a community that encourages both its leaders and members to share and examine the social meanings of their experiences within the community and beyond it. A reflective community is further capable of taking responsibility as a socially situated and interpersonally bonded community.[38]

Wisdom leadership, or the capacity to create a reflective community, grounds my hope in making the classroom a site for knowledge production where all voices are welcome, including my own. In developing this form of leadership, I call particular attention to the use of stereotypes. Stereotypes are dangerous in that they mischaracterize the other and assume a "totalized fixity of the image," as described by postcolonial theorist Homi K. Bhabha. In other words, the concern is not simply whether the stereotypes represent "negative" and "disadvantageous" or "positive" and "favorable" images of the other. It is rather the repeated reproduction of stereotypes that becomes essentialized and accepted as "natural," "preconditioned," and "historical."[39] A deliberate attempt to reveal the misrepresentation of the stereotypes and discrepancy among them would dismantle the fixity and help us point out a larger structure. Instead of being framed and regressed into these stereotypes, Asian American women leaders and their communities can consciously turn them into a resource of knowledge that shifts realities and the gazes of others.

For example, I first shape the classroom as a site of sharing stories in order to draw on the lived experiences of students. I often begin by asking students what they know about Koreans and Korean Americans. Then I tell students my experiences of being a Korean woman, foreigner, lay feminist theologian of the Catholic Church, and English as a second-language speaker. This process surprises students by their lack of knowledge or misconceptions about Koreans and helps me teach about the connection between stereotypes and their social and historical apparatus.

As I do this, I also invite students to share their contradictory experiences through various pedagogical approaches such as performing a skit or creating a body sculpture. The college classroom intersects with a number of issues that students often struggle with including economic status, culture, language, sexual orientations, personalities, abilities, marital status, explicit and implicit forms of racism and sexism, and various stereotypes. I ask them to discuss questions such as, "When was the very first moment you felt you were 'different' from others, and what did you feel?"[40] "Do you think that you fit in the society's and Church's representations of a 'normative' human being? If not, why?" "As you listen to the struggles of your professor and peers, what are the shared struggles and overarching issues?" These questions usually sensitize students and challenge their assumptions, enabling them to recognize contradictory views between themselves and me, among themselves, in their church community, and finally in larger society. Through these questions, students reflect upon their discomfort and examine what is considered to be normative and familiar. This process leads them to a deeper level of critical consciousness that often enables them to "have a productive, rather than a defensive dialogue" with other students about their privileges and vulnerability.[41]

This strategic use of stereotypes discloses my marginality as an Asian woman as well as invites students to reflect on their own marginality and to further resist the forces that displace and depoliticize them. In other words, the stereotypes of Asian American women in theology and ministry can make the permeating force of *kyriarchy* in society and the church visible and tangible. Furthermore, it connects theology and ministry with social issues in the larger world. Eventually such a commitment will challenge students to view individual problems and social issues together, equipping them to understand the value and necessity of collective action for the transformation of the church and society.[42] That is what I envision for a reflective community built and led by wisdom leadership.

The wisdom leadership of Asian American women will encounter multiple forms of contradictions. The use of stereotypes will not necessarily offer a liberating experience at all times. It could be both an instrument and a hindrance, both a teachable moment and a stumbling block. It could even perpetuate the stereotypes, marginalization, and oppression of women of color in theology and ministry. Yet I believe we should worry less about the challenges or risks of creating opportunities and worry more about the consequences that would result when we stop reflecting on the wrongs of the church and society, avoid taking risks, escape from challenges, disguise our vulnerabilities, and settle for the status quo. The challenges may hinder us, but we can also utilize them as an indicator of the ideologies of "correctness" and "normativity" imposed on us by the church and larger society.

As I close this chapter, I stand in front of the mirror and look at myself. I see the Wisdom Woman. I see the Strange Woman. Looking closely, I see neither of them. I see a woman who strives to see herself among these varying images. I see a woman who ponders how her Asian identity brings her closer to people, instead of shunning her away. I also see a woman who eagerly wants to connect with others through a community of learning, reflecting, and growing together. The Wisdom Woman and the Strange Woman will never disappear from her. They will always interfere in her journey. However, they will point her toward paths—paths from the past, paths that intersect with others, paths that need to be paved. There, she will build and perform her wisdom leadership with both her Wise sisters and her Strange sisters.

12

One-Pot Menu

Korean American Women's Wisdom Leadership

HANNAH KA

During my six-year-old daughter's spring break from school in 2014, she accompanied me to a teachers' meeting at a church. Not too long after we arrived, our administrative director convened the meeting. Soon, taking turns, the volunteer teachers began to debrief, discuss, and plan their areas of responsibility. While they were going over the past semester and planning for the next one, my six-year-old, who was playing by herself, nudged me: "Mom, aren't you the leader of this group?" Although taken aback by this direct yet intuitive question, I could not help but smile, understanding where she was coming from. Her question reflects a six-year-old's perception of an organization's structure and her transient observation of her mom's leadership role. For much of her life, her experience of an organizational structure has been that of a classroom setting where there is a teacher (leader) above students. She has also seen her mom preach in worship, teach classes, and lead seminars and workshops, a few of the many aspects of my leadership practice. She must have assumed that her mom was going to lead this meeting as well.

So I whispered back to her quietly, "Yes, I am their pastor and spiritual leader. The one who is leading this meeting is an administrative director. That lady over there is in charge of AV. The teacher next to her is a praise leader. And the next person is a leader in charge of teachers' training. And we switch roles when we need to." A moment later, she responded to me, "Oh, I get it. So, everyone is a leader here. I thought there could be only one leader for each group."[1]

That's where our discussion about leadership began. From this personal conversation sprang my theological reflection on Korean American women's perceptions and practice of leadership within faith communities.

This leadership practice—"everyone is a leader"—has emerged out of this group of women over the past few years. It's a circular form of leadership that is shared in a nonhierarchical, horizontal way. It is particularly worth noting that these women fostered such a change even within the context of a Korean American immigrant church, where a hierarchical patriarchy is prevalent in every aspect of the faith community. This chapter elucidates how these women were able to affect such a change in their leadership paradigm. I will introduce the context of this leadership formation, followed by strategies and skills employed by these women. And lastly, I will offer the metaphor of "one-dish menu" for wise leadership.

CHECKING OUT THE SOIL: GROUNDING THE CONTEXT

In 2011, a mid-sized Korean American immigrant church launched an outreach program for an age cohort of thirty-to-forty-year-olds, after discovering that this demographic was missing from active participation. This outreach program invited families with infants and toddlers to weekday worship and free classes. The leadership of the program was comprised of one male cleric and a few core women leaders who had special training in preschool education, children's psychology, and spiritual formation. To implement the program, laywomen were recruited to participate.

Although highly educated with college degrees in various disciplines, the recruited volunteers, who were all first-generation Korean American immigrant women, were unable to channel their education outside of the Korean American immigrant context. Because of their spouses' incomes, however, most of them were financially secure. Yet, despite their financial stability, the intellectual and political agency of these immigrant women did not correspond to their economic reality. Within their families, they were not financial contributors, but many of them nurtured and supported their households emotionally and spiritually. As reflected in the church database system, some of them were indicated as "the spiritual head of a household." Although they had some things in common—gifts in ministry and availability during weekdays—they were indeed very diverse with complex identities. Regardless of their differences, however, each woman supported this outreach ministry with guidance and direction from the core leaders.

Shortly after the first year, the male cleric was reassigned to another pastoral role, leaving the group without a pastor. Although they had become more experienced in this specialized outreach program by then, they still felt uncomfortable about leading it by themselves. In January 2013, some of the women approached me, then a stay-home mom with theological education, to see if I would join their outreach ministry in the role of their pastor. They discussed with me the importance of having a theologically trained pastor. They wanted the pastor to preach, teach, and mentor teachers theologically and spiritually, to guide them in their administrative decisions, and to legitimize their gatherings with a pastoral authority and presence.

Through these conversations, I learned that these laywomen, although highly gifted in various aspects of ministry, did not see themselves as leaders of the church. They were more inclined to passively receive guidance from male clergy and other leaders. When nominated for leadership roles, most of them expressed uneasiness and hesitancy and frequently declined leadership positions, not only because of their own lack of confidence but equally because of the established cultural expectations of women in the church. They often sought approval from others whose position they felt was superior to their own. Their perception and practice of leadership was a clergy-centered, top-down leadership model. I felt more uncomfortable after hearing about these women's practice of leadership and their expectation of a pastoral leader. Having been raised in and accustomed to the clergy-centered (mostly male) and hierarchical leadership structure and practice within Korean and Korean American churches, I remembered how burdensome it was when I felt positioned at the bottom of that pyramid. Yet I felt equally uneasy about having others positioning themselves at the bottom of a top-down leadership pyramid and looking up to me as their leader. The more I heard their stories, however, the more closely I could identify with them in many ways; my own uneasiness and hesitancy along with my tendency to seek approval from other leaders did not deviate from theirs. So I reluctantly agreed to join them on a short-term basis.

IDENTIFYING INGREDIENTS
AND NUTRITION FACTS

In Eric Carle's children's storybook *The Mixed-Up Chameleon* the protagonist is a chameleon whose life seemed very tedious.[2] When the chameleon saw a zoo full of beautiful animals, it wished to be like other animals—to be big, white, handsome, smart, strong, and funny, to be one who could swim well, run fast, and see from afar. Each wish came true, but the chameleon was still unhappy with itself. After a while, this chameleon had become such a mixture of other animals it could not catch a fly when it was hungry. In being like others, the chameleon lost one of its most essential gifts—the ability to feed itself. So the chameleon wisely wished to be reverted back to itself. And as a chameleon, it was able to catch a fly.

"Catching the fly" requires finding and affirming one's own identity. Embracing one's own identity and gifts is not only a matter of great import but necessary to survive and thrive. Juxtaposing this story with 1 Corinthians 12, I underlined the importance of having various gifts when offering the devotion on my first day with this group. The church, as one body of Christ, cannot function without other parts that constitute the whole. Each plays an important role with her strengths and weaknesses within the faith community simply by being a part of it. Therefore, everyone stands as an equally important part of the whole. Closing this devotion, I highlighted how differently gifted everyone is and why each one should embrace her own identity and unique contributing gift. Then I encouraged everyone to play their own roles as equally important parts of the church, leading the rest with their own gifts while respecting others with different gifts. I, too, offered to bring my gift of theological insight to the group.

Two years after that first day, as a part of this anthology project, I asked about ten volunteers to share their practice and understanding of wisdom and leadership in our Korean American church context. They identified cultural practices, values, and liabilities that continued to challenge their leadership. Patriarchal cultural expectations of women in the Korean American church implicitly and indirectly diminish women's leadership roles, limiting them to women-only, or women-specific contexts, such as women's ministry, children's education, caring ministry, and hospitality. The outreach ministry was not an acceptable exception. This cultural practice often results in further diminishment of women leaders' confidence, formal leadership training, and being a leading presence in the church. One core leader stated that the "saving face" culture of Asian Americans can cause disparity between the public and the private self, severely limiting women's lives in the public spheres. These cultural practices and liabilities often trigger uneasiness in women when asked to accept leadership positions in the larger church context.

An example of this dynamic is that when this outreach ministry began to bear fruit, the leaders of the church began to pay attention. They recognized that these women in leadership resulted in the growth of the church. And more importantly, they recognized the personal and communal transformation of these women as leaders. Nevertheless, some male leaders continued to disparage their contribution and insist that it was meaningful only in women-only contexts. Given the cultural atmosphere of this church, there was no immediate and direct way to address this. Instead, these women began to witness how their small group provided leadership for the church.

Despite these cultural obstacles, these women bravely shared their understandings of wisdom and leadership. How did these women understand wisdom and leadership? Wisdom and knowledge are different. Knowledge involves acquiring information objectively through intellectual learning. Therefore, knowledge can be attained through (formal) education and can be articulated in words. The attainment of knowledge often results in exercising intellectual, economic, and political power over others in a hierarchical fashion. In contrast, the wisdom these women acquired is from their foremothers. Wisdom is engrained in their hearts and embodied through their life experiences. Wisdom leads them to a deeper understanding of themselves and of others, allowing them to embrace others within complex relationships beyond the restrictions of a hierarchy.

For these women, leadership is closely associated with wisdom. Wisdom and leadership, acquired from family members and friends, are first and foremost grounded in their life experiences and are therefore communally practiced. Wisdom and leadership are intertwined as each inspires and refines the other, while remaining grounded in culture and tradition. Thus, genuine wisdom is often associated with sound leadership, and vice versa. The women gathered had struggled to articulate the meaning of wisdom and leadership because, for them, knowledge resides in the mind and can be spoken, but wisdom and leadership reside in the heart and are expressed in daily interactions with others. They were able, however, to identify common crucial characteristics of wise leaders of the church. Wise leaders are able to (1) recognize, embrace, and organize others' diverse gifts and (2) respect all members equally. From reflecting on this gathering, here is my attempt to encapsulate what I think women's practice of wisdom leadership looks like in a Korean American context.

While it would be too simple to tie any element to any specific tradition, I have identified influences of a few cultures and traditions—Confucian, Taoist, and Christian—interwoven in the life experiences of these women that ground their practice of wisdom and leadership. In the early church in Corinth, the community struggled with varying gifts and priorities among those gifts (1 Cor. 12). After discerning "greater" and "lesser" gifts in 1 Corinthians 12:28, Paul urges the church to seek "greater" gifts regardless of their social status.[3] In doing so, he unintentionally endorses a new hierarchical order even as he dismantles the previous rigid social structure prevalent in the early Christian community. A new hierarchy remains, because an emphasis is placed on the gifts (roles) of a person. From the beginning of their outreach ministry, this was what the women inherited from Christian tradition, and for that reason they automatically placed their pastoral leader and administrative director above others in a hierarchical order. Recognition of the diverse gifts within each other was an important aspect of their community formation. It enhanced their confidence in the roles they played. Yet it was not the whole of their community-building process.

The second crucial characteristic of leadership is respecting all members equally. In their further elaboration of this leadership quality, the women articulated that leaders must be able to acknowledge everyone's dignity and respect all members equally. A wise leader must regard people's presence as the most valuable gift to the community, regardless of other gifts each brings. If one is not present, one's gift cannot be utilized. These characteristics of wise leadership have been concretely conveyed in the respectful interactions the women have with the infants, toddlers, and adults whose presence continues to sustain this outreach ministry. Theologically, I draw on the Christian concept of human beings being created in the image of God and therefore called to embody God's all-embracing love for the least of the least; however, the women's understanding of personhood and community draws from a different well.

Beyond the likeness of God and beyond playing an important role for the body of Christ, these Korean American women's understanding of personhood is in their genuine appreciation of others' presence in the communal life. The root of this can be traced to the long-lasting Confucian tradition within Korean and Korean American cultures. Despite the criticism that Confucian and neo-Confucian tradition has been the backbone of patriarchal hierarchy in Korea, Confucius' understanding of humanity, as opposed to the polarized notions of individual vis-à-vis society, provides the underlying support for these women's respect for everyone's presence within the community. In a didactic conversation with his disciple, in the Analects, Confucius elaborates his notion of humanity with a metaphor of "a sacrificial vessel of jade" used for holding grains in a holy ceremony. In this, the sacredness of "a sacrificial vessel" lies neither in its material, aesthetic, or functional value of the vessel nor in the edible value of the grains placed in each vessel. Rather, the sacredness is conferred by its participation in holy ceremony.[4] Likewise, the significance of a person lies not in her functional contribution, but in her respectful participation in the communal life, rendering whatever roles she plays secondary to her presence within the community.

The women's acknowledgment of equal dignity of all and their subsequent appreciation of everyone's presence finds a home in this particular metaphor of Confucius. These women emphasize presence over functionality, deviating from the early Christian emphasis on a variety of gifts and responsible stewardship. One cannot actualize one's gift unless one exists first. For them, being together as a community is a prerequisite for recognizing, affirming, and utilizing diverse gifts. Hence what leaders must value first and foremost is not how well one plays one's role but that the presence of all is what constitutes community.

Prioritizing presence over gifts (the existential significance over the functional value) of people rearranges the relationship that we have, or the leadership we share, with others within the community. Before we can depend on each other's functional contributions, we are radically indebted to each other's presence, without which community does not begin to exist; we are equally indebted to each other's presence for the continuation of life. Taken in that light, there can be no one above or below others. Therefore, our leadership should be exercised in horizontal, rather than hierarchical relationships. This existentially horizontal relationship leads us to a functionally shared leadership. When we value the presence of each person, we can truly welcome the diverse gifts each one brings to the community and wholly embrace complex identities within diversely indebted life contexts without conforming to a hierarchical leadership structure.[5] Our functional indebtedness is so diversified beyond any singular measure throughout different phases of our life that we cannot confine our relationship to a unilateral hierarchical power structure; we are functionally indebted to others in a variety of ways: intellectually, emotionally, physically, artistically, philosophically, and spiritually. Finally, when we recognize these complexities of inevitable indebtedness among persons both existentially and functionally, we cannot help but respond to each other with respectful grace and graceful respect.[6]

Besides this primary emphasis on presence over roles, the gathered women also listed a few other important qualifications of leaders in the church: a leader listens deeply to the community and sets the tone and direction. In a sense, good leaders are also good followers, leading in and amongst the followers. Leaders acquire deeper understanding of others through empathetic listening, and they respond to the needs of the community holistically. They do so by doing rather than speaking. These women's understanding of wisdom and leadership is more ingrained and practiced than simply articulated. Leaders should be available, prayerful, considerate, sincere, genuine, content to be where they are, and willing to fill in for vacant positions.

This understanding of wisdom and leadership is influenced by Taoism, more explicitly voiced in Lao-tzu's teaching: "The Master has no mind of her own. She works with the mind of the people," "the Master is content to serve as an example and not to impose her will," and "the best leader follows the will of the people."[7] The women volunteers' practice of leading embodies the *Tao Te Ching's* description of wise leadership: it collaborates and deflects attention from itself; it leads from behind and by example; and most importantly it engenders a sense of accomplishment in others.[8] The wisdom these laywomen acquired from their life experiences rooted in their cultures and traditions has enabled them to fashion a new leadership model: a shared and circular leadership in a horizontal relationship. This new model of leadership would rectify their cultural liabilities—their lack of confidence and the cultural expectations of women in taking on the responsibility of conventional leadership—that have accumulated in their life-long experience of patriarchal hierarchy in family, church, and other Korean American or Asian American contexts.

Over the past few years, the women have come to embody this circular and shared practice of leadership. It is shared because each leader takes full responsibility for a particular task area. It is also circular, because their roles do not remain rigid but are fluid and interchangeable when necessary—indeed, these women circulate their roles periodically, which makes this outreach ministry more sustainable. Second, through their practice of switching leadership roles, they are now not only more multi-gifted in various areas within this outreach ministry but also more understanding of other leaders within the larger faith community. Through this new leadership practice, these lay-women are formed and recognized as highly competent leaders within the church, granting them more opportunities to lead outside this small group. They are now more willing to do so, trusting that others will be there to offer support. Third, they inspire, empower, and thus lead others within this faith community, whether in task forces, committees, or in discipleship classes.[9] These women feel confident in the circular and shared leadership model they have nurtured, and, in the process, they have slowly yet persistently transformed the rigid and hierarchical tone of other small communities within the church.

As these women fully embodied this collective and collaborative leadership, they went beyond circular and shared leadership toward servant leadership. While servant leadership may be criticized as a dangerous reiteration of women's submission within the traditional patriarchal hierarchy of the Korean American church, this particular form of servant leadership has been enlightened by the exercise of wisdom leadership, whereby leaders allow wisdom to guide their willingness to embrace others. These women move toward servant leadership, rather than being placed at the bottom of a top-down, male-centered hierarchy; the community is better served when these women are positioned in a horizontal relationship to embrace and serve others because they have the wisdom to understand.

This particular model of servant leadership draws on the Christian virtue of humility as it was embodied by Christ Jesus, who emptied and humbled himself to become like human beings, even to the point of bearing the cross.[10] During his lifetime, Jesus modeled genuine servant ministry by washing his disciples' feet. As a teacher, he lived among his disciples. The ideal of servant leadership these women wish to embody, as exemplified in Jesus' life, also parallels the Taoist teaching of humility: just like the sea receives all streams of water because it is lower than they are, if a leader wants to govern and lead people, the leader must first place herself below others and learn to follow them.[11] As grounded in both Taoist and Christian traditions, humility gives these women's servant leadership power to lead.

SECRET RECIPE TO DEVELOPING AS KOREAN AMERICAN WOMEN LEADERS

Surprisingly, during the meeting in 2014, when asked whether they consider themselves to be leaders of the church, all of those gathered identified themselves as leaders. Each had her own description of leadership—understanding, empathetic, accepting, prayerful, embracing, relating, communicating, attentive, and approachable. It was an astounding change that had occurred in these women's self-perception since I joined the group two years earlier. Back then they were going through major changes in leadership positions, all occurring under the old pyramid form of leadership. Hereafter, as I unpack their stories, I will use the pronoun "we" instead of "they" to reflect our shared reality as Korean American immigrant women, to highlight our communal and mutual mentoring, and to include myself in the formation of wisdom leadership in the context of this Korean American church.

Most of the new leaders in this group felt uneasy about leading in the conventional sense. It was the new director's first time directing this program, overseeing several dozen young children and their parents. It was the new volunteers' first time teaching in the church. It was also my first time returning to church leadership after several years of graduate studies, time spent far removed from church leadership roles. Feeling uncomfortable in the new hats we were wearing, all of us were busy doing what each of us was assigned to do; the new director was fully occupied with managing the program, newly recruited teachers were busy preparing their class materials, and I was fully focused on story telling in worship. Lacking confidence, none of us was able to fully exercise our agential capacities even within our assigned roles. Rather, we were heavily dependent upon each other's support. It was a spirit—not specifically skills—that was essential for our leadership development, one that was attentive, affirming, embracing, empowering, and most importantly willing.

In the midst of our insecurity was the rising leadership of a newly joined assistant teacher, who was relatively freer than others during the preparation time. She volunteered to help other teachers by visiting each classroom to see if anyone needed help. When help was needed, she extended her hand, always leaving with positive affirmation for everyone. Although the newest addition to this group, she was able to lead us with her attentive and affirming spirit; her affirmation was thoroughly grounded on her gift of attentiveness. And her gifts in both soon led the whole group to follow her leadership.

Through this spirit of attentiveness and affirmation, we were able to embrace and empower each other. Due to the lack of experience, many of the volunteers were likely to make mistakes and were in need of additional growth. Yet what nurtured our growth was not harsh criticism and challenge, but the spirit with which we affirmed, embraced, and empowered each other that enabled us to develop as Korean American women leaders. I was not an exception to this development. Although my skills for children's story time needed much improvement, my fellow volunteers embraced my weakness and empowered me with their truthful but affirming support. My development as a leader was just one among many other cases. We affirmed the new director in her leadership in worship, new teachers' assistants in their gift of teaching, and the new pianist in her gift of responding to our needs in musical praise. We also affirmed and embraced different developmental stages of all attending children and the various parenting philosophies of their parents, empowering them to be who they are.

This uplifting spirit encouraged us to be less conscious of how well we performed our roles and more willing to step up. Many of us began to fill in when others could not perform their routine roles. As mentioned earlier, we were willing to switch roles when necessary, which provided more opportunities to develop additional leadership skills. Through it all, everyone became mutually empowered. Those who were once hesitant to take on leadership roles began to grow in willingness to serve not only within the confines of this outreach program but also in the larger church context. Now, many of us are frequently being asked to lead in other areas of ministry in this church, and we more willingly accepted these invitations to lead.

OUR MENUS: *KIMBOP* AND *BIBIMBOP*. WHAT'S YOURS?

As we have reflected on our journey in this ministry together, images of one-dish meals best described our leadership style: *kimbop* (Korean sushi rolls) and *bibimbop* (Korean mixed vegetable rice bowls). These images were initiated by the creativity of one attentive teacher. After witnessing the director's servant leadership—her generosity and hospitality—in providing lunch every week after the program, the music leader wanted to share the director's self-imposed responsibility by bringing ingredients to make sandwiches. Leading by doing, she inspired each of us to bring an ingredient to make a communal dish—a one-dish menu. Unlike a potluck where everyone would bring her own signature dish, we created a one-dish menu where each brought a different ingredient that highlighted the importance of our presence in the community and the gifts we bring to the table. In doing so, we celebrated our being a church together in horizontal relationships, because no single ingredient could make the whole dish.

This practice of making a one-dish menu with various ingredients allows us to take each of our life situations into consideration. Those who have more time would bring time-consuming ingredients while those who are more financially stable would provide costlier ingredients. When one of us had a busy week and was unable to bring an ingredient, we would just come to enjoy the lunch. I define this image of a "one-dish menu" as "radically yet unequally indebted" leadership; we are radically indebted because we cannot make the dish without others' participation, yet unequally indebted because we bring disparate gifts to make the dish communally. Whatever gifts or limitations we bring to the table define our dish by allowing us to create variations of the dish. The true value of our one-dish menu lies in the spirit of both constituting community with our presence and contributing to a meal with our gifts.

Several ingredients and secret recipes have been put together to create these one-dish menus—*kimbop* and *bibimbop*. As in these one-dish menus, this particular Korean American women's wisdom leadership model—a shared and circular leadership in a horizontal relationship—nurtures and nourishes many Korean and Korean Americans within their faith communities. However, these menus may not be nutritious or organic to other Asian and Asian American women and their respective contexts. By introducing this one-dish menu metaphor, however, I invite others to share their variations.

13

"Working to Make the World a Little Better Place to Live"

An Interview with Helen Kim Ho

JUNG HA KIM

When Sara Lawrence-Lightfoot set out to chronicle six storytellers in her book *I've Known Rivers: Lives of Loss and Liberation* (1994), she successfully demonstrated an alternative to the long-held objectivity-subjectivity debate in social sciences. She argued for love. "For a portraitist to see her subject clearly, she must fall in love. This love has many dimensions: respect, advocacy, intimacy, and admiration, and the curiosity and skepticism required to penetrate layers of image toward the essence."[1] Ever since, I tried to decipher various manifestations of love when I conduct interviews. My interview with Helen Kim Ho, which took place in summer 2015 in her home, became yet another testimony of love, both expected and unexpected.

I had asked Helen Kim Ho for an interview soon after the PANAAWTM (Pacific Asian and North American Asian Women in Theology and Ministry) group decided to celebrate its thirtieth anniversary by producing an anthology to showcase women leaders. Not only had Helen participated in the annual conference of PANAAWTM when it was held in Atlanta by leading the discussion on the documentary *9500 Liberty*, but Helen had also recently founded Asian American Advancing Justice–Atlanta (AAAJ), previously known as the Asian American Legal Advocacy Center (AALAC). I had approached her for an interview several times, but community mobilizing for the elections, the national regrouping of her organization, and personal circumstances prevented us from scheduling an interview until we met at her house for the interview that follows.

At the time of this interview, Helen had been Executive Director at the AAAJ–Atlanta for five years, and I had just walked out of a grassroots non-profit organization that I worked with longer than twenty-five years. Both of us were going through significant changes. And five months after this inter-view was conducted, Helen decided to leave the AAAJ and asked me to serve on the transitional committee to hire the new executive director. Helen Kim Ho left the position effective December 2015 and is currently "taking a year off to rest and reflect" to see where her next chapter in life will lead.

Our interview was a bit over three hours long and generated forty-one pages of single-spaced texts in verbatim. What I share in this chapter are slices of excerpts from a much longer conversation around various topics, includ-ing leadership models, identity politics, the relationship between local and national civil rights organizations, community mobilization strategies, reli-gion, balancing family and advocacy work, and Asian Americans in the South.

KIM: Thank you for your willingness to participate in this interview. And I'd like to congratulate you again on becoming the head of the South East regional chapter of Asian American Advancing Justice. You are the founder of AALAC (Asian American Legal Advocacy Center) and have led it as the executive director for years before taking on this regional and national lead-ership position. What are key differences in your leadership responsibilities then and now? How do you see your work in terms of making a difference in the community, then and now?

HO: About the transition. . . . It's both the same and different. Because [AAAJ] is into co-branding now. What I mean is that all [regional] affiliates are with independent 501(c)3 status and have their own board of directors. And they've been talking about co-branding for the last four or five years until they officially changed their name last year. And that's when the invitation came to us to join. At that time, I honestly thought that we'll be more robust with more coordinated strategies to work together. And it goes to the truth, you know since you've been working with us, that for collaborative and coalition work to become really something transformative, it takes a lot of time. So, I think that as soon as we joined, that's when the talk became very earnest: How do we connect the dots. And of course, really candidly, they got one of the first joint affiliation grants through Ford [Foundation]. And you just have to do a lot of affiliative work even if there is other community work to be done.

As you know, a lot of organizations don't move until we have money. . . . You know, D.C. is the capital. So when they hear about some bills, they send it out to all of us and ask whether we align with them or not. That's easy: we sign on. . . . We do citizenship work now. And we just started a direct-legal service program. So it's very easy to connect with San Francisco and L.A., since they have already established with direct legal service programs. And [I can] say, "Hey, could you share with me your intake forms and stuff, all that information." And that's easy. But most of the projects that I'm now working on as an affiliate, I've already done it.

KIM: Yes. So being part of the national affiliates can be more cumbersome at times. How does it work? I mean, you have been your own "boss." In a way you're still the boss, but now you're connected [to the affiliates]. How does that feel? How does . . .

HO: It's *hard*! You know, even when I ran the Advancing Justice, it really was run by the same first generation people that you know. And when we fought against the English Only Driver's License Bill [in Georgia], many of them felt so empowered. When they went to the capitol, it was their very first time that they were doing advocacy work in their lives. And they were saying, "Wow, I can make a difference." And, and . . . they wanted us to start a group. And then, as you know, [a local organization] didn't move [to organize]. So I left and started the work independently. And even before the affiliation, there were always these circles, the networks of groups, leaders, donors that I've always worked with in collaboration. I never felt autonomous, you know. So, our organization started with this coalition spirit, it was always there. Now with this [national] affiliation, it's a whole new coalition work again. [*soft laughter*] It's a whole new network. It's a whole new environment. You know the coalition's culture.

Now I am learning about the new culture of this affiliation. And how do we fit into it? How does it work? How does it not work? See, honestly, Dr. Kim, the older you get, the more you realize like the whole idea of how you can control people is never true. [*laughter*]

Right? I think that when you come into deeper faith in God and deeper understanding that God is in control, then you surrender the outcome to God. Only God knows the future. Doing as best I can with what I can do as a person in the situation is important. You know, the reality is that I am only one out of five [regional groups]. If I want to go in one direction, I can't just do that by myself. I mean, I guess, in my younger days, I might have said, *leave me* or *lead me*! But I'm too tired of that, Dr. Kim . . . I am now trying to be honest and authentic in all my dealings—mean what I say and do what I can really do.

KIM: Yes. With all these years of experiences, I hope we become mature too. We come to know what to compromise and what to hold fast and try to figure out what ways we can also accomplish the goal together.

HO: Yeah. So I am hopeful that things will work out, but yet. . . . Every time I talk with you, Dr. Kim, I just can't help it. I'm just not going to give the expected answer. The fact of the matter is that the transition had taken up so much of my personal and my professional time. And it's not just the strain of how does this affiliation work, but all EDs [Executive Directors] and staff are all in this process together, you know, and . . .

KIM: And at the national level, I think, they are beginning to realize the importance of the Southeast region, the American South, at least from my perspective.

HO: Yeah, exactly.

KIM: And when I think about you in the context of this national network, I'm thinking it must be extra work for you to educate and share . . .

HO: Yes! It's a lot of work. As you know so well, the non-profit world is about consensus building, dialogue, negotiation....

You know what's really funny? Years ago, I actually called a person who works in the D.C. office and I also called a person who I knew at NAKASEC [National Association of Korean American Service and Education Consortium]—these national groups—and asked whether they can start an office here. And I said, "Please, please, we're working on the English-only driver's license [campaign] here. Please, you guys, I know you want to work on civil rights and that there is a community here that can be moved and that can be engaged. But nothing here in the South. Would you open an office here? Something needs to start here." And the person who worked in D.C. told me that "It's just not a priority now." And I also heard through grapevines that in general they didn't think Asian Americans can be moved.

KIM: I think it also has to do with us being in the South.

HO: Yeah. The South is the lost cause. And Asian Americans are a hard-to-reach community. And Asian Americans are not moveable in a way, from a typical community organizing perspective.

And I was very frustrated. But it's funny that four or five years later the same organizations are asking us to join them. So you already know that non-profit organizations' dealings are a lot of times tied to funding. So really I think over the years, two things worked for our benefit. The funders have become more interested in the South. And that's a benefit. That's part of why the affiliates are like, "ooh, okay." Two, the immigrant civic engagement work that we've been doing is very methodical.

You know, immigrant organizing was just rallying. Right? Or just civil disobedience. All those tactics were extremely important, but the whole spectrum of organizing immigrants has been rarely about voting and political participation. And we're doing it from 2010, and now there is an interest from funders. And thankfully, out of all affiliates, we do it the best. And I think they know that.

KIM: Yes, I think that's thankfully because of you, your work. Speaking of which, I saw one of your "get out to vote" video campaigns some time ago on a Korean cable network . . .

HO: The 2013 video about how to vote?

KIM: I think so. And there was Mayor Reed [of Atlanta]. . . .

HO: And John Lewis [congressman].

KIM: Yeah. And I was thinking as I was watching that you must had fun making the video. But I was also wondering if you had any difficulty contacting the mayor and asking him to participate in the promotional video.

HO: No, actually, he had called me. He invited me to join his Immigrant Welcoming Board.

KIM: Wow, that's great.

HO: It's really cool to be called by the mayor. Of course, I had seen him on many occasions, and I'm sure he doesn't remember me so I would introduce myself again and again. Uh, but, I guess through his staff or somebody has said to him something about Helen Kim Ho and she should be on the board.
[A brief pause, then, imitating him] "Hi, this is Kasim Reed, your mayor. I want you to be on the board." Like, wow. [loud laughter]

KIM: How did you ask him to be on that promotional video?

HO: Oh, so I am on his Welcoming Atlanta Board. And I helped to launch that Welcome to Atlanta Initiative. So I got to work with some of his staff. So when we did that get-out-to-vote video, I called the staff and told them this is what it's going to be about, this is where it's going to be, and tied all that into what Atlanta wants to be—a kind of great place of civil rights. So he agreed. I mean the connections, I guess.

KIM: That's great. I saw the video repeatedly for almost a month or so leading up to the election. And you also had John Lewis involved! I mean people like the Mayor Reed and John Lewis are very public and important figures. So my question is, as an Asian American and Korean American woman, how do you approach these politicians? How do you approach these and other national figures? Do you think being an Asian American and a woman matter? Or has any of your racial or gender identity. . . .

HO: Oh, I wish…. I wish that I was more strategic. I mean, with these people, I was at some events with them. I mean, there are not many groups who work on immigrant rights and there aren't that many groups, period, that focus on civic engagement. So since there're not a lot of groups doing it, you just stand out. You know, Dr. Kim, I tested on the job personality test and I am an introvert.

KIM: Hmm. I don't think people would see you as an introvert.

HO: Well, I love people. I think being an introvert has to do with where you get energy from [being around/with] people or that you love people but need to get alone time away from people.

KIM: Yes. I fully understand. I am an introvert, too. But people who see me at community functions just don't believe that.

HO: Yeah. Introvert is not antisocial. It's about where you get your energy from. Often times I get invited, because I guess, I would accept that our organization is doing great work. But it also shows how so few groups are doing this kind of work. With Congressman John Lewis, literally, I reached out to his office to help us do the IRS tax forms because it was delayed. And sometimes, it's just authentically connecting with staff members, like being respectful and kind. Like our mission [statement]: there is nobody better than or less than anyone. And I feel that way about speaking with administrative staff who assist John Lewis. They are not unimportant. In fact, they are usually the most important people, honestly.

KIM: Yes, that's so true.

HO: Yeah. From there, it's just getting to know some of these staff people. And it was the District Manager who pitched the get-out-to-vote, the Gangnam style, video. So I just pitched my idea about doing the video with the district manager and he talked with others. Then I had to convince the communication director. And obviously, her job is to be very protective of John Lewis's reputation. And we worked with her, that we'll do everything right and that we would not do anything to hurt his reputation, and it worked!

I mean, we didn't know anyone. But I think as women and also as Asian American people and as immigrants, we don't have the benefit of embedded institutional relationships. Like, "oh, I have a friend or my uncle is on the board of trustees of such and such foundation." Like, "I, my father is on the board of trustees of the Georgia State University."

KIM: Exactly!

HO: So I feel different. I mean, my parents don't even live here. There is no ready-made connection. So I really just have to work to hopefully spark the interest and engagement of those people that I talk to and convince that this idea or this cause is worth it. And hopefully I can prove that it was worth their effort to come along with me. Clearly, that video was great for John Lewis and it was great for our campaign. So now it is, like, way easier. And they know me and they are always open to help me.

KIM: When they, different communities of people, work with you, do they see you and relate to you as an Asian American? Or Korean American? How do you think they see you, how do they treat you racially and ethnically?

HO: . . .

KIM: I noticed, for instance, your work in writing [of editorial pieces in newspapers] and some public speaking engagements, you usually identify yourself as Korean American, rather than Asian American.

HO: Yes.

KIM: But from an advocacy perspective, I wonder if people would identify you as a member of a racial minority group, or Asian American. So I'm wondering how do people see you? I mean it also has to do with how you negotiate your identities at different times and in different contexts.

HO: I honestly have not thought much about that. I think, I think in a kind of very broad way, like Asian, in the eyes of elected officers and nonprofit peers of non-Asian organizations. I think they probably see me as Asian. And a woman. And young. [*laughter*]. I'm not that young. But boy, we have that great young Asian genes. [*more laughter*]. So I am Asian, woman, and young. Or maybe not that much young, but our groups are young, you know.

Our community is young. You know how it is. I've been seen as an immigrant. And that intersects gender. And there is this additional intersection of a perception of our community as weak, not powerful, not important, not engaged and very conservative. And this progressive work that I do. . . . And sometimes I hear this in black-brown circles. You know I used to get mad. I know sometimes people are wondering if there's any commonalties among these three groups. Umm, there is this perception that Asians are conservative. [But] Latinos are conservative [too]. There are conservative black people, too. My experience is that there are a lot of commonalities [among the three groups]. I mean, these are things that they layer when they look at me. I don't know how I navigate. Sometimes, I . . . I use it to my own advantage.

KIM: Yeah, there is an "advantage" for being seen as an underdog.

HO: I agree. People are assuming less of, less from you. You're not as great or powerful as you are. Or your community [is seen] as less impactful as they actually can be. Because when you prove them wrong, you know, I'm not doing it to prove them wrong, but often times the results just prove. And there is nothing better than to prove, prove them wrong.

KIM: I agree. This brings me to the next question I have for you. You as a leader. I'd like to delve more into what kind of leader you are.

HO: Okay.

KIM: For instance, some of us are good facilitators, some of us are good managers, good visionaries, and so forth. So some of the questions are to figure out what kind of leader you are. And the other part of this leadership question deals with how you became a leader. The process and the history of becoming a leader. Like who influenced you? What kind of early childhood or adolescent memories that had led you to see and understand yourself as a leader? How did you get here? Do you have a person or maybe an incident in your life that triggered you to think about what it means to be a leader?

HO: Yeah, I think so. I mean . . . [*a pause*]. I think, I am not sure if I think of myself as a leader, but choosing to lead the Asian American or immigrant rights, I think definitely one of the core things and that's due to my parents. You know, just like many Koreans, my parents, they immigrated in 1975. I, I was about to turn four . . . I can't remember. I think I was three, because I think we moved, like in March. In March, I was 3.

We moved to L.A., because my aunt put my mom with the sibling visa. And they were working there through a friend of a friend, working at someone's sewing shop. But my aunt and her husband were professors at University of South Carolina and they were so lonely that they asked my mom to please move to Columbia. So after nine months [in L.A.], my family moved to Columbia, South Carolina, still in 1975 or maybe in early 1976, I am not sure. It was so different. There were virtually no Koreans there. Most of the Koreans that were there at the church were either there to get postdoctoral degrees at USC or were wives of military [personnel].

KIM: Yes, I can imagine, especially in Columbus, South Carolina, in the 1970s.

HO: My parents at that point were a little bit odd, because there were not that many immigrants like them then. They were adult immigrants that didn't come to go to school with a lot of money. So the only job my parents were able to find was at the cotton mill, you know? My mom, my mom actually told me this when I visited her two years ago. And at the cotton mill factory, there was no ventilation. And the machines were very steamy and hot. And my dad's job was to keep all dust down and apparently he lost thirty or forty pounds of weight in the first month of the job.

We grew up, or I grew up, very poor. Not that I grew up poor at my heart. You know, growing up in a trailer, sleeping on a sleeping bag, because we didn't have beds. Visiting my parents at work at the factory, you know.

[*Wiping tears*] You know, my mother told me that if she knew what it will be like [in the U.S.], they would have never come. . . . You know that I know their strength, intelligence of my parents, and . . . [*crying*] You know, as you get older, you get so much more grateful for your parents.

KIM: Yes. And you know, I think you were too young to remember what they went through.

HO: Yeah. I think I remember some, but when I visited mom with [her husband] two years ago when I heard all these stories from her . . . and I'm crying my eyes out here. . . . Yeah, my mom shared some stories with me. But I do remember how we were treated bad. People assume that we're stupid and bad. Like, growing up, my oldest brother was beaten up because he wore shoes from Kmart, things like that. And being the only Asian kids in the school and also being very poor. And . . . uh . . .

KIM: You have one older brother?

HO: I have two older brothers. So I do believe at the core of my heart the fundamental dignity, the human dignity, and worth of all people and that everyone should have equal access . . . umm, umm, to the civil rights. And in terms of actually working with community members that we worked with, I mean I don't look down on them as just clients, because really, they provide the insights and motivations for us to do the work that we do. So, I guess, I try to honor everyone like my parents. Even like immigrants, whether documented or not, just think about all their struggles and sacrifices. If there is anything that our group can do to integrate them better, integrate people like my parents, to know that there is a group that's there to help and to fight for them too.

Another was when I was going through the law school and practiced the corporate law, I was involved in an Asian group. After a year in Huston in Harrison County, we realize, there were enough Vietnamese that they were supposed to put all ballots in Vietnamese, according to the Voting Rights Act. As lawyers, we knew this. So we tried to talk to insiders, like elected officials of the county and others, but they did nothing. So after a couple of years, we reached out to the Voting Rights office of the Justice Department and asked them to investigate the case. And we were told, "we need you guys to do the work before we can do anything and you guys need to organize the people and survey the people as they come out from the voting polls." And we were to go to each and every voting site. And check and ask Asian people if they had any language help. . . . And we were just one small group. You know, we were just three of us. One worked at a government firm, I worked for a law firm . . . and another colleague . . .

KIM: When was it? Was it a long time ago?

HO: Yeah. That was a long time ago. This was about 2002 or 2003. And this was before Facebook and all that. So we sent out e-mails to Vietnamese people in the county who we helped in the [legal] clinic. We said, "We really need your help. Can you come out for training? We are asking for a whole day [of training] and come to a poll site and take information." And I didn't think anybody would come. Well, sixty-eight people showed up! And these are all limited English proficiency people. And I was so moved! I mean, fundamentally the change that forced the Harris County to comply the law of the ballot could fundamentally have been ignored without those community leaders, no, those community members. That's when I realize that that's how I want to practice the law.

KIM: Yes, it's a powerful story!

HO: Yes, they were so moved and wanted to contribute.

KIM: But the people had to be informed about what they can actually do. So the matching of the resource, information, and education is very important.

HO: Yes, that is true. That is true. So that was my formal experience of organizing work. And at the same time I was like, "Oh, I don't know. I need to work on becoming a partner [in the law firm] in Houston, but I don't know." I wasn't really passionate about it. [*laughter*]

I was talking to the partner and the mentor who really cared about me. They were guiding me with my career but also being very honest about themselves. [They told me,] "You know, not everyone, and you don't have to be a partner." You know, I used to jog every morning, running at 5:30 around Rice University.

KIM: You were so disciplined.

HO: During the forty-five-minute jogging and praying in my mind, "God, what is your will for me? What is your will for me? I read the *Purpose Driven Life* like a hundred times. What is your will for me?" I specifically remember one morning I was walking my dog and I just felt the answer coming from inside of me. You know, my debts were paid. It's not like I have children.

I was single. I was in a very privileged place of my career, and that maybe God wants to use my being a lawyer for somehow, you know, for public interest.

[Helen came to Atlanta, got married, and worked at CPACS (Center for Pan Asian Community Services, Inc.) before she founded her own nonprofit organization, AALAC.]

I used to work a lot. I pretty much used to work until 11 or 11:30 every night, the fear of failing was soooooo great. . . .

KIM: I really don't know how you started AALAC. I mean, after you left CPACS, what was the process like? Was it difficult to start something of your own from scratch?

HO: Oh, I was terrified. The fear of failure . . . I was so terrified.

KIM: How did you do it?

HO: You know, Dr. Kim, I wish I can give you an easy answer, but I won't. It was *hard*. I hate, like, a ready-made answer. Like, if this book comes out . . . I'm so honored and I hope that if any other person reads about me and who considers taking risks, I don't want that person to sound like, I felt so good and everything was great. Like God has rewarded you for being able to do the things that you did. And you know what I'm saying?

KIM: Yes.

HO: I was terrified. Honestly, I had no choice but to leave and start my own.

KIM: And you just got married then, too. [*laughter*]

HO: Yes, that was supposed to be really romantic and all. And I felt like I was trapped. And [her husband] convinced me and he said "Look, we can survive on my income for a year." I mean, he's a reporter. So he doesn't get paid that much. But he said, "We can survive on my income for a year and we have to be very tight. But I know you can do this." He told me, "Look, just one year and try it. And if it doesn't work, at least, you know you tried. Then we will consider moving." You know, then we will consider.

KIM: I guess you knew you married the right person, then, for sure.

HO: Yeah, but I wished we'd moved to New York or D.C. Then it would have been a completely different story. That's what I mean. That year, like, oh my God, if this [her own nonprofit] didn't work, I would have completely destroyed my résumé. I would completely, I mean, it was like going so far on left that it wasn't even in the ballpark any more. I mean, so far out of nowhere.

KIM: Well, from my perspective and looking back, you had that vision even when you're in the law school. It wasn't like you were lost. You had the vision. It's just that the institution that you're hired to work didn't fit. And you felt confused and lost for a while at that time.

HO: That's true. By the time I was at [a nonprofit organization], I really knew what God would want me to do during that period of time. I think, it's so funny. Being raised in the church that sometime you think you see some signs of God's guidance and love. But I was consumed with worries, just one challenge after another and another. Um, I'm not, I don't see myself as an entrepreneur. Because I grew up with parents that owned a small business that I never wanted to do that. I mean I always had to work all the time, since my parents ran a small business. It's that . . . I did not want that life for me. So from my childhood, and throughout all my upbringing, I did not want that risk for me. God, God has very interesting ways to push you . . . into the direction that you're meant to go.

[*Soft laughter*] But it's really through a lot of failures and sometimes just working through the fear. Now, you know I still worry all the time, and just being an anxious person.

KIM: Do you worry mostly because you have responsibilities as a leader? When you go to bed, do you worry about things of tomorrow? What do you worry about? Do you worry about whether you would be able to pay your staff? What do you specifically worry about?

HO: I worry about, honestly . . . now that I am where we are, I want to help create an organization with the right kinds of leadership and for staff. To me, when I move on, I want to see a lot of leadership there, with staff and the board. And . . .

KIM: Helen, you're not thinking about leaving [the organization]. Are you?

HO: No.

KIM: Do you always entertain the possibility of what if, what if I . . . ?

HO: I always think it's dangerous when an organization is too founder-heavy. When the organization is more about the founder's personality than [about] the mission, it's not right.

KIM: Right.

HO: Again, the coalition work. Ah, it's so annoying. [*Laughter*] Everything takes forever. But in a way, it's also a good reality-check. Ideally, no one person in collaborative work dominates. And of course, I am a dominant person. I did the leadership style test in the work place. And my primary trait is "dominant." Like the leader-driver-doer. I am also "cautious and observant" as the secondary traits. With all stakes and no matter what, the buck stops with me. Right?

KIM: Yes, that's another responsibility of being a leader.

HO: Yes, but in terms of developing leadership, I really want to get that clear. It's only literally just last year that I was feeling comfortable enough with the funding. But you know how it is. You want it to be multiyear funding. So since last year, I was like, I don't need to worry about hiring people, then let them go [for lack of funding]. It takes a lot of funding to hire and train the right people. So I have now six staff. And all of them have been with me less than a year. This is what I mean. Now I have this team. I know it doesn't happen overnight. Now I have a lot of work as I need to think about my staff. And I'm actually trying to hand over a lot of relationships to her. I have a deputy director. And hand over a lot of community relationships to her and [other] staff.

JKH: I think you're right about sharing responsibilities with staff, because people are not just filling the position to carry out certain job, but to develop their own career as they work.

HO: Yeah. I think also this is a good retention tool. Some days I'm like, uh, you promised to do this. Then they would say, "Oh, I was going to do this and that but . . ." You know what I mean? I think you did this too and that's how you lasted at [an organization] all these years with your staff, and your board and . . .

KIM: Yes, and the community.

HO: Yeah, the community. You know it's more than a job. Actually being part of this community. They have invested in you, and you invested in them. So wish me luck. You know nonprofits. There is a lot of turnover. You know, the nonprofit world is all about turnovers.

KIM: Yes. That's a fact of life, fact of organizational life. I now want to direct our attention to what you shared with me earlier already—about religion. I was going to ask about religion in general. Like do you have a religion? But you talked about God already, and talked about growing up in the church. So I am assuming that you define yourself as a Christian. Right?

HO: Yeah, yeah. Christian.

KIM: So, as a Christian . . .

HO: I'm Buddhist, too.

KIM: What? You're Christian *and* Buddhist? Wow, please, tell me more. This is fascinating, because I grew up in a Buddhist temple.

HO: Oh, wow! What was it like?

KIM: I think being in the temple probably is some of my earliest recollection of Korea. I mean, I remember the sound, the scent, and the feeling of being in the temple. Very early in the morning, maybe not even morning hours, [but] at dawn, young men, I mean, they were boys in their early teens, I guess, they would sweep the yards. That was the first sound and activity of the day as I remember.

HO: Wow.

KIM: So when people talk about remembering the "homeland" and describing city scenes, I'm thinking, my recollections are a bit different. And after I became a Christian, I'm a first-generation Christian in my family, I noticed that my way of experiencing and understanding Christianity was also different.

HO: Yeah.

KIM: So I am a Christian, but I'm also Buddhist in some way. That's why it's really fascinating to hear that you're a Christian and Buddhist, too. And you say that without any hesitation.

HO: Wow. Good! What I know is that my dad's side of family are pretty much all Buddhists, but my memory of growing up is definitely at the church. As immigrants, we went to the church. As Koreans, the church was where all Koreans used to go to, right? [*laughter*] And my mom's family were all Christians.

I used to talk and walk with my dad. My dad likes to walk, walk with me, and we used to talk a lot about religion. And when I was at college, I was so close to double majoring in religion. I just loved studying religion. I think Buddhist is nontheistic and Buddhism is more about reading. I love reading. It's more about reading and meditating. There is a Buddhist center in Decatur.

KIM: Yes, I know.

HO: I used to go there fairly regularly and meditate. The Zen Center.

I think a lot of it is so similar. I mean, a lot of it is about what's within. Starting from within, it's like a ripple effect of moving out and how you're in the world. I think a lot of Christian core teaching of the Christ is about compassion and nonjudgment. And my middle brother is a pastor. And when he was young, he was very fundamentalistic. My parents are elders of the church.

And I was in high school already when I realized what the church is saying is what I didn't agree with. It really came to a head when I was in college when I met those Campus Crusade for Christ and I was so turned off.

[*Soft laughter*] For me, religion is always like love and action. And in the church, I was like, the community service chair or something like that. You know I always was like, do something. But I didn't even claim my religion as Christianity for many years. College through . . . I don't know when. I think I just came back to being comfortable with not just my faith, but as my cultural identity too.

KIM: Yeah?

HO: And that's okay. It's like you can be a good person, a compassionate person in multiple religions.

KIM: Yes, I agree. You talked about how your brother used to be fundamentalist. I think political activism and spirituality don't mix well in the Korean American church. I mean, especially in the evangelical and fundamentalist churches, they often draw clear boundaries between religion and society.

HO: Yeah.

KIM: So I think you're probably one of those few people who experienced positive relations with the church when organizing Korean American community.

HO: Yeah. I feel lucky. And I wish that the working relationship would be much, much deeper. But just to give you an example, the bottom line is, regardless of my belief, as an organizer, I try to think of how I connect and partner with other leaders to have reach into different populations and to disseminate different information and hopefully to mobilize people into action for the common cause, whatever that is.

Of course, pastors or priest or monks, faith leaders have the most credibility in the ethnic community, have a captive audience in their congregation. They just need to put the information and announcements in the *jubo* [church bulletin] or in the prayer requests, which will carry so much more power than me saying over and over again. Yeah, it took, it took time. Organizing people and developing relationships always takes time. But I'm just really, I don't know why, I'm fortunate that when they hear about my work, they trust me or . . . You know, the KCPC (Korean Central Presbyterian Church)?

HK: Yes.

HO: Again, it was just asking pastors at the KCPC specific things, like would you please allow us to do voter registration at the church? We will do all the work of filling out the forms. They said sure. And the next time, we asked, would you allow us to pass out these T-shirts inside the church office? Sure. Could you please pass out this information on your *jubo*, next time? [*Soft laughter*]

Then I asked as many *moksanims* (pastors) to be on this billboard. We did this billboard in Korean at the corner of Pleasant Hills and Steve Reynolds. It says ten thousand Korean voters. I don't know if it's the billboard or by asking things little by little at the church. But when we were actually at the polls doing exit surveys, actually two people said, "I'm from Jones Creek, and I go to this church, and I decided to come out to vote." And one woman said that she's been a citizen for twelve years but never voted before. "But my pastor kept bringing up at the adult Bible study at Wednesday night and on Sunday to vote, and how important it is to vote. So I finally registered to vote. And I am voting for the first time." Wow, I was so happy! I don't know which pastor it was, but this pastor clearly did more than what I asked him to do. That's like, so it's working! I mean, the pastor deeply felt that it's important to vote. That's why he persistently talked about it at the church. If this person feels [that it's] important, and I think it's important, then it's a ripple effect. I was so pleased. In fact, with the "10,000 Koreans vote" campaign, we looked at the whole state. I mean, nobody votes in the midterm. When we crunched the data and did the research, our estimate is that 17 percent of all Koreans who could have voted had voted. That's not so good. The state average was like 38 percent. So Asians still lag and immigrants in general are low. But we caught all the Koreans we directly touched by setting up the registration to vote or we mailed out letters in Korean and English, or we knocked on the door. Based on our estimate, I think it was 78 percent of Koreans we directly touched went out to vote.

KIM: Wow, 78 percent is incredible! This is a powerful story. This also means that we have a lot more work to do to personally contact the church, send out reminders and call people and knock on their doors. I think your story about working with the church will be a helpful and welcoming reminder for many people, Koreans or not, to build partnerships and collaborations with religious organizations when working with the community at large.

HO: It's still a few thousand. But percentage-wise, it can make a big difference!

KIM: And that also means your advocacy work is really working. Helen, I have a few last questions. If you have all the resources and power to solve one problem in the world, what would you like to do? Which problem do you want to resolve?

HO: [*Laughter*] Oh, this is one of your Barbara Walters-esque questions.

KIM: [*Laughing*] Perhaps. I also want to conclude the interview with a positive note, you know. Something that can lighten up our spirits and energy. . . .

HO: I'd like to work to eradicate hunger.

KIM: Oh!

HO: I mean, this may sound so out of the blue, but I'd like to address the problem of hunger, especially ending hungry children in the world.

KIM: Do you think your next work will have something to do with ending hunger of sorts?

HO: I don't know, but eradicating hunger comes to mind if I have all means to end one social problem.

KIM: One more last question. How would you like to be remembered? I mean, when you have gone to the next world and when people want to remember you later, what would you like them to know about you?

HO: I'd like the people to know . . . that I tried and tried my best to make the world a little better place to live. That when I'm gone, I'd like to know that the world I left behind is a better place because we all tried to make it better.

14

Wisdom Crying Aloud in the Street

DEBORAH LEE

"Oh, so you're a pastor?" someone asks inquisitively. "So where's your church?"

I *am* a pastor; that is true. But pastoring thus far hasn't landed me in a church. In the past decade as an ordained minister, I have mostly presided over interfaith prayer services outside immigration detention centers, in front of courthouses or banks, or on the steps of the state capitol or the Pentagon. I have learned to invoke the Spirit through traffic and honking horns. Together with the people of God, particularly undocumented youth, the homeless, immigrant families, and peace activists, we have reclaimed contested public spaces as holy and sacred. We sing, confess, hear testimony, and pray. We feel hope, offer reassurance, march, and sometimes get arrested. In the streets and many places outside the church, something holy is happening. God and Spirit are present and crying aloud in the streets. Proverbs 1:20–21 states, "Wisdom shouts in the street; in the public square she raises her voice. Above the noisy crowd, she calls out. At the entrances of the city gates, she has her say."[1] How do we do ministry in the streets? How do we discern what Wisdom is saying there? What are the practices of Wisdom? In this chapter, I explore the value of wisdom and leadership for ministries in the streets. I offer three practices of wisdom leadership born out of my experience as an activist pastor: manifesting the Sacred in the streets, inspiring the leadership of others, and being artists of wisdom leadership.

PRACTICE #1: MANIFESTING THE SACRED
IN THE STREETS

I knew early on in my life that it was possible to experience God outside the church. My immigrant parents, who landed in northeastern Ohio, loved parks and nature. Not only was it free, but the woods where I grew up was where my Indonesian mother experienced awe, serenity, and the divine. I remember many Sunday afternoons after church where we wandered through the trees and caves, places where Native Americans who lived for millennia along the Cuyahoga River had also experienced the Sacred. For my father, who emigrated from Hong Kong, the soccer field was his outdoor temple. Soccer had paid his way through college in the United States, and he passed on that love to his daughters. Saturdays were spent on grassy soccer fields, where I experienced the transcendence of being embodied, empowered, and part of a community working toward a collective goal. I knew in my being that the holy could be experienced in many places outside the church, and soon it became a deep hunger to find a faith practice that connected to the realities and struggles of the wider world.

As a young adult, I began to question the evangelical church I was raised in. It did not seem to address the pressing issues in the world around me: hunger, poverty, racism, and sexism. My church had few answers beyond saving souls and explaining injustice as God's will. Then I moved to California. As a student at the University of California at Berkeley, I was exposed to political activism. People organized in compelling ways to speak out and to right the wrongs of society. Where was the church, I asked? Here were secular people doing the work of Jesus—feeding the hungry, marching for peace, restoring and seeking justice for the marginalized and the outcast. I soon discovered that alongside these secular activists was a dedicated community of spiritual activists, inspired by faith and politically engaged in social change. In fact, I discovered that there was a long history of faith-inspired activists, revolutionaries, and reformers in the United States and around the world. I learned about liberation theology, feminist theology, creation spirituality, black theology, and Asian theology.

This awakened my heart and intellect, and after college, I went to Brazil for several years to see how liberation theology worked in practice on the ground. I was inspired by Catholic religious sisters called *Irmãs Inseridas*. *Irmãs Inseridas* literally means "Sisters Inserted" and are religious women who live outside the convent and are embedded in the community. In Brazil, they lived and worked in favelas, the slums and the streets, practicing a holistic form of ministry that cared for people's minds, bodies, souls, leadership, and the future of their communities. It was a ministry *with* and *among* poor people to solve social problems and alter history. They were doing more than "saving souls." They were performing "saving works . . . the saving of the earth, of the oppressed, of humankind."[2]

Several years later when I returned from Brazil and entered seminary, I learned what this could look like in the United States. As a seminarian my field placement was to shadow Rev. Glenda Hope of San Francisco Network Ministries, who for forty-one years has holistically served and walked the streets of San Francisco's Tenderloin neighborhood, which is home to many homeless, mentally ill, and very poor people. Rev. Glenda's ministry and leadership in the streets of the Tenderloin were both pastoral and prophetic. As a pastor, she accompanied people who wandered the streets and conducted the memorial services for those who died alone. As a prophet, she powerfully advocated in City Hall for policies and funding to support the housing, dignity, and opportunities for the poor and homeless. It was a ministry of presence and structural change. Rev. Glenda gave me a charge on my last day: "I hope your ministry every day allows you to be in contact with poor people." I continue to pray that God blesses me with the courage and wisdom to respond to that charge. Wisdom leadership knows the deep value of doing ministry in the street, slums, and favelas, witnessing the sacred among the marginalized. It was where Jesus did his ministry. It is in the edge of struggle, in the issues of life and death, in the streets, where wisdom stirs.

In the last few years, the streets of our nation and world have erupted with ordinary people spilling out into public spaces to express the need for life over death. In the United States, unemployed young people, moms with kids in strollers, fast food workers, and folks representing the 99 percent showed up in town squares across the country in the Occupy Wall Street Movement. And in the current minimum wage fights, people protest, decrying the immoral economic system that privileges the wealthy few over the many who face underpaid jobs, poverty, and foreclosure. The wisdom has cried out in the streets with mass protests and unprecedented actions of undocumented young people, immigrant workers, and families, risking everything by calling for an end to harsh deportations and immigration policies that criminalize and keep immigrants in the shadows. And today, even as I write this, towns across the United States are exploding with black youth, families, pastors, and allies protesting that "black lives matter." They are calling for an end to the epidemic of police killing unarmed black men, women, and children. They are crying out for black lives to be treated with equality, value, and sanctity. Wisdom stirs on these streets.

In Spanish, the word used for a demonstration or a street protest is *manifestación*. The word comes from the root word, "to clearly reveal." Demonstrations, street marches, and public activism are ways to clearly reveal and lay bare the moral and ethical questions before us. Like the prophets of old, wisdom leaders reveal and expose the lies that are perpetuated to justify suffering, inequality, and separation. They point to the truth of human sacredness, resistance, and resilience. They shine a light on what is good, what is God, and where our hope lies.

I took my teenage sons to a people of faith march to honor the black lives lost: Michael Brown, Eric Garner, Tamir Rice, Trayvon Martin, Oscar Grant, and young Latino/a lives: Andy Lopez, Yanira Serrano. They were gunned down by law enforcement officers without accountability and prosecution.[3] The march was held after church on a Sunday, and people gathered from various congregations across town, across races, ethnicities, and generation. Together we marched several miles starting from a predominantly white "downtown" church to an African American church in the "flats." The differences between the two churches were stark: the building infrastructures, the surrounding neighborhoods, and even the cars in the parking lots reflected the deep racial and class inequality and separation that exists in every part of our daily life in the United States. And our faith communities are not exempted from this divide. As we marched across town together, we chanted and sang.

When we arrived in front of the African American church, we heard testimony from young African American teens about their own experiences, their fear of leaving the house and walking down the street, their determination to no longer accept the status quo, to demand that our nation do better. I took my teenage sons, who question the value and relevance of church and Christianity. I was hoping they might witness what faith is about. Faith is about my own spirit touching the spirit of my brother, my sister. It is about being connected to humanity and a life-force greater than all of us. Lying down in the middle of the street, blocking traffic in the "die-in," we stare at the clouds in the sky while hearing the names of those young people who will never be able to see another beautiful blue sky. This is spirituality. This is faith. It is about making connections between my life and the life taken too soon, and collectively making our lives count for something.

The march that day was a "manifestation," exposing for all to see the moral contradictions in our society that perpetuates that lives of some are worth more than lives of others. That day, we also reimagined our cities and streets as places where all people are afforded the most basic human rights of respect, safety, nutrition, housing, education, and healthcare. We reimagined who the police could be, a nonviolent force for community safety and genuine security. When we make the Sacred manifest in the streets, we are revealing the coming of a new day, the revelation of a truth, a new way of being the beloved community.

Wisdom leadership in the street sees the street as holy ground. It is holy because it is where people live and die. It is where their hopes, frustrations, and deepest sufferings are spoken. The street is where faith speaks to the pressing and critical issues that shape our lives and future. It is where my faith in a living and loving God speaks to the realities of racism, sexism, homophobia, inequality, mass incarceration, migration, environmental sustainability, and militarism. Our faith calls us into the street, walking with others to shape the future. The wisdom is crying out in the street and the Sacred and holy one is there too, shouting for all to hear.

PRACTICE #2: INSPIRING THE LEADERSHIP OF OTHERS

Our world needs many wise leaders. Wisdom leadership needs to multiply by awakening and inspiring wisdom leadership in others. Wisdom and leadership are not reserved for the elite, the enlightened, or the ordained. They are not obtained only through academic degrees or study. Wisdom and leadership are not something one is innately born with. Wisdom, like faith itself, can be accessed by the young and the old. With nurture and practice, wisdom can be cultivated and developed. Anyone can become a wisdom leader if she is awakened, inspired, and developed.

One of my favorite biblical stories about ministry is the familiar story of Jesus feeding the five thousand. This story is found in all four Gospels. However, one important detail is found only in the Gospel of Mark and the Gospel of Luke.[4] In the Markan and the Lukan accounts, Jesus instructs the disciples to direct the crowd that has gathered for healing and preaching to sit in groups of fifty or one hundred. He then gives thanks, breaks the bread, and distributes the five loaves and two fish to all gathered. After all had eaten, there were twelve baskets left over to spare. Dividing into groups of fifty or one hundred could be seen as an insignificant instruction, but it is at the heart of the miracle. Perhaps, by sitting down and facing each other in groups of fifty or one hundred, the crowd discovered that there was a lot more food among them to share—a little here, a little there. Perhaps by sitting in groups and looking into each other's eyes, they took their eyes off of Jesus and started dialoguing with each other. Perhaps they shared what they hungered for and what they feared. Perhaps they talked about their dreams for the future. Perhaps they discovered that they suffered common problems and ailments under the Roman Empire, and perhaps they developed solutions for their own emancipation. They broke bread, and perhaps they told stories, shared suffering, prayed, and found ways for community healing and libera-tion. They were full. And there were leftovers. They practiced church.

From 2000 to 2009, I was the program director of the Institute for Lead-ership Development and Study of Pacific Asian North American Theology (PANA). PANA operated a seminary-based youth leadership program spe-cifically dedicated to the theological and leadership formation of Asian and Pacific Islander (API) American youth.[5] Like in the story of the Feeding of the five thousand, many came to be fed but left as leaders, having uncovered their own power to transform the world. Over the course of the program, 150 high school and college-age API, Latino/a, Native American, and African Ameri-can youth participated in the residential program called Represent to Witness (R2W). R2W was rooted in the unique cultural and historical experiences of API and other working class youth in the United States. The participants ranged from first generation immigrants to fourth generation API Americans, and were equally split between middle-class and working-class young people. Different faith traditions were represented. They were Buddhist, Catholic, mainline Protestant, Evangelical, Mormon, and indigenous religions.

The curriculum was called "Critical Faith," and it synthesized liberation theology and grassroots pedagogy. It did not begin with religious material but began with the narratives and experiences of the youths' own lives and their communities. From that starting point, the popular education curriculum focused on raising critical consciousness and leadership development.[6] One of the youth participants, Lei, who was sixteen years old when she entered the program, came from an immigrant American Samoan family in Hawaii. She was a shy young woman who had never been encouraged to speak her thoughts or opinions in her family, her church, school, or neighborhood. She did not have the words to articulate the complexity of her identity as a young woman, resident of a U.S. colony, and an immigrant. She was seeking to make sense of her people's struggle to thrive in the United States. She had not come to grips with who she was—the power, intellect, and capacities that God had gifted her.

One of the core components of the "Critical Faith" curriculum is the prac-tice of Social Biography, which is a practice of critically examining and deep-ening one's understanding of one's life. It is a process of telling your personal story in the context of the larger economic, political, historical, and social events and forces in the world. It helps students understand how the external world shapes their personal story and how their personal story can transform the external world. It is a way of making meaning out of one's story and using it to teach others about that truth and reality; "The social biography is an 'annunciation'—an act of public declaration of oneself and one's agency to the world. It is a social, political and spiritual claim."[7]

Through Social Biography participants discovered what they knew and did not know about their own story and the story of their people. They developed skills of social and historical analysis to understand why things were the way they were. They taught each other about their various lived experiences, the conditions of the communities they lived in: colonization and migration from Pacific Islands, immigration journeys and separated families, being undocumented, living in public housing, community violence, racism and unequal treatment, LGBT discrimination, sexism in the church, loss of identity and culture. They learned to ask critical questions. For example, what does poor health and rampant funerals in the community have to do with our history of colonization? What critical reflection of the historical, social, political, economic, spiritual dimensions of this problem do I need to know to understand this problem? How does religion and culture interplay and address this complexity? One youth declared, "You enter with one question and you come out with ten, twenty . . . How does all this fit in the wider social context, the social frame?"[8] Like in the story of the feeding of the five thousand, the instruction for the youth was to take their eyes off something external, even "Jesus," and to look deeply within and to speak and listen to each other.

The object of the leadership development was a "moral and spiritual project"[9] of humanization, for them to see themselves in new light, as active agents in a process of freedom and liberation. The students learned to speak authoritatively about their own knowledge and to recognize that they have knowledge to share. They learned about empathy, how to share in another's suffering, and what it means to be an ally.

Through intentional "community crawls" into specific API and other neighborhood settings, students began to see how other youth, grassroots organizations, and faith communities organized and tackled real concerns in the community. They experienced spirituality and faith in new ways that integrated who they were and the narrative of their people in the world. The youth in R2W were inspired to be participants in the movement for freedom and liberation. Like Jesus' crowd of five thousand, they became awakened to help make miracles happen.

Lei is just one of the many miracles I witnessed in the program. After participating in the program for several years, she became a leader. She found her voice, her power, and is confidently pursuing her distinct path as a bridge-builder of cultures and people. She has become a teacher of her people's history, with a deep yearning for the thriving of Pacific People's and powerful women. She is a researcher in the community oral history project called "API Women, Faith, Action." In this role, she researched and documented the first Samoan woman to be ordained in the Congregational Christian Churches of American Samoa, an inspiration to her.[10] Lei is now an inspiration to others in the Pacific Islander students club she co-leads at her university, committed to issues of justice for all peoples, and helping to encourage and empower others on their path as leaders.

Wisdom leadership is never about just one leader but about inspiring the leadership of many. By inspiring, literally *breathing into*, wisdom leadership can *breathe in life* to people who may not yet see themselves as leaders. Wisdom leadership offers space to *breathe* for those who may feel suffocated by oppression, self-doubt, or fear. Inspiring leadership means rekindling the passion and purpose of others, stirring up possibility, hope, and conviction. In Ezekiel 37, God breathes life into dry bones and the bones rise up from the dead, not just one, but a multitude. Inspiring leadership is not a one-time event but an ongoing process of sustaining and deepening, just like breathing itself.

Awakening leadership is a mutual endeavor, and the youth in the R2W program have been some of my greatest teachers about the API community. Not only was their leadership awakened, but they called me to deepen my own leadership and seek formal ordination as a minister. Several of the other API immigrant young women, including Lei, wrestled with their own calling to ministry. Some were in church denominations that did not yet ordain and fully recognize the leadership of women. As I watched them grapple with the structural and internalized sexism, racism, classism, and colonialism, I recognized that I too was internally grappling with similar barriers and doubts shaped by my experience as an API woman. I had been undecided about ordination because of my commitment to the notion of the priesthood of all believers, but I had to recognize my own internalized sexism and racism as I questioned: Could I be a leader *beyond* my own racial people? What was I asserting by pushing myself forward for ordination? Do I believe that I have leadership to offer and contribute in my predominantly white denomination? It was the youth who helped me answer those questions. To those young women, I was a woman in religious leadership, and they wanted me to be fully recognized, not just for me, but also for them. They called and awakened me into ordination through *their* wisdom leadership.

PRACTICE #3: ARTISTRY OF WISDOM LEADERSHIP

When I was getting ready to leave home for college, my dad wanted to make sure I knew some self-defense, so he taught me some basic Bruce Lee kung fu moves. Fortunately, I never had to put it to use, but it did inspire me to start learning wushu, an exhibition version of traditional Chinese martial arts and tai chi chuan. It was a way for me to be around my people. And since I cannot speak the language, it was some way for me to connect to my culture by learning an ancient art form. Learning a martial art form meant literally forming my body into a "form," or series of movements, developed over millennia, to increase the flow of chi, develop strength, balance, and power. There is a method, a discipline, a correct way. It takes time and a lot of practice. You practice the same forms—twenty-four movements, thirty-two movements, forty-eight movements—over and over again for years. I remember it was only after five years that I was able to completely relax my shoulders. After ten years, I could move from the waist. In my twentieth year, I am still discovering new things.

Like martial arts, wisdom leadership is an art form. It cannot be learned on the Internet, in a one-day workshop, or by reading a book. Rather, it demands the day-to-day exercise and praxis of leadership. The form requires intentionality, practice, and mastery. It may even require a *sifu*, or a teacher. It requires conscious cultivation and reflection on leadership. How am I leading? What kind of leadership am I practicing? What are the values, principles, and deeper goals I am embodying?

One way I cultivate this art form is to reflect daily and be conscious of my body and my presence in the world. It is asking, "Am I free?" Wisdom leadership means tapping into the wisdom in our bodies, to heal wounds of oppression so that we can be authentically free, be fully human and be wisdom leaders. Each day, I breathe and take a moment to notice how fear, oppression, and notions of my own authority are physically lodged in my body, in my posture, in my voice, and in my very way of being in the world. I ask, "Am I speaking and moving," as my friend, dancer, and healer Coke Nakamoto calls it, "as 'a free body moving in space?'" What does that feel like? If yes, when? If no, why? Freedom and conscious leadership requires intentionality and focused development, as one would master an art form.

Wisdom leadership as an art form suggests that leadership is more about craft and creativity than command and control. It employs aesthetics, beauty, and Spirit in the way we work with people and communities to build collective purpose. Wisdom leadership is curating sacred space, like crafting liturgy each time we gather and convene people for a meeting, a conference, or even a demonstration. Every gathering is an opportunity to hold space, to deeply honor and value each person, to create a humanizing and life-giving moment and way of engaging. One important contribution we can make to social movements is to be artists of wisdom leadership, bringing our gifts of ritual and liturgy into the street to nourish the soul and spirit of the movement.[11]

For the past six years, I have directed the Interfaith Coalition for Immigrant Rights, a project of the Interfaith Movement for Human Integrity,[12] bringing the moral and spiritual power of faith communities together to engage in the movement for immigrant justice with undocumented students, immigrant workers, and community members engaged in a struggle for the dignity and full personhood of all immigrants. At different seasons of the year, the immigrant community has asked us to lead several public rituals in connection with immigrants' lives. During Holy Week, we perform a public foot washing ritual of immigrants in front of the Immigration Customs and Enforcement (ICE) office. To wash the feet of those wearing ankle monitoring bracelets and facing deportation is to honor the dignity and lives of immigrants. During Holy Week, we also offer a prayerful stations of the cross ritual retold as stations of deportation. At the end of the year, we organize a Christmas Posada with recent immigrants reenacting the story of their own perilous migration stories, connecting the terror and rejection of the Holy Family and their journey.

For over four years now we have gathered each first Saturday of the month for a prayer service in front of the nearest immigration detention center, one of 250 detention centers across the country.[13] Each month a different congregation, school, or organization has led the service where the "homily" is given by those people who have been most impacted by the broken immigration system: immigrants who have been released, family members of those detained, immigrant workers unjustly fired from their jobs by ICE raids, those fighting their deportation. From them, we have witnessed the suffering caused by our immigration system. We have also seen their courage to act and speak the truth in spite of fear, despair, and loss. The testimonies are followed by the prayers of the people and then a cacophony of hollering, cowbells, ram's horns, tambourines. We make a "joyful noise to the LORD" (Ps. 98:4) as loud as we can, so that those inside the detention center will know that they are not forgotten. This is our "church." It is made up of people from various congregations and people who are not in any faith community. We are "doing church," praying and hollering, crying and laughing in the parking lot of a prison. People creating a network of pastoral care and solidarity, using our faith voices to change public policy and build community between immigrants and nonimmigrants so that all can live with respect and dignity. As artists of wisdom leadership, we bring our street liturgies and the power of truth to confront systems of injustice and to sustain the spirit and hope of those struggling for peace.

WISDOM CRYING OUT IN THE STREET

We are at a time and place in the United States where the relevance of Christianity and our religious institutions is being seriously challenged. We are at a crossroads, wondering *if* and *how* we will continue to exist. And if we continue to exist, for what purpose? Perhaps the question for us must be, not how do we stay alive as a church but *how do we keep hope and meaning alive for others?* We have much to offer as wisdom leaders: making manifest the Sacred in the streets, inspiring the leadership of others, and being artists of wisdom leadership. The streets are where we will witness and see with our own eyes that God *is* alive and that faith is powerfully stirring in the world. The streets are where Jesus sent forth his disciples to be among the people, to announce to them, "God is with you. God is within you. Right here, right now. The reign of God is at hand." We are sent forth to testify and witness to the Spirit of the living God; to see the people outside the church as God's people; to ask not how do we stay alive as a church but how do we keep hope alive for others? Pope Francis has repeatedly said, "I prefer a church which is bruised, hurting and dirty because it has been out on the streets, rather than a church which is unhealthy from being confined and from clinging to its own security."[14] Our job as religious leaders is to help people step off the curb into the streets, to let go of our own notions of security, to grapple with fear, and to encounter God in the other, to see God where they would least expect. In so doing, in spite of ourselves, we just may find renewal and new answers to our questions of purpose. If we are successful in inspiring the wisdom leadership of God's people to organize for the sacred dignity of each person, and for peace, we will be the resurrected people bringing forth a hopeful and resurrected world.

15

Fitting Nowhere

Meditation on Ministry, Wisdom, and Leadership

LAURA MARIKO CHEIFETZ

The beginning of wisdom is this: Get wisdom, and whatever else you get, get insight.

—*Proverbs 4:7*

Ancient Mesopotamia influenced the biblical Wisdom tradition. In Mesopotamian mythology, "Wisdom belongs to the gods and there must be a process that it can be given to others. . . . Wisdom comes to human beings mediated by authorities in the community such as kings, teachers, and parents."[1] Wisdom comes through community. And my community consists of leaders in ministry.

Ministry is more than a profession. It is a life. It is a life prone to isolation, which we counter-act with layers of community and accountability. My community looks like a sisterhood. I have sisters in ministry. We spot each other across convention center halls and hotel ballrooms. We schedule visits in between church meetings. We e-mail each other about challenges in ministry, pictures of food, photos of us holding one another's babies. One of my Korean American friends came to guest preach at the church I attend. The white pastor of the church asked me how we knew each other. I said, "We're both Asian American women pastors. There aren't that many of us." These sisters I gained through my vocation.

I did not grow up with a sister. I have one younger brother. Growing up, I would get so angry over nothing with him; we also had our better moments, when he came to my tea parties and I played with his electric racing car tracks. Now he is married to a brilliant woman, giving me a sister who gives good book recommendations, sends funny e-mails, and makes sure we know what the niece and nephew are up to. And my partner gave me another; her sister welcomed me into the family. When she was having babies, I did her laundry, took care of the older kids, accompanied the kids to birthday parties and the playground. She gives me hand-me-downs more stylish than I know what to do with. I have sisters through family, and I have sisters through ministry.

Just as we can't choose our family of origin, I can't choose my sisters in ministry. They arrive in ministry through any number of paths, and it is rare that I meet an Asian American woman in ministry that I do not already know. We have diverse experiences of anti-Asian racism. We have diverging interpretations of incidents of racism and sexism. We do not necessarily affiliate with each other; some Asian American women prefer communities not defined by ethnicity or race, and almost all of us serve white or multiracial churches and constituencies. But in a relatively small white-dominant church whose ministers are disproportionately white, male, and over fifty, those of us that do not fit into these categories encounter each other simply because we are the "others." The racism of the United States and in our church, in which "all Asians look alike," brings us together whether or not we want to be together. At large conferences, people get us confused, calling one of us by the name of another. We have kept tallies of these incidents at more than one event, texting the funnier stories to those who are not in attendance. At one event, I was sitting next to a Korean American pastor with short hair, approaching middle age. The person across from her called her the name of another Korean American pastor with long hair, who is in her early thirties. The pastor next to me said, "How can you confuse me with her? We don't even look alike!"

We arrived in each other's lives because we are in this church, bound together by race, gender, and vocation. Even when we resist this connection or do not see it as important, we are still seen by others as Asian American women.

This community of Asian American women in ministry holds wisdom. Proverbs 4:5–6 says,

> Get wisdom; get insight: do not forget, nor turn away
> from the words of my mouth.
> Do not forsake her, and she will keep you;
> love her, and she will guard you.

I am not always so wise, even though my hair is turning salt-and-pepper. The list of foolish things I have said and done is far too long, and plenty cringe-worthy, to say nothing of the list of things I have done without realizing it. I hate these moments of foolishness, weakness, ignorance, and carelessness. I hate my moments of poor decision making and apathy. "I'm sorry for the things I said when I was hungry," says the meme online. I might as well make that my mantra, but you could add a few things for me. "I'm sorry for the things I said when I was paying attention only to the goal and not to the process." "I'm sorry for the things I said when I was tired." "I'm sorry for all those times I sat back and didn't say anything." "I'm sorry for all those times I said too much."

I have a habit of going back to dwell on these things. The Buddhism of my ancestors dies hard. I live a works-based faith, even though I know intellectually, as a good Reformed Christian, that you and I are God's beloved no matter what we do or what we leave undone.

Do not forsake Wisdom. Wisdom surrounds me. She has always surrounded me. Wisdom has many faces. She gives the bread of understanding. She is harsh to the undisciplined. Those who love her love life. It is she who deploys her strength from one end of the earth to the other. She is a breath of the power of God, emanation of the glory of the Almighty.

She also taught my mother how to make wontons, real ones, savory with chopped vegetables and meat, while learning the arts of ministry.

She endured discrimination and cruel, unthinking comments by the ignorant while baptizing their children, burying their parents, leading them Sunday after Sunday in worship.

She brought a congregation barely limping along into full flower, into a group of people determined to love all the world.

She helped a congregation develop a culture of welcome to people of faith who have been shaped by different religions.

Wisdom is frequently ignored, until she has proven how much she loves those around her.

And it is Wisdom who guides the women who care for her people. She clucks her tongue and shakes her head when one of the good servants of the church falls into exhaustion even before she has a chance to turn her phone off while on vacation.

Wisdom shows her face only occasionally. I saw her the other day, when I stood in front of a group of good church people, smiled, thanked them, shared information appropriate to my role. I know they vote against my interests at church assemblies and at the ballot box. They told me so, without knowing quite who I am. A different me would have been angry. But instead I smiled, and I asked them about their congregations. Because we are not so different, they and I. We love God. We love our church. I am to love them no matter their actions, their votes, or my convictions.

I only know this because of Wisdom.

Do not forsake Wisdom. Wisdom surrounds me. She has always surrounded me.

She is my mother. My colleague. My friend. My classmate. My rival. My sister in Christ.

I first encountered Wisdom among Asian American women in ministry at home. I grew up biracial and multicultural in primarily dominant culture communities and churches. My Japanese American mother went from a pastor's wife to an ordained minister and spiritual director, noting along the way that she could be for me the Asian American woman in the pulpit she never saw as a child. My mother and many other Asian American women saw to it that I was surrounded by Wisdom, whether or not they knew they were her mediators. There was Betha Hoy, a Chinese American woman who served as a seminary intern with my (much younger) father pastor. There was Annie Wu King and Unzu Lee, national church staff, who mentored generations of younger women into leadership. There was Mary Paik, who has mentored more young people into ministry than any of us can count. Stacy Kitahata mentors a diversity of leaders with great patience. It is a long list of women who have made it their work to encourage Asian American women's leadership.

Wisdom has a way of creating accidental leaders.

Leadership is accidental, particularly in my experience as an Asian American woman. I am aware that many people felt they shaped me into a leader, but it is as though I fell into it. I have many traits, I suppose, that predispose me to be a leader. I work well with diverse people. I am not afraid to jump in and help facilitate a process. Speaking in front of crowds doesn't bother me. I am capable of having challenging one-on-one conversations, even if they scare me. I am able to "read" the culture of an organization and work within it. I learn quickly. I know when to say I don't know something, and I have plenty of opinions.

What is most accidental, I believe, about my leadership, is that I fit nowhere. I'm an ordained Teaching Elder in the Presbyterian Church (U.S.A.), but I have never served in a parish. My cultural heritage is embedded in the West Coast and in the Northeast, but I have lived most of my professional life somewhere in the middle. I am a multiracial Japanese American/Eastern European woman of Jewish descent. In an Asian American context that is relatively young, with most Asian Americans having arrived post-1965, I am a fourth and fifth generation Asian American. Of Jewish descent, I am Christian. I have upper-middle-class tastes, identify with the middle class, and was a MediCal[2] baby. I am of childbearing age and love children but have decided not to have any of my own. I am a church bureaucrat, but I long for the days when my job meant I had to be out somewhere, marching, protesting, petitioning, talking with those most marginalized by our own society's economic system and cultural norms. I am aware of the ways in which I rely on the labor of others who are women, working class, and immigrants, to keep my life together so that I can do my job.

I am not the only Asian American woman leader, of course. Wisdom literature shows a diversity of what it means to have a personification of wisdom. Reflections on my own journey and leadership are an interesting exercise but leave me curious to learn about others. Wisdom reminded me she has many faces, and within my sisterhood, I have found this is true.

I am reminded by wise women that my experience is just that: my experience. And to learn more about Asian American women's leadership, I need to hear the experiences of my sisters, especially when my sisters have very different or contradictory experiences and interpretations of experiences than my own.

I thought of some influential Asian American women in leadership in the church. Within their diversity, they share certain qualities. They challenge the church to more fully reflect God's love in the world, and they love the church deeply. They are not satisfied with how the church is, quite yet, even as they have given their lives to the call of serving the church. Most serve outside of Asian American communities, holding influence because they have earned authority through their work, not just through their positions or job descriptions.

I sent a short survey to a group of women who I recognized as leaders in ministry. My intent was not to do a comprehensive survey that would test a true sample of Asian American women in ministry. My intent was to ask questions of Asian American women I know to be leaders, whom I respect, who have interesting stories to tell that might provide a contrast to my own story.

Eight women responded. They were from three mainline denominations: the Christian Church (Disciples of Christ), the Evangelical Lutheran Church in America, and the Presbyterian Church (U.S.A.). The respondents are Korean American, Taiwanese American, Chinese American, Japanese American, Filipina American, and multiracial (South Asian/hapa), ranging in age from early thirties to mid-sixties. All but one is an ordained minister. Most serve as associate or solo pastors in churches, with two serving in the nonprofit sector and one serving in campus ministry. The ten-question questionnaire on leadership follows at the end of this chapter.

The respondents grew up in majority white or majority Asian contexts. Some feel connected to the community in a comprehensive way, some feel connected to the community only individually, and some do not feel they are part of the community. This diversity, I believe, is inherent to what it means to be Asian American women in leadership: we all have different ways of being and leading.

I consider them part of my sisterhood of Asian American women leaders.

Like me, some of these women also found themselves to be accidental leaders, falling into leadership by virtue of passion or place. One pastor, a Chinese American woman, said she realized she had become a leader while working to end racism at seminary. Another said she felt affirmed as a leader only upon seeing an Asian American woman in the pulpit. A Filipina pastor said, "I am the eldest of six siblings. I was 'in charge' of my siblings' care and safety. . . . So from the age of twelve to sixty-five, I have realized that I have entered a leadership role at different times." A Korean American pastor said she felt like a leader when she was elected to be the moderator of her judicatory.

Leaders can be cultivated. I have been given opportunities to grow, take charge, learn from my mistakes, and absorb the wisdom of other leaders. I have been given permission to speak (which I do too often, and too freely). I have access to leaders in multiple sectors and institutions. Knowing the areas in which my own leadership training was limited, I went back for more training, this time in business. I have watched where other leaders fail and where they succeed.

In the midst of this cultivation, I have often fallen into the trap laid by well-meaning mentors of emulating them instead of growing into my own leadership. As all those who mentored me communicated their own style and best practices, I, the ever obedient firstborn daughter, tried to follow what they said and did, even though what I learned was a hot mess of contradictions. I was taught to look out primarily for members of my community, without regard for my own physical and spiritual well-being. I was taught to protect myself at all costs, a philosophy I have understood as "playing the long game," while others paid the price for being in their jobs at the wrong time in the life of an organization or standing up for the right thing at the wrong time. I was taught by example to give tough love, while another example taught me to let people fail instead of addressing the issues at hand. I was taught by some that the finances would work themselves out and taught by others (and my business training) that financial success requires multiple parties pay close attention to income and expenses.

For other women, leadership was cultivated. A multiracial South Asian pastor was encouraged to think of herself as a leader as soon as she began ministry after seminary. A Japanese American lay leader was given leadership responsibilities long before she grew into the identity of leader.

At some point, I learned from yet another mentor that all experiences teach me something. Mentors and leaders may teach me practices and philosophies that fit who I am and what I am called to do. And they definitely teach me styles of leadership that I hope I never emulate, lest I participate in the slow destruction of an institution or the spirit of another person.

Because I have worked with many leaders shaped by the individualistic forces of U.S. society, and because those same forces shape me, I sometimes forget. Sometimes I think I have earned where I am, when in fact where I am is the result of others investing in my leadership development. I forget the ways in which leadership is forged in and recognized by a community. But I never forget who has my back. When I take risks or make decisions or work within institutions facing significant criticism, I remember there are many who will support me even when they disagree with me. I remember my call to ministry is more than my job, or any job I have ever held. I remember that people who have my back will someday tell me what I'm doing wrong, giving me the chance to change. This, above all else, has shaped my sense of leadership.

Again, I find myself curious about the experiences of my sisters. How did they come into leadership? How did we all end up here?

Of the Asian American women I surveyed, most came into leadership through their roles or through the authority of their persons. Some were told early about their leadership by others around them and were encouraged to take on leadership. One respondent said, "Early on, as a teenaged young person, I noticed that people came to me with problems. And then some-one suggested it wasn't . . . because I had fewer [problems], rather it showed [they trusted me]." Some understood they had become leaders after entering a particular role or job. A respondent said she could cite instances of seeing herself as a leader previously, "but the one that stands out is 2012 when I was the Moderator of my presbytery." Another said racist experiences at seminary fueled her organizing for change at the institutional level, which contributed to the creation of an office for multiculturalism on campus.

The role of others in bestowing leadership was mentioned explicitly by at least three respondents. One said, "I recognize that I am a leader when others turn to me for leadership and when others entrust me with more leadership responsibilities."

Another respondent realized she had become a leader because of her work in the church in high school, and in her role as a firstborn daughter, but she remembers most significantly that her leadership was affirmed in the first church she served. She said, "It seems like a little thing, but the first time [I was called] *moksanim* (Reverend), I felt the shift in my very being and knew that I had entered into a position of leadership in a way that I had not experienced before."

Like many Pacific Asian and North American Asian women in leadership in the church and society, I am an anomaly, upsetting expectations largely shaped by white patriarchal assumptions of church leadership. We are women of color in largely white churches. We are women of color ministers in denominations or traditions where white men are disproportionately represented as ministers. We are Americans who are fluent in English and hold U.S. citizenship, even though the stereotype is that Asians and Pacific Islanders are forever foreign.

A Japanese American lay leader who works for a foundation, and who previously served an institution of theological education and on the staff of her denomination's national offices, said,

> I've been fortunate to have been a first of something in each of my full-time employment positions—Asian American woman, person of color, person under thirty, woman, layperson, in this new position . . . or combination of some or all of those! That has been tremendously empowering and has shaped my leadership orientation and expectations!

A Korean American pastor offered:

> I am always mindful and aware of the other Asian American women who went the road ahead of me when the path was much more difficult. On my path into ministry, I got so much crap about being a woman and becoming a pastor, so I cannot imagine the cultural and societal hell those who went before me went through. I recognize that being an Asian American woman in ministry is rare, but I also recognize that to some extent, I do feel free to be who I am authentically in ministry and in my role.

Instead of bemoaning this series of "firsts," and their attendant challenges, they have the wisdom to find opportunity. They have been able to shape and define their work and the work of the institutions they serve. Indeed, it can be a distinct advantage in one's ministry to be different. The hapa South Asian minister said,

> In my current ministry, my focus is on creating a culture of faith-rooted organizing embedded with systemic anti-oppression analysis. Because I'm a minister in a secular organization with a religious organizing arm, I get away with nudging us in that direction. . . . My voice is not infrequently turned to in the majority culture in the denomination as a known quantity around anti-oppression and social justice issues, largely because I have located myself in a position of not relying on denominational funding or resources to do my work—also a little inside/outside.

Finally, a Chinese American pastor reflected, "when I served in a predominately white congregation, I felt as though I was treated as if I were white *unless* a marginal perspective was needed. Yet now I am serving in a multicultural, multiethnic congregation and my identity is of high importance."

Being the one upsetting expectations, being in the minority in almost every way, has made me more aware of those on the outside, those experiencing some kind of marginalization. I find myself paying attention to who is not in the room, and finding ways to hear those voices. In my survey, I found that many of the women also pay attention to marginalization. In noticing their own experiences of being other than the norm, they see when others experience exclusion and marginalization. When we fit nowhere, we can find ways to contribute to a multitude of communities. We can have an affinity for those on the edges of the communities we serve. The Filipina pastor surveyed was called to her current church to either close it or change it. In fifteen years of her ministry, she has prayed a great deal and repeatedly declared that she would "'love' to do a hell of a memorial service for the church if they didn't want to think outside the walls." Now, the church "is a thriving community focused on outreach [rather than itself]." Their ministries include a Spanish-language worship service, partnering to support services for people with limited resources and those impacted by domestic violence, and hosts the largest food pantry in the county.

A Korean American associate pastor illuminates a skill specific to being in the minority that she believes is important. She said,

> When I am in the midst of Asian American women, I become more aware of how important it is for people to learn to be comfortable being uncomfortable. Minorities who have learned the skill of being comfortable outside their comfort zones have this valuable skill to contribute to people who haven't needed to learn this skill.

I have found, like her, it is invaluable to my ministry to feel comfortable with being uncomfortable. My comfort level with feeling I am on the outside, or feeling a little different, has made my capacity to walk into and work in unfamiliar spaces a skill that is helpful in national church work.

Being a leader looks different for different women. Said one, "Being a leader is about improvising and thinking on your feet—soaking in what is being thrown at you and using it to your advantage." A pastor who does community work said her leadership "has had much more of a facilitation style, bringing together partners engaged in the work of creating peace and justice." One pastor intends to serve as an example, saying, "I hope my leadership style can demonstrate that leadership comes in different forms." Another said, "I just want to be thought of as a pastor who did her best to follow God and brought the faith community along with her, deepening their faith, changing hearts to love their community."

This diversity, to me, shows a fundamental truth about leadership among Asian American women. We are deeply committed to ministry and the church, and we have as many different approaches to this commitment as women in leadership.

Wisdom has her many, diverse ways.

Upsetting expectations is not enough for us. I asked each woman what kind of long-term influence she wants her leadership to have. A Chinese American college chaplain said, "I hope that I model a different way of leading and a different face. I am very conscious of being an Asian American woman, and a mother as well, and let those identities infuse my pastoral leadership. . . . I hope that expands people's expectation and upends assumptions." A Chinese American parish pastor, also engaged in national church work, said, "I would love to be seen as a bridge-builder." Another says she hopes her leadership has long-term influence, because that would mean "that my vision was big enough for an expansive horizon and that I created a stable and generative foundation for the vision to be realized."

Many of the Asian American women leaders mentioned being one of the only or one of the few Asian American women in ministry in their regions. They are aware of the difference they symbolize, the potential for living in discomfort, the knowledge they may not quite fit, even as they fit into the spaces of where ministry is done. A Filipina pastor said she believes people see her leadership as unique to her, not specifically Filipino, but, in her words, "I have always said to the people I serve or work with to recognize I am a brown woman and come with different life experiences than they do but am on the same journey of faith calling us to share our stories with each other."

Like many of these women indicated in their surveys, I also grew up in settings that nurtured my leadership, particularly in church. I was generally treated as just another white person, unless someone felt the need to point out my otherness. My church experience did little to contribute to my racial identity formation. Instead, my family and mentors socialized me. My Asian American women mentors, in particular, helped me to see many ways of being an Asian American. It was my mother, attending seminary and serving a church, who explicitly told me that my identity as an Asian American woman was important in the church context. By reflecting on her own racial and gender identity in the context of church leadership, she taught me to bring my whole self. I began to consider my own racial and gendered identity in the church after my mother began to point out she never grew up with an Asian American woman in the pulpit, something she wanted me to see.

She was among the first wise women I saw in leadership; she and others form this sisterhood.

We may not exactly fit what society, or the church, expects. We might be the first in any given place. We have our own ways of leading in the midst of this marginal space. Wisdom has many faces. They are my sisters. They are leaders.

A QUESTIONNAIRE ON LEADERSHIP

Name:

Ethnicity:

Age Bracket: 20–29, 30–35, 36–40, 41–50, 51–60, 61–70

1. Do you see yourself as a leader? If not, how do you see yourself?

2. If you do see yourself as a leader or having leadership responsibilities, what does that mean to you and for your ministry?

3. When did you realize you had entered into leadership?

4. Do you hope your leadership has long-term influence? What kind of influence?

5. Do you feel people treat you differently because you are an Asian American woman? Or do you feel people treat your leadership as particular to you, and not to a group identity?

6. Do you feel your leadership reflects on Pacific/Asian/North American Asian women?

   a. If so, do you ever modify your behavior as a result?

7. Are you interested in changing the system of the place where you are in ministry? If so, how do you see yourself creating that change?

8. Do you think you "rock the boat" as an Asian American woman in leadership? How do you feel that impacts your relationship with your Asian American community, if at all? With the majority community?

9. Tell me a story about a time when your leadership made an impact. That impact could be on the system, on an individual, a small group within your community, your community, or a group of people outside your community.

10. Anything else you want to share?

Appendix

This *Leading Wisdom* anthology project explored various venues to generate question that we used for the anthology. There were various focus groups, meetings, and conferences where we met to discuss the theme and solicit reflections. And we identify three distinct phases:

Phase 1

We have asked all potential contributors to read *Leaving Church: A Memoir of Faith* by Barbara Brown Taylor (2007) to generate discussions (and more questions) around the following questions:

I. What is leadership in ministry?
II. How do women lead and minister?
III. In particular, how do Pacific Asian and North American Asian (PANAA) women experience leadership?
IV. If we place our experiences at the center of the inquiry, would conventional ways that we think about leadership in churches and communities change?
V. Can this exploration help imagine other ways of "being" and "doing" church?

Phase 2

We have used the following questions for the selected contributors of this anthology to participate in the "Leadership Round-table" session and the "Setting the Table: Wisdom Leadership of Pacific Asian and Asian North American Women in Theology and Ministry" session at the ANAATE (Association of Asian/North American Asian Theological Educators) conference in 2014:

• Looking back on your own experiences, what can you say about the nature of leadership? How do you see yourself as a leader?

- Can you name one incident/biblical passage/person/experience (in the church, community or academy) that contributed to your own understanding of wisdom leadership?
- What have you learned from your experience of becoming a leader that you would like to share as key life lessons with young striving Pacific Asian and Asian North American women and men today?
- If we take "the call to ministry" outside the church (and seminaries), what would that look like?

Phase 3

We have used other prompts, such as "metaphor for leadership" exercises as well as "word play" to generate reflections and insights about wisdom and leadership in focus groups. The following questions are a collection of questions from all three phases categorized by function and role of wise leadership.

Definitions

- What is wisdom for you? How do you understand it?
- What is leadership?

Context

- What is your context for leadership?
- What does wisdom look like in the context of leadership?
- What are our cultural values and cultural liabilities?
- What challenges and opportunities do PANAA women leaders face?

Skills/Characteristics

- Who is one wisdom leader you have encountered? What aspect/characteristic of hers did you experience as special?
- If you could meet any wisdom leader (past or present) for thirty minutes, who would it be and why?
- What are two or three traits that are essential for wisdom leaders?
- What training is needed for or contributes to leadership capability?
- How do you negotiate power and responsibility?
- How do you manage conflicts?

Practices/Experiences

- Generational question: What has been your experience as a mentee with a role model? When have you been a mentor?
- What three pieces of advice do you have for young women?
- What spiritual practices inform and enhance your leadership?
- How do you care for yourself?

Metaphors and Images

- What are metaphors and images for leadership?

• How would you describe/categorize your leadership (i.e., mentor, coach, pioneer, nurturer, prophet, bridge-maker, etc.)?

Metaphor for Leadership Exercise

This exercise is designed to assist writers to articulate their understanding of leadership and engage it theologically.

Step One: Image/Metaphor

Read "The Movement Toward Insight: The Human Process of Coming to Wisdom" from *The Art of Theological Reflection* by Patricia O'Connell Killen and John de Beer. Reflect on your experience of leadership (either your own or someone else's). It could be an experience that awakened you to ministry, teaching, or social service. It could be a "Paul on the road to Damascus" blinding experience that gave you conviction. It could be gentle urgings, discomfort, un-ease with the way things are that led you to explore something more. Sit with that experience and let an image or metaphor emerge. For example, your metaphor might be "riding the subway," or "dinner party on $10 budget" or "dying daily" or "extravagant hospitality." Let something emerge for you.

Share/write a brief description of that experience. And share what your image or metaphor is.

Step Two: Questions

What (theological) questions would you bring to your metaphor? For instance, if your metaphor was "dinner party on $10 budget," you might ask: (1) what is the purpose of gathering? (community, church); (2) why only $10? (economic justice); (3) who is invited? (inclusion, hospitality); (4) what's for dinner? Who's cooking? (substance and context of ministry); (5) party suggests fun, grace-filled event (scarcity vs. abundance); (6) who's not coming and why? (discord, conflict, war). As much as possible, theologically engage the questions that might arise from these questions. Are there other theological concepts like sin, forgiveness, liberation, salvation, creation, revelation, death, heaven, hell that need exploring as you probe your metaphor/image? What are they?

Share/write questions that you bring to the metaphor/image. Also share/write questions that your metaphor/image poses for you.

Step Three: Saying Yes and Saying No

Saying yes and saying no are another way of understanding discernment. Sometimes, saying yes to something might necessitate saying no to something else. As you ponder, sit with and reflect on your image/metaphor, what are you saying yes to? What are you saying no to? What are some "not yet" and "don't know" and "both/and"?

Share/write your "yes's," "no's," "not yet's" "both/and's." Share insights and future explorations. What skills, development, and understanding would you need in order to lead as the metaphor/image opens up for you?

Step Four: Bringing It All Together

Write a paragraph statement on your understanding of your theology/ philosophy of leadership.

Themes and Questions for the Writers

We have asked all committed contributors to address the following themes and questions in their writing:

1. Describe your context and development as a leader. What challenges and opportunities do you face as a PANAA women leader?

2. What definitions and traditions ground your understanding of both wisdom and leadership?
   - You might bring in theological, biblical, cultural, tradition sources to bear on this question.

3. What skills have proved to be necessary for you to develop as a PANAA women leader?
   - If you could meet any wisdom leader (past or present) for thirty minutes, who would it be and why?
   - What are two or three traits/skills that are essential for wisdom leaders?
   - What training is needed for or contributes to leadership capability?

4. Which practices, cultural values, and cultural liabilities inform, sustain, and challenge your leadership as PANAA women?
   - Do women lead differently? Do PANAA women lead differently? If so, how?
   - How do you negotiate power and responsibility?
   - How do you manage conflicts?
   - What spiritual practices inform and enhance your leadership?
   - Who is one wisdom leader you have encountered? What aspect/ characteristic of hers did you experience as special?
   - Generational question: What has been your experience as a mentee with a role model? When have you been a mentor?
   - What three pieces of advice do you have for young women?

5. What metaphors and images describe your leadership style?
   • How would you describe/categorize your leadership (i.e., mentor, coach, pioneer, nurturer, prophet, bridge-maker, etc.)?

Notes

Introduction

1. Hal Taussig, "The Thunder: Perfect Mind," in *A New New Testament: A Bible for the 21st Century Combining Traditional and Newly Discovered Texts* (Boston: Houghton Mifflin, 2013), 183.
2. Rita Nakashima Brock, et al. eds., *Off the Menu: Asian and Asian North American Women's Religion and Theology* (Louisville, KY: Westminster John Knox Press, 2007).
3. Kwok, Pui Lan and Rachel Bundang, "PANAAWTM Lives!," *Journal of Feminist Study in Religion* 21:2 (2005).
4. Rita Nakashima Brock and Nami Kim, "Asian Pacific American Protestant Women," in *Encyclopedia of Women and Religion in North America*, edited by Rosemary Skinner Keller, Rosemary Radford Ruether, Marie Cantion (Bloomington: Indiana University Press, 2006).
5. Laura Mariko Cheifetz and Stacy D. Kitahata, "Forming Asian Leaders for North American Churches," Sharon Callahan, ed. *Religious Leadership: A Reference Handbook* (Los Angeles: Sage Reference, 2013), 709–20.
6. As per the title of Cherríe Moraga and Gloria Anzaldúa book, *This Bridge Called My Back: Writings by Radical Women of Color*, 4th ed. (Albany: State University of New York Press, 2015).
7. Lois P. Frankel, *Nice Girls Still Don't Get the Corner Office: Unconscious Mistakes Women Make That Sabotage Their Careers* (New York: Business Plus, 2014); John P. Kotter, *Leading Change* (Boston, MA: Harvard Business Review Press, 2012); Tracy Brian and Peter Chee, *12 Disciplines of Leadership Excellence: How Leaders Achieve Sustainable High Performance* (New York: McGraw Hill, 2013); David L. Van Rooy, *Trajectory: 7 Career Strategies to Take You from Where You Are* (New York: American Management Association (AMACOM), 2014).
8. Brita I. Gill-Austern, "Love Understood as Self-Sacrifice and Self-Denial: What Does It Do to Women?" in *Through the Eyes of Women: Insights for Pastoral Care*, ed. Jeanne Stevenson Moessner, 304–21 (Minneapolis, MN: Fortress Press, 1996); Deborah M. Kolb, Judith Williams, and Carol Frohlinger, *Her Place and the Table: A Woman's Guide to Negotiating Five Key Challenges to Leadership Success* (San Francisco, CA: Jossey-Bass, 2010); Chanequa Walker-Barnes, *Too Heavy a Yoke: Black Women and the Burden of Strength* (Eugene, Oregon: CASCADE Books, 2014).
9. Parker Palmer, *The Courage to Teach: Exploring the Inner Landscape of a Teacher's Life*, 10th anniv. ed. (San Francisco: Jossey-Bass, 2007), 9–33.

10. Sheryl Sandberg, *Lean In: Women, Work and the Will to Lead*. (New York: Knopf, 2013).
11. Ariana Huffington, *Thrive: The Third Metric to Redefining Success and Creating a Life of Well-Being, Wisdom, and Wonder*. (New York: Harmony Books, 2014, 2015).
12. Sheri Parks, *Fierce Angels: Living with a Legacy from the Sacred Dark Feminine to the Strong Black Woman* (Chicago: Chicago Review Press, 2013).
13. Callahan, *Religious Leadership, Vol 1*, xv.
14. Alice Eagly and Linda Carli, *Through the Labyrinth: The Truth about How Women Become Leaders* (Cambridge, MA: Harvard Business School Publishing Corp., 2007).
15. Pew Forum on Religion and Public Life, *Asian Americans: A Mosaic of Faiths* (Washington, DC: Pew Research Center, 2012).
16. Rita Brock, "Cooking without Recipes: Interstitial Integrity" in *Off the Menu*, 136.
17. Hal Taussig, *The Thunder: Perfect Mind: A New Translation and Introduction* (New York: Palgrave Macmillan, 2010).
18. Ibid., 185, 183.

Chapter 1: Crumb-Gathering Wisdom Calls Out for Pacific Asian and North American Asian Women Historians

1. On theological commentaries on the Syrophoenician woman, see Kwok Pui-lan, *Discovering the Bible in the Non-Biblical World* (Maryknoll, NY: Orbis Books, 1995), 71–83; and idem, "Overlapping Communities and Multicultural Hermeneutics," in *A Feminist Companion to Reading the Bible: Approaches, Methods, and Strategies*, ed. Athalya Brenner and Carole Fontaine (London and Chicago: Fitzroy Dearborn Publishers, 2001, 1997), 203–15. Also see Raymond Apple, "The Two Wise Women of Proverbs Chapter 31," *Jewish Bible Quarterly*, vol. 39, no. 3 (2011): 175–80 on Wisdom; and Hisako Kinukawa, *Women and Jesus in Mark: A Japanese Feminist Perspective* (Maryknoll, NY: Orbis Books, 1994), 59, on an analogy of the Syrophoenician woman and Korean Japanese women.
2. Kwok Pui-lan, *Postcolonial Imagination and Feminist Theology* (Louisville, KY: Westminster John Knox Press, 2005), 46.
3. *New York Times*, 4 January 2013, obituary. Note Lerner's experiences as a Jewish refugee.
4. Gerda Lerner, *Teaching Women's History* (American Historical Association, 1981), 60, 65. Also see her epoch-making *The Creation of Patriarchy* (1986) and *The Creation of Feminist Consciousness* (1997).
5. See such works as *In Our Own Voices: Four Centuries of Religious Writings by American Women*, ed. Rosemary Skinner Keller and Rosemary Radford Reuther (Louisville, KY: Westminster John Knox Press, 2000).
6. See Joan Kelly-Gadol, "Did Women Have a Renaissance?," in *Becoming Visible: Women in European History*, ed. Renate Bridenthal and Claudia Koonz (Boston: Houghton Mifflin, 1977), 137–64.
7. Her first editions were quickly outdated. See the third edition of *Women and Gender in Early Modern Europe* by Merry E. Wiesner (Cambridge and New York: Cambridge University Press, 2008); and the second edition of Merry E. Wiesner-Hanks, *Christianity and Sexuality in the Early Modern World: Regulating Desire, Reforming Practice* (London: Routledge, 2010).

8. Kirsi Stjerna, *Women and the Reformation* (Malden, MA: Blackwell, 2009), 1.
9. See Merry Wiesner-Hanks, "Gender and the Reformation," *Archive für Refromationsgeschichte/Archive for Reformation History*, v.100 (2009): 363–4.
10. *Documenta Indica* [*DI*], ed. Josef Wicki (Rome: Monumenta Historica Societatis Iesu, 1948–), 4:365–66 (Luís Fróis, 10 Nov. 1559) and *DI*, 4:654 (Luís Fróis, 13 Nov. 1560). The citations from *DI* are translated into English by me. Also see Haruko Nawata Ward, "Good News to Women? The Jesuits, Their Pastoral Advice and Women's Reception of Christianity in the Portuguese East Indies; Goa and Japan," in *Jesuits in India: History and Culture*, ed. Délio de Mendonça (Goa: Xavier Centre of Historical Research, 2007).
11. *DI*, 4:207 (Pero Almeida, 26 Dec. 1558).
12. *DI*, 4:654 (Luís Fróis, 13 Nov.1560).
13. *DI*, 4:366 (Luís Fróis, 10 Nov. 1559).
14. *DI*, 5:607 (Barthasar da Costa, 4 Dec. 1562).
15. See *DI*, 4:655, 5:609, 6:286, 6:367, 6:618. See also António da Silva Rêgo, ed., *Documentação para a história das missões do padroado português do Oriente* (Lisbon: Agência geral do ultramar, Divisão de publicacões e biblioteca, 1947–1958), 10:97.
16. Also see Haruko Nawata Ward, "Nait Julia and Women Catechists in the Jesuit Mission in Japan and the Philippines," in *Putting Names with Faces: Women's Impact in Mission History*, ed. Christine Lienemann-Perrin, Atola Longkumer, and Afrie Songco Joye (Nashville: Abingdon, 2012); and idem, *Women Religious Leaders of Japan's Christian Century: 1549–1650*, Women and Gender in the Early Modern World (Aldershot, England and Burlington, VT: Ashgate Publishing, 2009).
17. See Luís Fróis's annual report (13 December 1596) in John Hay, *De Rebvs Iaponicis* (Facsimile. Nara: Tenri Central Library, 1977), 454.
18. The sixteenth- and seventeenth-century spellings are retained for Miyaco and bicuni.
19. See Archivum Romanum Societatis Iesu (ARSI), *Philippinarum 7I* (Juan de Salazar, annual letter 1634–35), 197v–198; also see Francisco Colín, *Labor Evangélica, ministerios apostolicos de los obreros de la Compañía de Jesús, . . . en las Islas Filipinas* (Madrid, 1663; repr. ed. Pablo Pastells, Barcelona, 1992), 3:500–501.
20. Daniello Bartoli, *Istoria della compagnia di Gesú il Giappone: Secunda parte dell'Asia* (Naples, 1857–58), 4:196–97.
21. See Marcelino A. Foronda, *Mother Ignacia and her Beaterio: a Preliminary Study* (Makati, Rizal: St. Paul Publications, 1975); and Horacio de la Costa, *The Jesuits in the Philippines 1581–1768* (Cambridge, MA: Harvard University Press, 1967).
22. See Luís Fróis, *Historia de Japam*, ed. José Wicki, 5 vols. (Lisbon, 1976), 5:457.
23. See Diego Pacheco, *Kyūshū Kirishitanshi kenkyū* (Tokyo: Kirishitan Bunka Kenky kai, 1977).
24. See Colín, *Labor Evangélica*, 3:503–4. Its partial translation in English is available in Juan G. Ruiz-de-Medina, *The Catholic Church in Korea: Its Origins 1566–1784*, trans. John Bridges (Rome: Jesuit Historical Institute; Seoul: Korean Branch of the Royal Asiatic Society, 1991), 245–47.
25. See Juan G. Ruiz-de-Medina, "Historia y Ficcion de ta Julia," *Hispania Sacra* 41 (1986):529–43; and "History and Fiction of ta Julia," *The Kirisutokyo-shigaku* 42 (1988): 49–67. See also Ruiz-de-Medina, *The Catholic Church in Korea*.

26. The following citations come from *Archivum Romanum Societatis Iesu, Jap.Sin. 62*, 3, Cristóbal Ferreira (20 August 1631). English translation is mine.

27. The following information on Candida is based on Claudia von Collani, "Lady Candida Xu: A Widow between Chinese and Christian Ideals," in Jessie Gregory Lutz, ed., *Pioneer Chinese Christian Women: Gender, Christianity, and Social Mobility*, Studies in Missionaries and Christianity in China (Bethlehem: Lehigh University Press, 2010), 224–45.

28. Von Collani, "Lady Candida Xu," 232.

29. See Gail King, "Christian Women of China in the Seventeenth Century," in Lutz, ed., *Pioneer Chinese Christian Women*," 55–86 (citation from 78).

30. On the Chinese Christian virgins (nuns), see chapters by R.G. Tiedemann, Robert Entenmann, and Eugenio Menegon in Lutz, ed., *Pioneer Chinese Christian Women*. Also see Eugenio Menegon, *Ancestors, Virgins, and Friars: Christianity as a Local Religion in Late Imperial China*, Harvard-Yenching Institute Monograph Series 69 (Cambridge, MA: Harvard University Asia Center for the Harvard-Yenching Institute: Distributed by Harvard University Press, 2009).

31. See Peter C. Phan, *Mission and Catechesis: Alexandre de Rhodes and Inculturation in Seventeenth-Century Vietnam*, Faith and Cultures Series (Maryknoll, NY: Orbis Books, 1998). See also Tara Alberts, *Conflict and Conversion: Catholicism in Southeast Asia, 1500–1700* (Oxford University Press, 2013).

32. A study on Asian women in New Spain can begin with Catarina de San Juan, a Mughal Indian woman, sold as slave to Manila and became a mystic in Mexico. See Ulrike Strasser, "A Case of Empire Envy? German Jesuits and an Asia-born Saint from Colonial America," *Journal of Global History* (2007): 23–40.

33. On different interpretations of boundary crossings of the Syrophoenician woman, see Jane E. Hicks, "Moral Agency at the Borders: Rereading the Story of the Syrophoenician Woman," *Word and World*, vol. 23, no. 1 (Winter 2003): 76–84; and Surekha Nelavala, "Smart Syrophoenician Woman: A Dalit Feminist Reading of Mark 7:24–31," *Expository Times*, vol. 118, no. 2 (2006): 64–69.

Chapter 2: Taiwanese American Women Pastors and Leaders

1. All four of our interviewees belong either to the Presbyterian Church (U.S.A.) (PCUSA) or the RCA; three of the four have family roots in the Presbyterian Church in Taiwan (PCT), and one grew up in a PCUSA Taiwanese American church.

2. See Timothy Tseng et al., "Asian American Religious Leadership Today: A Preliminary Inquiry," (Durham, NC: Pulpit & Pew Research on Pastoral Leadership, 2005), 29–34 at 31 and Su Yon Pak, "Women Leaders in Asian American Protestant Churches," in *Religious Leadership: A Reference Handbook*, ed. Sharon Henderson Callahan, 287–96 (Thousand Oaks, CA: Sage, 2013) at 298–99.

3. Tseng, "Asian American Religious Leadership Today," 34.

4. Charlene Jin Lee, "Response #2," *Society of Asian North American Christian Studies* 2 (2010): 63–67 at 65. See also Jung Ha Kim, "Cartography of Korean American Protestant Faith Communities in the United States," in *Religion in Asian America*, eds. Pyong Gap Min and Jung Ha Kim, 185–13 (Lanham, MD: AltaMira Press, 2002) and Grace Ji-Sun Kim, ed. *Here I Am: Faith Stories of Korean American Clergywomen* (Philadelphia, PA: Judson Press, 2015).

5. For a condemnation of sexism from Korean male theologians, see Sang Hyun Lee, *From a Liminal Place: An Asian American Theology* (Minneapolis, MN: Fortress Press, 2010), 107–8, 138–41 and Andrew Sung Park, *Racial Conflict and Healing: An Asian-American Theological Perspective* (Eugene, OR: Wipf & Stock, 2009), 43–44.

6. The Rev. Dr. Fu-Ya Wu, the president of Tainan Theological College and Seminary and an ordained minister in the Presbyterian Church in Taiwan (PCT), published her DMin thesis in 1996 under the direction of Kwok Pui-lan titled "Women in the Christian Church: The Taiwanese Case." She concluded that Taiwanese Christian women (in Taiwan) face the triple burden of (1) Taiwanese cultural patriarchy, (2) androcentrism and male domination of Christianity and Christian churches, and (3) foreign domination. Wu found that women's service and contributions to the church were longstanding but largely invisible. She understands that Taiwanese women have long been "dominated under patriarchal teachings of womanhood as reflected in obedience, submission, and docility." Though she observed there has been some progress with educating women and training them to become evangelists, there has been very little effort to create equality between men and women. To be sure, note that Wu's work is (to date) two decades old and is based on the Taiwanese, not Taiwanese American context. See Wu Fu Ya, "Women in the Christian Church: The Taiwanese Case," DMin thesis, Episcopal Divinity School, 1996, especially p. 92, 96.

7. Carolyn Chen, "A Self of One's Own: Taiwanese Immigrant Women and Religious Conversion," *Gender and Society* 19.3 (2005): 336–57, at 343.

8. Ibid., 342.

9. As Simon Wang, one of Chen's male respondents, observed: "Before my word used to be her Bible. . . . Now she has the Bible, and she can disagree with me!" (Ibid., 351).

10. Chien-Juh Gu, *Mental Health among Taiwanese Americans: Gender, Immigration, and Transnational Struggles* (New York: LFB Scholarly Publishing, 2006), 242.

11. Ibid., 173.

12. Ibid., 173.

13. Ibid., 178–79.

14. Please see the list of questions at the end of this chapter that we asked each interviewee.

15. We recognize that women's leadership positions can be found elsewhere in the church but chose to focus on positions of leadership that either govern the entire congregation or are elected by them.

16. Consistent with best practices, we have used pseudonyms to protect our interviewees' identities.

17. Grace's father served one term as a deacon and one term as an elder; Grace's mother served several times as the women's group leader. Both of Grace's parents were part of the original church plant.

18. When commenting on a Facebook post about male-dominated leadership in Asian and Asian American churches, Grace's friend Nick Liao, who had grown up attending EFC NASA in Texas, wrote the following: "[I was] grateful to have grown up in the EFC, where woman pastors were never an issue, and my parents never taught me otherwise! It was a funky blend of conservative

evangelical theology and egalitarian ministry." Nick Liao, private Facebook discussion with author, February 20, 2015.

19. Pak, "Women Leaders in Asian American Protestant Churches," 300.

20. Rev. David Shinn, private Facebook message to the author, September 18, 2014.

21. Chinese immigration to Taiwan began in the sixteenth century. The Taiwanese people were then ruled briefly by the Spanish, Portuguese, and the Dutch from the late sixteenth to the mid-seventeenth century; came under Chinese rule for the next 250 years until China ceded Taiwan to Japan in 1895 in their loss in the Sino-Japanese War; then became a colony of Japan until World War II when the Allies forced Japan to give up Taiwan. The second major wave of immigration from China in the aftermath of loss of the Nationalists (KMT) to the Chinese Communist party is explained below in note 28. In the 1950s during the Korean War, the United States also supported and influenced Taiwan in the areas of defense and economics, part of its containment strategy. See Carolyn Chen, *Getting Saved in America: Taiwanese Immigration and Religious Experience* (Princeton, NJ: Princeton University Press, 2008) 17–18 and Gu, *Mental Health among the Taiwanese*, 98–99, 120.

22. See Gary Marvin Davidson, *A Short History of Taiwan: The Case for Independence* (Westport, CT: Greenwood Publishing Group, 2003) who describes such cultures as "highly egalitarian" and Pao-tsun Tai, *The Concise History of Taiwan*, trans. Ruby J. Lee (Nantou: Taiwan Historica, 2007), who uses the more common descriptor "matriarchal." In fact, the "dominance of the female gender" in aboriginal cultures apparently "had become so much a part of the popular imagery of Taiwan" that certain writers had established the stereotype of "the supremely capable wife" by the nineteenth century. See Emma Teng, "An Island of Beautiful Women: The Discourse on Gender in Ch'ing Travel Accounts of Taiwan," in *Women in the New Taiwan: Gender Roles and Gender Consciousness in a Changing Society* (Armonk: ME Sharpe, 2004), 48.

23. By the 1920s, urban residents, male or female, could receive six years of primary school education in Japanese, and eventually middle- and upper-class boys and girls could receive a middle and high school education as well. Catherine S. P. Farris, "Women's Liberation under 'East Asian Modernity' in China and Taiwan: Historical, Cultural, and Comparative Perspectives," in *Women in the New Taiwan*, 340.

24. Gu, *Mental Health among Taiwanese Americans*, 120.

25. According to Ya-chen Chen, these early feminist efforts included an end to foot-binding, the establishment of prestigious girls' high schools, and the organization of women's professional associations. See her "Taiwanese Feminist History: A Sociocultural Review," in *Women in Taiwan: Sociocultural Perspectives*, ed. Ya-chen Chen, 15–30 (Indianapolis, IN: University of Indianapolis Press, 2007) at 16–17.

26. For instance, Farris in "Women's Liberation" observes that the professionalization of midwives became "part of the public health and educational policies of the Japanese for Taiwan" (p. 341). An example of consciousness-raising can be found in one writer's call in a Taiwanese magazine, *Taiwan Youth*, for "the establishment of an egalitarian 'mutually responsible family.'" See Farris, "Women's Liberation," 342.

27. Gu, *Mental Health among Taiwanese Americans*, 120.

28. The Taiwanese people are ethnically distinct owing to a host of political issues. *Wàishĕngrén* refer to post-1945 Chinese immigrants or so-called mainlanders: they primarily speak Mandarin and are the ones who fled the mainland after the end of WWII, especially after the Nationalists lost to the Communists in 1949. *Bĕngshĕngrén*, or the so-called Taiwanese, refer to pre-1945 Chinese who had been emigrating from China since the sixteenth century and who speak *Hokkien* or *Hakka*, in addition to Mandarin if they have been formally educated. Approximately 2 percent of the Taiwanese population is indigenous.

29. The majority of the churches we interviewed were Presbyterian or Reformed. A few were independent churches and one was the Salvation Army, the latter which encourages spouses to pastor churches together rather than alone as both husband and wife are ordained together as a couple. We had no Baptist churches in our sample—the one denomination Sarah (our senior pastor) had reported disapproving of female clergy.

30. The Women's Ministry Committee of the Presbyterian Church in Taiwan, http://women.pct.org.tw/aboutus.aspx.

31. Luca Pisano, "Taiwanese Composers and Piano Works in the XX Century: Traditional Chinese Cultures and the Taiwan Xin YinYue," *Kervan: Rivista Internazionale di Studii Afroasiatici* no. 1 (gennaio 2005): 49–71 at 50.

32. http://www.laijohn.com/archives/pc/Li/Li,Pchou/brief/Niu,Uchin.htm.

33. Worldwide Guide to Women in Leadership, Chronology of Women's Ordination, http://www.guide2womenleaders.com/Chronolgy_Ordination.htm.

34. We owe the following insight, that the church is disincentivized to be choosy genderwise when Christians only represent a small percentage of the total population, to Rachel Lei and Gloria Hu—two Taiwanese North American Christians with deep family histories in the Presbyterian Church in Taiwan (PCT). We are grateful for other helpful feedback they gave on our chapter; any mistakes that remain, of course, are ours.

Chapter 3: Neither the Suffering Servant nor the Syrophoenician Woman

1. Sun Ai Lee Park, "A Theological Reflection," in *We Dare to Dream: Doing Theology as Asian Women*, eds. Virginia Fabella and Sun Ai Lee Park (Maryknoll, NY: Orbis Books), 75.

2. Chung Hyun Kyung, *Struggle to Be the Sun Again: Introducing Asian Women's Theology* (Maryknoll, NY: Orbis Books), 53–54.

3. Haejoang Cho, "Male Dominance and Mother Power: The Two Sides of Confucian Patriarchy in Korea," in *Confucianism and the Family*, eds. Walter H. Slote and George A. DeVos (Albany, NY: State University of New York Press, 1998), 192.

4. Elaine H. Kim, "Men's Talk: A Korean American View of South Korean Constructions of Women, Gender, and Masculinity," in *Dangerous Women: Gender and Korean Nationalism*, eds. Kim, Elaine H. and Chungmoo Choi (New York and London: Routledge), 70.

5. Ibid., 85.

6. Ibid., 83.

7. Rita Nakashima Brock, *Journeys by Heart: A Christology of Erotic Power* (New York: Crossroad, 1988), 90.

8. Ibid., 93.

9. Elisabeth Schüssler Fiorenza, *Jesus, Miriam's Child, Sophia's Prophet* (New York: Crossroad, 1985), 102.

10. Ibid.

11. Geena Davis, Public Lecture at Boston University on 23 March 2011. For more resources, see Geena Davis Institute on Gender in Media at http://www .seejane.org/research/2011.

12. Henning Graf Reventlow, "Basic Issues in the Interpretation of Isaiah 53," in *Jesus and the Suffering Servant: Isaiah 53 and Christian Origins*, eds. William H. Bellinger, Jr., William R. Farmer (Harrisburg, Pennsylvania: Trinity Press International, 1998), 35.

13. Ibid., 34.

14. Ibid., 35.

15. R. E. Clements, "Isaiah 53 and the Restoration of Israel," in *Jesus and the Suffering Servant: Isaiah 53 and Christian Origins*, eds. William H. Bellinger, Jr., William R. Farmer (Harrisburg, Pennsylvania: Trinity Press International, 1998), 42.

16. Ibid., 52.

17. Ibid., 48.

18. Stephenson Humphries-Brooks, "The Canaanite Women in Matthew," in *Feminist Companion to Matthew*, eds. Amy-Jill Levine and Marianne Blickenstaff (Sheffield, England: Sheffield Academic Press, 2001), 142–43.

19. Surekha Nelavala, "Liberation beyond Borders: Dalit Feminist Hermeneutics and Four Gospel Women" (PhD diss., Drew University, 2008), 82.

20. Aristotle and H. Rackham, *Aristotle. 19* (Cambridge MA: Harvard University Press, 1934.1102b), 14–17.

21. Eugene Garver, "The Contemporary Irrelevance of Aristotle's Practical Reason," in *Rereading Aristotle's Rhetoric*, eds. Alan G. Gross and Arthur E. Walzer (Carbondale: Southern Illinois University Press, 2008), 58.

22. Susan J. Brison "Relational Autonomy and Freedom of Expression," in *Feminists Rethink the Self*, ed. Diana T. Meyers (Boulder, CO: Westview Press, 1997), 28.

23. Ibid., 27–31.

24. Musa W. Dube, *Postcolonial Feminist Interpretation of the Bible* (St. Louis, MO: Chalice Press, 2000), 177.

25. Surekha Nelavala, "Liberation beyond Borders," 78.

Chapter 4: Returning to the Source

1. A part of this story was published in my article, "The Tao of Great Integrity" *Journeys: The Magazine of the American Association of Pastoral Counselors* 11, no. 2 (2009).

2. Lao Tze, the founder of Taoism, once taught that people can live contentedly in justice when they observe the Tao, or "Great Integrity," in Chinese. We inherit weapons and armor but no need to use them. We return to honest forms of relationships and the simple enjoyment of an ecological way of life. We may live so close to each other that we hear the barking of each other's dogs and the crowing of each other's cocks. Yet we live contentedly, that we will have no need to guard each other's space.

3. Paula Ellen Buford, "The Lost Tradition of Women Pastoral Caregivers from 1925–1967: A Dangerous Memory" (PhD diss., Atlanta Theological Association at Columbia Theological Seminary, 1997).

4. Buford, "The Lost Tradition," vi, 1, 2, 18.

5. Yoke Lye Kwong, "Spiritual/Pastoral Care in Worlds Beyond: Ministry to International and Immigrant Patients," in *Professional Spiritual and Pastoral Care: A Practical Clergy and Chaplaincy Handbook*, ed. Stephen B. Roberts (Woodstock, VT: SkyLight Paths Publishing, 2001), 252.

6. Letty Russell, *Church in the Round, Feminist Interpretation of the Church* (Louisville, KY: Westminster/John Knox Press, 1993).

7. It is interesting to see the correlation of my grandmother's story with Proverbs 31:16, which describes a woman of wisdom as one who plants a vineyard. Often I find myself describing my ministry as growing a vineyard in the healthcare field.

Chapter 5: "While There Is Life, There Is Hope"

1. Mary John Mananzan, *Nun Stop: A Pilgrim's Tale* (Manila: Institute of Women's Studies, St. Scholastica's College, 2015), 263.

Liturgical Interlude: "We've Come This Far by Faith"

1. For a more detailed history of PANAAWTM, see Pui Lan Kwok and Rachel Bundang, "PANAAWTM Lives!," *Journal of Feminist Study in Religion* 21:2 (2005)

2. Ibid., 151.

Chapter 6: "I Shall Not Bow My Head"

1. Ronald A. Heifetz, *Leadership without Easy Answers* (Cambridge, MA: Belknap Press of Harvard University Press, 1994).

2. Manh Thuong and Quang Thuy, "Tu Dien Viet-Anh: Vietnamese-English Dictionary," (Ha Noi: Nha Xuat Ban Van Hoa Thong Tin, 2003).

3. Arnold van Gennep, *The Rites of Passage* (Chicago: University of Chicago Press, 1960), 18.

4. See David Ng, *People on the Way: Asian North Americans Discovering Christ, Culture, and Community* (Valley Forge, PA: Judson Press, 1996). Ng traces the Asian American consciousness of "the Way" to the Confucian concept of "Tao" (xxvii).

5. See Rubén G. Rumbaut, "Vietnamese, Laotian, and Cambodian Americans," in *Contemporary Asian America: A Multidisciplinary Reader*, ed. Min Zhou and James V. Gatewood (New York: New York University Press, 2000).

6. See Choan-Seng Song, *Third-Eye Theology: Theology in Formation in Asian Settings* (Maryknoll, NY: Orbis Books, 1979).

7. Charles F. Melchert, *Wise Teaching: Biblical Wisdom and Educational Ministry* (Harrisburg: Trinity Press International, 1998), 4. Citing Michael V. Fox, *Qohelet and His Contradictions*, Journal for the Study of the Old Testament Supplement Series (Decatur: Almond, 1989), 83.

8. Melchert, *Wise Teaching*, 5. Citing James L. Crenshaw, *Old Testament Wisdom: An Introduction* (Atlanta: John Knox Press, 1981), 25.

9. Melchert, *Wise Teaching*, 2, 5.

10. Ibid., 2–3.

11. Barbara Brown Taylor, *Learning to Walk in the Dark*, 1st ed. (New York: HarperOne, 2014).

12. Stephen D. Brookfield describes the capacities for "assessing, appraising, and action" to be constitutive of a skillful teacher's "practical reasoning." See

Stephen Brookfield, *The Skillful Teacher: On Technique, Trust, and Responsiveness in the Classroom*, 2nd ed., Jossey-Bass Higher and Adult Education Series (San Francisco: Jossey-Bass, 2006), 6–8.

13. Achille Mbembe, "Necropolitics," *Public Culture* 15 (2003).

14. Arlene Eisen Bergman, *Women of Vietnam* (San Francisco: People's Press, 1974), 30.

15. Sun Tzu, *Sun Tzu and "The Art of War": The Oldest Military Treatise in the World*, trans. Lionel Giles (Champaign, IL: Project Gutenberg, n.d.). E-book Collection (EBSCOhost), 34.

16. Stephen Brookfield and Stephen Preskill, *Learning as a Way of Leading: Lessons from the Struggle for Social Justice*, Jossey-Bass Higher and Adult Education Series (San Francisco: Jossey-Bass, 2009).

17. Ibid.

18. Ibid., 171.

19. Ibid., 173.

20. "The arc of the moral universe is long, but it bends toward justice." Versions of this saying have been attributed to multiple figures, notably Theodore Parker and Martin Luther King Jr.

21. Brookfield and Preskill, *Learning as a Way of Leading: Lessons from the Struggle for Social Justice*, 176.

22. "The Ferguson Commission is an empowered, independent and diverse group that will study the underlying social and economic conditions underscored by the unrest in the wake of the death of Michael Brown." It is composed of sixteen St. Louis-area residents of diverse make-up and professional backgrounds, all appointed by Missouri's Governor Jay Nixon. "Stl Positive Change: Official Site of the Ferguson Commission," http://stlpositivechange.org/.

23. "HuffPost Religion's People of The Year Are the Religious Leaders of Ferguson," *Huffington Post*, December 29, 2014, http://m.huffpost.com/us/entry/6373064.

24. "More than 50 Arrested at Ferguson Police Station on 'Moral Monday,' Other Events Elsewhere," *St. Louis Post-Dispatch*, October 13, 2014, http://www.stltoday.com/news/local/crime-and-courts/more-than-arrested-at-ferguson-police-station-on-moral-monday/article_c1752132-9731-542e-8525-1885fae7fd10.html.

25. Yonat Shimron, "NAACP's William Barber Emerges as Leader of Moral Monday Protests," *Religion News Service*, June 24, 2013, http://www.religionnews.com/2013/06/24/naacps-william-barber-emerges-as-leader-of-moral-monday-protests/.

26. Margaret J. Wheatley, *Leadership and the New Science: Discovering Order in a Chaotic World*, 3rd ed. (San Francisco: Berrett-Koehler Publishers, Inc., 2006), 76.

27. Ibid., 83.

28. Ibid., 108.

29. A portion of this chapter, used with permission, can be found in Mai-Anh Le Tran, *Reset the Heart: Unlearning Violence, Relearning Hope* (Nashiville: Abingdon Press, 2017).

30. Anne Streaty Wimberly, "Daring to Lead with Hope," *Religious Education* 98, no. 3 (2003).

31. Ibid., 283–84. See Mary Elizabeth Moore, *Teaching as a Sacramental Act* (Cleveland: Pilgrim Press, 2004).
32. Wimberly, "Daring to Lead with Hope," 287.
33. Ibid., 281.
34. Jas. 3:1.
35. Matt. 10:16.

Chapter 8: *Phronēsis*, the Other Wisdom Sister

1. I limit my discussion to wisdom leadership of women in Asia, particularly in East Asia, and Asian American women in the United States in the context of Christian theology and ministry because this combined context constitutes my social location.
2. The Greek term *logos* has a variety of meanings, such as language, speech, thought, reason, and so on. Logocentrism in Western culture promotes rational thought in which language is based and which produces speech. Andrologocentrism denotes a cultural system that privileges man as the norm and as the producer of truth and meaning in language.
3. Elisabeth Schüssler Fiorenza coined the term "kyriarchy," which derived from the Greek words "lord" (*kyrios*) and "to rule" (*archein*) to indicate a complex social system that maintains all intersecting oppressions in place. Elisabeth Schüssler Fiorenza, *Wisdom Ways: Introducing Feminist Biblical Interpretation* (New York: Orbis Books, 2001), 211.
4. The references to Old Testament books (Proverbs and 2 Samuel) and deuterocanonical books (Judith, Wisdom, Sirach, and Baruch) in this chapter are taken from the Septuagint (LXX). The deuterocanonical books are the texts considered by the Roman Catholic Church and some Orthodox Churches to be canonical parts of the Christian Old Testament but are not found in the Hebrew Bible.
5. For example, Wis. 7:25 reads, "For she (*sophia*) is a breath of the power of God, and a pure emanation of the glory of the Almighty (*Pantokratoros*)." Also see Sir. 24:1–3: "Wisdom (*sophia*) praises herself, and tells of her glory in the midst of her people. In the assembly of the Most High (*Hypsistou*) she opens her mouth, and in the presence of his hosts she tells of her glory: 'I came forth from the mouth of the Most High. . . .'"
6. I cannot but agree with Schüssler Fiorenza, who has already argued that the feminist emphasis on the female gender of the divine *Sophia* "divinizes the sociopolitical patriarchal gender notion of cultural femininity modeled after the image and likeness of the White Lady." Elisabeth Schüssler Fiorenza, *Sharing Her Word: Feminist Biblical Interpretation in Context* (Boston: Beacon Press, 1998), 177. I am going to show how feminist theologians "reproduce this ideological framework."
7. Such a wise woman in the Bible is described as "an independent thinker" or "a smart lady." Linda Day, "Wisdom and the Feminine in the Hebrew Bible," in *Engaging the Bible in a Gendered World*, ed. Linda Day and Carolyn Pressler, 114–27 (Louisville, KY: Westminster John Knox Press, 2006), 119.
8. In Wis. 8:21 the narration, which is attributed to Solomon, says, "But I perceived that I would not possess her unless God gave her to me. . . ." The editors of *Wisdom's Feast* would assume "her" as wisdom but omit these last verses of the text in the list of Sophia passages. Susan Cady, Marian Ronan, and Hal

Taussig, eds., *Wisdom's Feast: Sophia in Study and Celebration* (San Francisco: Harper & Row, 1989), 204.

9. Schüssler Fiorenza traces the sophialogical shift from the open-ended connection of *Sophia*-prophet-Jesus-followers to the more exclusivist frame of Father-Son-*Logos* (Matt. 11:25–27) in early Christian discourses. See Schüssler Fiorenza, *Sharing Her Word*, 172.

10. Ibid, 162.

11. Cady, Ronan, and Taussig, *Wisdom's Feast*, 13.

12. While *sophia* is a translation of the Hebrew word *chokmah*, *phronēsis* is a Greek rendering of Hebrew words, *biynah* or *tabuwn*, in the Septuagint and is most often translated as "understanding" in English.

13. Michael Pakaluk, *Aristotle's Nicomachean Ethics: An Introduction* (New York: Cambridge University Press, 2005), 209, 228.

14. For a more detailed discussion, see Chapter 3 in Jin Young Choi, *Postcolonial Discipleship of Embodiment: An Asian and Asian American Feminist Reading of the Gospel of Mark* (New York: Palgrave Macmillan, 2015), in which the author has developed an Asian and Asian American feminist hermeneutics of *phronēsis*.

15. A brief discussion of women speaking in silence in Mark appears in Choi, 117–18.

16. But even when this woman is presented as speaking her voice, her embodied knowing is highlighted (7:24–30). She perceives and argues for Jesus' body to be broken for many, including the poor, the sick, and the migrants across the border, just like her and her daughter. After this conversation, Jesus, who has asserted that bread should be provided for children (Jews), not dogs (Gentiles), moves into the Gentile territory.

17. The word *diakonein* is used in 10:45 when Jesus says, "For the Son of Man came not to be *served* but to *serve*, and to give his life a ransom for many." Additionally, this word is applied to women who followed and *served* Jesus when he was in Galilee (15:41).

18. King-Kok Cheung, *Articulate Silences: Hisaye Yamamoto, Maxine Hong Kingston, and Joy Kogawa* (Ithaca, NY: Cornell University Press, 1993), 33.

19. Hisaye Yamamoto, *Seven Syllables and Other Stories* (New York: Kitchen Table Press, 1988).

20. Cheung, 128; Joy Kogawa, *Obasan* (New York: Anchor Books, 1994).

21. Kogawa, 71.

22. Ibid.

23. Ibid., 291.

24. Ibid., 288.

25. Ibid., 289.

26. Cheung, 82; Maxine Hong Kingston, *The Woman Warrior: Memoirs of Girlhood among Ghosts* (New York: Vintage/Random House, 1989).

27. Cheung, 84.

28. Kwok Pui-lan, *Postcolonial Imagination and Feminist Theology* (Louisville, KY: Westminster John Knox Press, 2005), 37, quoted in Choi, 36.

Chapter 9: Foolishness of Wisdom

1. Carolyn McDade, *Sorrow and Healing* (Wellfleet, MA: Surtsey Publishing, 1993), 16.

2. "Eastern Religions #3," https://quizlet.com/109399862/eastern-religions-3-flash-cards/

3. http://britannica.com/EBchecked/topic/585059/de.
4. For discussion on water-like leadership, see Yueh-Ting Lee, Heather Haught, Krystal Chen, and Sydney Chan, "Examining Daoist Big-Five Leadership in Cross-Cultural and Gender Perspectives," *Asian American Journal of Psychology* 4, no. 4 (December, 2013): 267–76; 268.
5. Miriam Therese Winter, Adair Lummis, and Allison Stokes, *Defecting in Place* (New York: Crossroad, 1994), 39.
6. Lee et al., "Examining Daoist Big-Five Leadership," 269.
7. Elizabeth Smythe and Andrew Norton, "Leadership: Wisdom in Action," *Indo-Pacific Journal of Phenomenology* 11, no. 1 (May, 2011), 1.
8. Ibid.

Chapter 10: Three Tales of Wisdom

1. All the interviews were conducted in San Diego, California, during the annual meeting of American Academy of Religion from November 20 through 25, 2014. Some interviews were conducted in Korean and would be translated into English by me and some were in English. All unreferenced quotations that follow come from these interviews.
2. Kwok Pui-lan, *Postcolonial Imagination and Feminist Theology* (Louisville, KY: Westminster John Knox Press, 2005), 46.
3. Ibid.
4. Jane Iwamura, *Virtual Orientalism: Asian Religious and American Popular Culture* (New York: Oxford University Press, 2011), 20.
5. Ibid., 21.
6. Kwok, *Postcolonial Imagination and Feminist Theology*, 30.
7. Ibid.
8. Ibid., 37, 40.
9. Ibid., 50.
10. Ibid., 37.
11. Following up with this initial gathering, on February 22 and 23, 1985, the first AWT conference was held at Mercy Center in Madison, Connecticut. Few years before the initial gathering of AWT on the East Coast, Asian Pacific American women in theology and ministry had met in California and developed resources for their studies and ministries. They had the conference at Berkeley, California, in 1981 (*Sisters Long Before the Struggle: Pacific and Asian Women Resources for Ministry*), and Rita Nakashima Brock was a coordinator for this conference.
12. Jin Young Choi, Panel of PANAAWTM Wisdom-Leadership, Asian North American Theological Educators, Princeton, New Jersey, October, 2014.
13. Andrea Smith, *Conquest: Sexual Violence and American Indian Genocide* (Cambridge, MA: South End Press, 2005), 187.
14. Rita Nakashima Brock, "Dusting the Bible on the Floor: A Hermeneutics of Wisdom," in *Searching the Scriptures: A Feminist Introduction*, vol. 1, ed. Elisabeth Schüssler Fiorenza (New York: Crossroad Publishing Company, 1993), 71.

Liturgical Interlude II

1. The term "Ricing Community" comes from the work of Su Yon Pak, Unzu Lee, Jung Ha Kim and Myung Ji Cho, *Singing the Lord's Song in a New Land: Korean American Practices of Faith* (Louisville, KY: Westminster John Knox Press, 2005).

2. A common English title of Tokuo Yamaguchi's Japanese hymn "Kekai no Tomo" is "Here, O Lord, Your Servants Gather."
3. "Here O God, Your Servants Gather" *United Methodist Hymnal* #552 (Nashville, TN: United Methodist Publishing House, 1989). "Servants" was changed to "daughters" for the purposes of this liturgy.
4. The Litany of Coming Together, evolving around the ingredients for a rice cake, which is a must-have celebration food in Korean American culture, was adopted from a prayer of thanksgiving from the Diocese of Bath and Wells website: http://www.bathandwells.org.uk/.
5. Kim Chi Ha, "Rice is Heaven" from *Gold Crowned Jesus and Other Writings* (Maryknoll, NY: Orbis Books, 1978).

Chapter 11: Becoming Wisdom Woman and Strange Woman

1. Claudia V. Camp, *Wise, Strange, and Holy: The Strange Woman and the Making of the Bible* (Sheffield, England: Sheffield Academic Press, 2000), 344.
2. I define leadership as a "negotiated process of mutual influence." I borrow this definition from Mary B. McRae and Lee L. Short, *Racial and Cultural Dynamics* (Thousand Oaks, CA: Sage Publication, 2009), 95.
3. *Mise en abyme* is originally from French meaning "placing into infinity" or "placing into the abyss"; a placement at the center of an escutcheon of a smaller copy of the same escutcheon; containment of an entity within another identical entity; image of an image, *Merriam-Webster Online Dictionary* at http://www.merriam-webster.com/dictionary/mise%20en%20abyme.
4. Claudia V. Camp, "'Wise and Strange: An Interpretation of the Female Imagery in Proverbs in Light of Trickster Mythology," in Athalya Brenner, ed., *Feminist Companion to the Wisdom Literature* (Sheffield, England: Sheffield Academic Press, 1995), 135.
5. Camp, *Wise, Strange, and Holy*, 344.
6. For the problems of both positive and negative stereotypes, see Mia Tuan, *Forever Foreigners or Honorary Whites?: The Asian Ethnic Experience Today* (Piscataway, NJ: Rutgers University Press, 1998), 30–36; Faye K. Cocchiara and James Campbell Quick, "The Negative Effects of Positive Stereotypes: Ethnicity-related Stressors and Implications on Organizational Health," *Journal of Organizational Behavior* 25 (2004), 782; Karen L. Suyemoto, Grace S. Kim, Miwa Tanabe, John Tawa, and Stephanie C. Day, "Challenging the Model Minority Myth: Engaging Asian American Students in Research on Asian American College Student Experiences," in Samuel D. Museus, ed. *Conducting Research on Asian Americans in Higher Education: New Directions in Institutional Research* (San Francisco: Jossey-Bass, 2009).
7. Angela Mae Kupenda shares her experience of being a black female professor in a predominantly white institution in her essay "Facing Down the Spooks." Although her experience differs from my experience, I see similarities in terms of how stereotypes affect the teaching, research, and campus life of women of color in academia. See her chapter included in *Presumed Incompetent: The Intersection of Race and Class for Women in Academia*, eds. Gabriella Gutierrez y Muhs, et al. (Boulder, CO: University Press of Colorado, 2012), 20–28.
8. Even though Title IX (a federal law enacted since 1972 that prohibits discrimination on the basis of sex in any federally funded education program or

activity) has played a significant role in creating access and equity for women of color in the academy, the institutions are still "less robust in advancing women of color to the highest levels in the institutions," including full professorship. Gaëtane Jean-Marie, "'Unfinished Agendas'": Trends in Women of Color's Status in Higher Education," Gaëtane Jean-Marie and Brenda Lloyd-Jones, *Women of Color in Higher Education: Turbulent Past, Promising Future, Diversity in Higher Education*, vol. 9: 10–11, 17.

9. At my institution, students are required to take one theology course along with one philosophy course.

10. Shirley Hune, "Asian American Women Faculty and the Contested Space of the Classroom: Navigating Student Resistance and (Re)Claiming Authority and Their Rightful Place," in Jean-Marie and Lloyd-Jones, 314.

11. Juanita Johnson-Bailey and Ronald M. Cervero, "Power Dynamics in Teaching and Learning: An Examination of Two Adult Education Classrooms," *International Journal of Lifelong Education* 17.6 (1998): 389–99.

12. By definition, internalized sexism refers to women's incorporation of sexist practices, and to the circulation of those practices among women, even in the absence of men. Janet K. Swim, Robyn Mallett, and Charles Stangor, "Understanding Subtle Sexism: Detection and Use of Sexist Language, *Sex Roles*, 51 (2004): 117–28.

13. Steve Berman, Neill Korobov, Avril Thorne, "The Fabric of Internalized Sexism," *Journal of Integrated Social Sciences* 1, no. 1 (2009):11.

14. Mary Crawford and Jessica A. Suckle, "Overcoming Resistance to Feminism in Classroom," in Sara S. Davis, Mary Crawford, and Jadwiga Sebrechts, eds., *Coming to Her Own: Educational Success in Girls and Women* (San Francisco: Jossey-Bass, 1999), 155–70.

15. By definition, "internalized" oppression is the incorporation and acceptance by individuals within an oppressed group of the prejudices against them within the dominant society. Suzanne Lipsky, "Internalized Oppression," *Black Re-Emergence*, no. 2 (Winter 1977): 5–10.

16. Karen D. Pyke, "What Is Internalized Racial Oppression and Why Don't We Study Acknowledging Racism's Hidden Injuries?" *Sociological Perspectives*, vol. 53, no.4 (Winter 2010): 553.

17. Donald L. Rubin and Kim A. Smith, "Effects of Accent, Ethnicity, and Lecture Topic on Undergraduates' Perceptions on Nonnative English-Speaking Teaching Assistants," *International Journal of Intercultural Relations* 14.3 (1990): 337–53. Quoted from Juanita Johnson-Bailey and Ming-Yeh Lee, "Women of Color in the Academy: Where's Our Authority in the Classroom?" *Feminist Teacher*, vol. 15, no 2 (2005): 115; Also see Shirley Hune's essay in Jean-Marie and Lloyd-Jones's book, 292–6.

18. Sheryl Sandberg, *Lean In: Women, Work, and Will to Lead* (New York: Knopf, 2013), 8.

19. Positional leadership is based on the rights granted by the position and title.

20. Alice H. Eagly and Linda Carli, *Through the Labyrinth: Truth about How Women Become Leaders* (Boston: Harvard Business School Press, 2007).

21. bell hooks, *Feminism Is for Everybody* (Cambridge, MA: South End Press, 2000), 4–7.

22. Johnson-Bailey and Cervero, "Power Dynamics in Teaching and Learning Practices," 389–99.

23. Grace Chang's chapter "Where's the Violence: The Promise and Perils of Teaching Women-of-Color Studies," in *Presumed Incompetent* resonates with my experiences, Gabriella Gutierrez y Muhs, et al., 198–218.

24. "Yellow peril" is a metaphor for race, namely "a danger to Western civilization held to arise from expansion of the power and influence of eastern Asian peoples." *Merriam-Webster Online Dictionary*, "yellow peril" at http://www.merriam-webster.com/dictionary/yellow%20peril.

25. I define feminist liberatory pedagogy as a teaching and learning method that encourages conscientization and activism by creating a safe, caring, and democratic teaching environment.

26. Juanita Johnson-Bailey and Ming-Yeh Lee, "Women of Color in the Academy," 111.

27. bell hooks, *Teaching to Transgress: Education as the Practice of Freedom, 13–22* and *Teaching Community: A Pedagogy of Hope* (New York: Routledge, 2003).

28. Lucila Vergas, "When the 'Other' is the Teacher: Implications of Teacher Diversity in Higher Education," *Urban Review* 31.4 (1998): 359–83.

29. My experience resonates with non-Asian women of color professors. See Rose Chepyator-Thomson, "Black Women's Experience in Teaching Euro-American Students in Higher Education: Perspectives on Knowledge Production and Reproduction, Classroom Discourse, and Student Resistance," *Journal of Research Association of Minority Professors* 4.2 (2000): 9–20.

30. For more information about the unique challenges faced by women of color in higher education, see Penny A. Pasque, "Women of Color in Higher Education: Feminist Theoretical Perspectives," in Jean-Marie and Lloyd-Jones, 21–41.

31. Kathleen Weiler, "Freire and a Feminist Pedagogy of Difference," *Harvard Educational Review* (November 1991): 4.

32. Kathleen M. O'Connor, *The Wisdom Literature* (Collegeville, MN: The Liturgical Press, 1988), 63.

33. Kyriarchy is neologism coined by Elisabeth Schüssler Fiorenza. It is derived from the Greek word for *kyrios* (lord) and *archein* (to dominate or rule) and seeks to redefine the analytic category of patriarchy in terms of multilayered intersecting structures of domination. For more information, see Schüssler Fiorenza's essay, "Introduction: Exploring the Intersections of Race, Gender, Status and Ethnicity in Early Christian Studies," in Laura Nasrallah and Elisabeth Schüssler Fiorenza, *Prejudice and Christian Beginnings: Investigating Race, Gender, and Ethnicity in Early Christian Studies* (Minneapolis: Fortress Press, 2009), 1–26.

34. Gale A. Yee, *Poor Banished Children of Eve: Woman as Evil in the Hebrew Bible* (Minneapolis: Augsburg Fortress Publishers), 135–58.

35. Ibid.,149–50

36. Camp, *Wise, Strange, and Holy*, 15.

37. Kathleen M. O'Connor, *The Wisdom Literature*, 19.

38. As I coined this definition, I was inspired by Seyla Benhabib's feminist perspective on self. Benhabib, et al., *Feminist Contentions* (New York: Routledge, 1995); Benhabib, "Sexual Difference and Collective Identities: The New Global Constellation." *Signs* 24 (1999): 335–61.

39. Homi K. Bhabha, *Location of Culture* (New York: Routledge, 2004), 162.

40. This question was proposed by one of my students who has struggled with her "otherness."

41. Mumbi Mwangi and Kyoko Kishimoto, "Critiquing the Rhetoric of 'Safety' in Feminist Pedagogy: Women of Color Offering an Account of Ourselves" *Feminist Teacher* 19, no.2 (2009): 95.

42. Henry A. Giroux: "Can Democratic Education Survive in a Neoliberal Society?" *Truthout* (Oct 16, 2012), http://truth-out.org/opinion/item/12126-can-democratic-education-survive-in-a-neoliberal-society#XI.

Chapter 12: One-Pot Menu

1. Hannah Ka, "A New Paradigm of Leadership," in *Leadership Is Discipleship* [in Korean] (Nashville: The Leadership Ministries of General Board of Discipleship, 2015), 12–13. Translated and reprinted by permission of The Leadership Ministries of General Board of Discipleship.

2. Eric Carle, *The Mixed-Up Chameleon* (New York: HarperCollins Publishers, 1975 and 1984).

3. First Corinthians 12:28 (Common English Bible). "In the church, God has appointed first apostles, second prophets, third teachers, then miracles, then gifts of healing, the ability to help others, leadership skills, different kinds of tongues."

4. Herbert Fingarette, *Confucius: The Secular as Sacred* (Prospect Heights, IL: Waveland Press, 1998), 73–74; Confucius, *The Analects* (Lun yü), trans. D. C. Lau (London: Penguin Books, 1979), 76 (V:4 and V:3).

5. Hannah Ka, "Respectful Grace and Graceful Respect: A Korean Feminist Ethic" (PhD diss., Claremont Graduate University, 2011), 122.

6. Ka, "Respectful Grace," 89–142, 227–46.

7. Lao Tzu, *Tao Te Ching* (New York: HarperCollins Publishers Inc., 1988), 55, 64, and 75.

8. Ibid., 19.

9. Letty M. Russell, *Church in the Round: Feminist Interpretation of the Church* (Louisville, KY: Westminster/John Knox Press, 1993), 54–58 and 65–74. The leadership practice of these Korean American women bears much resemblance to Letty Russell's feminist leadership model; Rosamund Stone Zander and Benjamin Zander, *The Art of Possibility* (New York: Penguin Books, 2002), 162. "Leadership is a relationship that brings this possibility to others and to the world, from any chair, in any role. This kind of leader is not necessarily the strongest member of the pack—the one best suited to fend off the enemy and gather in resources—as our old definitions of leadership sometimes had it. The 'leader of possibility' invigorates the lines of affiliation and compassion from person to person in the face of the tyranny of fear. Any one of us can exercise this kind of leadership, whether we stand in the position of CEO or employee, citizen or elected official, teacher or student, friend or lover."

10. Phil. 2:5–8.

11. Lao Tzu, *Tao Te Ching*, 73.

Chapter 13: "Working to Make the World a Little Better Place to Live"

1. Sara Lawrence-Lightfoot, *I've known rivers: Lives of loss and liberation* (Reading, MA: Addison-Wesley Pub., 1994), xv.

Chapter 14: Wisdom Crying Aloud in the Street

1. Common English Bible.

2. Rebecca Chopp, *Saving Work: Feminist Practices of Theological Education* (Westminster John Knox Press, 1995), 77.
3. http://thinkprogress.org/justice/2014/12/12/3601771/people-police-killed -in-2014/.
4. Mark 6:31–44; Luke 9:10–17.
5. The Institute for Leadership Development and Study of Pacific Asian North American Leadership (PANA) was a center at Pacific School of Religion in Berkeley from 2000 to 2009. It focused on the API theological intellectual tradition, congregational and youth leadership, and the API faith voice in the public square.
6. Critical Faith is the name of the R2W curriculum developed by popular educator Michael James who was the R2W Director from 2002 to 2009. Influenced by Brazilian educator Paulo Freire, it consisted of the following elements: Accords, Social Biography, Dialogue, Problem-posing/Invention, Research and Study, Personal Development, Praxis, and Critical Spirituality.
7. Michael James, "Liberation, *Conscientização*, and Pedagogy," thesis, San Francisco State University, 2014, 79.
8. Ibid., 75.
9. Ibid., 79.
10. Interviews, videos, and photos of this oral history project can be read at www .apiwomenfaithaction.blogspot.com.
11. For more on the unique gifts that the faith community brings to social movements, see *Faith-Rooted Organizing: Mobilizing the Church in Service to the World*, by Alexia Salvatierra and Peter Heltzel, (Downers Grove, IL: Inter-Varsity Press, 2014).
12. The Interfaith Coalition for Immigrant Rights (ICIR) began in 1993 organizing immigrant and faith communities in education and advocacy efforts to promote the rights, fair treatment, and dignity of all immigrants regardless of immigration status in California. ICIR is currently a program of the Interfaith Movement for Human Integrity, www.im4humanintegrity.org.
13. For a map of immigrant detention centers in the United States, see www .detentionwatchnetwork.org.
14. http://www.nytimes.com/2013/11/27/world/europe/in-major-document-pope -francis-present-his-vision.html.

Chapter 15: Fitting Nowhere

1. Richard J. Clifford, *The Wisdom Literature*, Interpreting Biblical Texts (Nashville, TN: Abingdon Press, 1998), 26.
2. MediCal is California's healthcare program for low-income families.

References

Alberts, Tara. *Conflict and Conversion: Catholicism in Southeast Asia, 1500–1700*. New York: Oxford University Press, 2013.

Apple, Raymond. "The Two Wise Women of Proverbs Chapter 31." *Jewish Bible Quarterly*, vol.39, no. 3 (2011): 175–80.

Aristotle, and H. Rackham. *Aristotle. 19*. Cambridge, MA: Harvard University Press, 1934.

Benhabib, Seyla, et al. *Feminist Contentions*. New York: Routledge, 1995.

Benhabib, Seyla. "Sexual Difference and Collective Identities: The New Global Constellation." *Signs* 24 (1999).

Bergman, Arlene Eisen. *Women of Vietnam*. San Francisco: People's Press, 1974.

Berman, Steve, Neill Korobov, and Avril Thorne. "The Fabric of Internalized Sexism." *Journal of Integrated Social Sciences*, 2009—1(1): 10–47.

Bhabha, Homi K. *The Location of Culture*, New York: Routledge, 2004.

Brecht, Bertolt. *Gesammelte Werke*. Frankfurt am Main: Suhrkamp, 1966.

Brison, Susan J. "Relational Autonomy and Freedom of Expression." In *Feminists Rethink the Self*. Edited by Diana T. Meyers. Boulder, CO: Westview Press, 1997.

Brock, Rita Nakashima. *Journeys by Heart: A Christology of Erotic Power*. New York: Crossroad, 1988.

Brock, Rita Nakashima, and Nami Kim, "Asian Pacific American Protestant Women." In *Encyclopedia of Women and Religion in North America*. Edited by Rosemary Skinner Keller and Rosemary Radford Ruether. Bloomington: Indiana University Press, 2006.

Brock, Rita Nakashima, Jung Ha Kim, Kwok Pui-lan, and Seung Ai Yang, eds. *Off the Menu: Asian and Asian North American Women's Religion and Theology*. Louisville, KY: Westminster John Knox Press, 2007.

Brock, Rita Nakashima. "Dusting the Bible on the Floor: A Hermeneutics of Wisdom." In *Searching the Scriptures: A Feminist Introduction*. Vol. 1. Edited by Elisabeth Schüssler Fiorenza. New York: The Crossroad Publishing Company, 1993.

Brookfield, Stephen. *The Skillful Teacher: On Technique, Trust, and Responsiveness in the Classroom*. Jossey-Bass Higher and Adult Education. 2nd ed. San Francisco: Jossey-Bass, 2006.

Brookfield, Stephen, and Stephen Preskill. *Learning as a Way of Leading: Lessons from the Struggle for Social Justice*. Jossey-Bass Higher and Adult Education. San Francisco: Jossey-Bass, 2009.

Buford, Paula Ellen. "The Lost Tradition of Women Pastoral Caregivers from 1925–1967: A Dangerous Memory" (PhD diss., Atlanta Theological Association at Columbia Theological Seminary), 1997.

Cady, Susan, Marian Ronan, and Hal Taussig, eds. *Wisdom's Feast: Sophia in Study and Celebration*. San Francisco: Harper & Row, 1989.

Callahan, Sharon Henderson, *Religious Leadership: A Reference Handbook*, New York: SAGA Publications, 2013.

Camp, Claudia V. *Wise, Strange, and Holy: The Strange Woman and the Making of the Bible*. Sheffield, England: Sheffield Academic Press, 2000.

———. "Wise and Strange: An Interpretation of the Female Imagery in Proverbs in Light of Trickster Mythology." In *Feminist Companion to the Wisdom Literature*. Edited by Athalya Brenner. Sheffield, England: Sheffield Academic Press, 1995.

Carle, Eric. *The Mixed-Up Chameleon*. New York: HarperCollins Publishers, 1975, 1984.

Chang, Grace. "Where's the Violence: The Promise and Perils of Teaching Women-of-Color Studies." In *Presumed Incompetent*. Edited by Gabriella Gutierrez y Muhs et al. Boulder, CO: University Press of Colorado, 2012.

Chen, Carolyn. "A Self of One's Own: Taiwanese Immigrant Women and Religious Conversion." *Gender and Society* 19.3 (2005): 336–57.

———. *Getting Saved in America: Taiwanese Immigration and Religious Experience*. Princeton, NJ: Princeton University Press, 2008.

Chen, Ya-chen. "Taiwanese Feminist History: A Sociocultural Review." In *Women in Taiwan: Sociocultural Perspectives*. Edited by Ya-chen Chen, 15–30. Indianapolis, IN: University of Indianapolis Press, 2007.

Chepyator-Thomson, Rose. "Black Women's Experience in Teaching Euro-American Students in Higher Education: Perspectives on Knowledge Production and Reproduction, Classroom Discourse, and Student Resistance." *Journal of Research Association of Minority Professors* 4.2, 2000.

Cheung, King-Kok. *Articulate Silences: Hisaye Yamamoto, Maxine Hong Kingston, and Joy Kogawa*. Ithaca: Cornell University Press, 1993.

Cho, Haejoang. "Male Dominance and Mother Power: The Two Sides of Confucian Patriarchy in Korea." In *Confucianism and the Family*. Edited by Walter H. Slote and George A. DeVos. New York: State University of New York Press, 1998.

Choi, Jin Young. *Postcolonial Discipleship of Embodiment: An Asian and Asian American Reading of the Gospel of Mark*. New York: Palgrave Macmillan, 2015.

Chopp, Rebecca. *Saving Work: Feminist Practices of Theological Education*. Louisville, KY: Westminster John Knox Press, 1995.

Chung, Hyun Kyung. *Struggle to Be the Sun Again: Introducing Asian Women's Theology*. Maryknoll, NY: Orbis Books, 1999.

Clements, R. E. "Isaiah 53 and the Restoration of Israel." In *Jesus and the Suffering Servant: Isaiah 53 and Christian Origins*. Edited by William H. Bellinger Jr. and William R. Farmer. Harrisburg, Pennsylvania: Trinity Press International, 1998.

Clifford, Richard J. *The Wisdom Literature*. Interpreting Biblical Texts. Nashville, TN: Abingdon Press, 1998.

Crawford, Mary, and Jessica A Suckle. "Overcoming Resistance to Feminism in Classroom." In *Coming to Her Own: Educational Success in Girls and Women*. Edited by Sara S. Davis, Mary Crawford, and Jadwiga Sebrechts. San Francisco: Jossey-Bass, 1999.

Crenshaw, James L. *Old Testament Wisdom: An Introduction*. Atlanta: John Knox Press, 1981.

Cocchiara, Faye K., and James Campbell Quick. "The Negative Effects of Positive Stereotypes: Ethnicity-Related Stressors and Implications on Organizational Health." *Journal of Organizational Behavior* 25, 2004.

Confucius. *The Analects* (Lun yü). Translated by D. C. Lau. London: Penguin Books, 1979.

Davidson, Gary Marvin. *A Short History of Taiwan: The Case for Independence*. Westport, CT: Greenwood Publishing Group, 2003.

Davis, Geena. A Public Lecture at Boston University on 2011. March 23. For more resources, see Geena Davis Institute on Gender in Media at http://www.see jane.org/research/.

Day, Linda and Carolyn Pressler, eds. *Engaging the Bible in a Gendered World*. Louisville, KY: Westminster John Knox Press, 2006.

De Guzman, Mila. *Women against Marcos: Stories of Filipino and Filipino American Women Who Fought a Dictator*. San Francisco: Carayan Press, 2016.

De la Costa, Horacio. *The Jesuits in the Philippines 1581–1768*. Cambridge, MA: Harvard University Press, 1967.

Dollaga, Norma P. "Subverting the Normalcy of Patriarchy, Stories of the Uppity Woman." *Pinays Doing Theology. Tugon. An Ecumenical Journal of Discussion and Opinions*. The National Council of Churches in the Philippines, edited by Revelation Velunta, vol. 16. no. 1 (November 2015).

———. "Of Femaleness My Body Speaks." *Pinays Doing Theology. Tugon. An Ecumenical Journal of Discussion and Opinions*. The National Council of Churches in the Philippines, edited by Revelation Velunta, vol. 16. no. 1 (November 2015).

Dube, Musa W. *Postcolonial Feminist Interpretation of the Bible*. St. Louis, MO: Chalice Press, 2000.

Eagly, Alice H., and Carli, Linda. *Through the Labyrinth: Truth about How Women Become Leaders*. Boston: Harvard Business School Press, 2007.

Fanon, Frantz. *Black Skin, White Masks*. New York: Grove Press, 2008.

Farris, Catherine S. P. "Women's Liberation under 'East Asian Modernity' in China and Taiwan: Historical, Cultural, and Comparative Perspectives." In *Women in the New Taiwan: Gender Roles and Gender Consciousness in a Changing Society*. Armonk, NY: M. E. Sharpe, 2004.

Fingarette, Herbert. *Confucius: The Secular as Sacred*. Prospect Heights, IL: Waveland Press, 1998.

Foronda, Marcelino A. *Mother Ignacia and her Beaterio: A Preliminary Study*. Makati, Rizal: St. Paul Publications, 1975.

Foucault, Michel. *The History of Sexuality*, vol. 1, *An Introduction*. New York: Vintage Books, 1978.

Fox, Michael V. *Qohelet and His Contradictions*. Journal for the Study of the Old Testament Supplement Series. Decatur, GA: Almond Press, 1989.

Freire, Paulo. *Pedagogy of Freedom: Ethics, Democracy, and Civic Courage*, New York: Rowan and Littlefield Publishers, Inc., 2001.

Garver, Eugene. "The Contemporary Irrelevance of Aristotle's Practical Reason." In *Rereading Aristotle's "Rhetoric."* Edited by Alan G. Gross and Arthur E. Walzer. Carbondale: Southern Illinois University Press, 2008.

Giroux, Henry A. "Can Democratic Education Survive in a Neoliberal Society?" *Truthout*, October 16, 2012.

Gennep, Arnold van. *The Rites of Passage*. Chicago: University of Chicago Press, 1960.

Groome, Thomas H. *Will There Be Faith?* 1st ed. New York: HarperOne, 2011.

Gu, Chien-Juh. *Mental Health among Taiwanese Americans: Gender, Immigration, and Transnational Struggles.* New York: LFB Scholarly Publishing, 2006.

Heifetz, Ronald A. *Leadership without Easy Answers.* Cambridge: Belknap Press of Harvard University Press, 1994.

Hicks, Jane E. "Moral Agency at the Borders: Rereading the Story of the Syrophoenician Woman." *Word and World,* v. 23, no. 1 (Winter 2003): 76–84.

hooks, bell. *Feminism Is for Everybody.* Cambridge: South End Press, 2000.

———. *Teaching Community: A Pedagogy of Hope.* New York: Routledge, 2003.

Huffington, Arianna. *Thrive: The Third Metric to Redefining Success and Creating a Life of Well-being, Wisdom, and Wonder.* New York: Random House, 2014.

Humphries-Brooks, Stephenson. "The Canaanite Women in Matthew." In *Feminist Companion to Matthew.* Edited by Amy-Jill Levine and Marianne Blickenstaff. Sheffield: Sheffield Academic Press, 2001.

Hune, Shirley. "Asian American Women Faculty and the Contested Space of the Classroom: Navigating Student Resistance and (Re)Claiming Authority and Their Rightful Place." In *Women of Color in Higher Education: Turbulent Past, Promising Future, Diversity in Higher Education,* vol. 9. Edited by Jean-Marie, Gaëtane and Brenda Lloyd-Jones. Bingley, UK: Emerald Group Publishing Limited, 2011.

Iwamura, Jane. *Virtual Orientalism: Asian Religious and American Popular Culture.* Oxford University Press, 2011.

James, Michael. *Liberation,* Conscientização, *and Pedagogy* (Thesis). San Francisco State University, 2014.

Jean-Marie, Gaëtane, and Brenda Lloyd-Jones, eds. *Women of Color in Higher Education: Turbulent Past, Promising Future, Diversity in Higher Education,* vol. 9. Bingley, UK: Emerald Group Publishing Limited, 2011.

Johnson-Bailey, Juanita, and Ronald M. Cervero. "Power Dynamics in Teaching and Learning: An Examination of Two Adult Education Classrooms." *International Journal of Lifelong Education* 17.6, 1998.

Johnson-Bailey, Juanita, and Ming-Yeh Lee. "Women of Color in the Academy: Where's Our Authority in the Classroom?" *Feminist Teacher,* vol. 15, no. 2 (2005).

Keller, Rosemary Skinner, and Rosemary Radford Reuther, eds. *In Our Own Voices: Four Centuries of Religious Writings by American Women.* Louisville, KY: Westminster John Knox Press, 2000.

Kelly-Gadol, Joan. "Did Women Have a Renaissance?" In *Becoming Visible: Women in European History.* Edited by Renate Bridenthal and Claudia Koonz, 137–64. Boston: Houghton Mifflin, 1977.

Killen, Patricia O'Connell and John de Beer. *The Art of Theological Reflection.* New York : The Crossroad Publishing Company, 1994.

Kim Chi Ha. "Rice." In *The Collection of Kim Ji Ha's Writings.* Waegwan, Korea: Bundo Book, 1984.

Kim, Elaine H. "Men's Talk: A Korean American View of South Korean Constructions of Women, Gender, and Masculinity." In *Dangerous Women: Gender and Korean Nationalism.* Edited by Elaine H. Kim and Chungmoo Choi. New York and London: Routledge, 1998

Kim, Grace Ji-Sun, ed. *Here I Am: Faith Stories of Korean American Clergywomen.* Philadelphia, PA: Judson Press, 2015.

Kim, Jung Ha. *Bridge-makers and Cross-bearers: Korean American Women and the Church*. Atlanta, GA: The Scholar's Press, 1997; New York: Oxford University Press, 1997.

———. "Cartography of Korean American Protestant Faith Communities in the United States." In *Religion in Asian America*. Edited by Pyong Gap Min and Jung Ha Kim, 185–13. Lanham, MD: AltaMira Press, 2002.

Kingston, Maxine Hong. *The Woman Warrior: Memoirs of Girlhood among Ghosts*. New York: Vintage/Random House, 1989.

Kinukawa, Hisako. *Women and Jesus in Mark: A Japanese Feminist Perspective*. Maryknoll, NY: Orbis books, 1994.

Kishimoto, Kyoko, and Mumbi Mwangi. "Critiquing the Rhetoric of 'Safety' in Feminist Pedagogy: Women of Color Offering an Account of Ourselves." *Feminist Teacher*, vol. 19, no. 2 (2009): 96.

Kogawa, Joy. *Obasan*. New York: Anchor Books, 1994.

Kupenda, Angela Mae. "Facing Down the Spooks." In *Presumed Incompetent: The Intersection of Race and Class for Women in Academia*. Edited by Gabriella Gutierrez y Muhs, Yolanda Flores Niemann, Carmen G. González, and Angela P. Harris. Utah: Utah State University Press, 2012.

Kwok, Pui-lan, *Discovering the Bible in the Non-Biblical World*. Maryknoll, NY: Orbis books, 1995.

———. "Overlapping Communities and Multicultural Hermeneutics." In *A Feminist Companion to Reading the Bible: Approaches, Methods, and Strategies*. Edited by Athalya Brenner and Carole Fontaine, 203–15. London and Chicago: Fitzroy Dearborn Publishers, 2001, 1997.

———. *Postcolonial Imagination and Feminist Theology*. Louisville, KY: Westminster John Knox Press, 2005.

———, and Rachel A. R. Bundang, "PANAAWTM Lives!," *Journal of Feminist Studies in Religion*, 21, no. 2, Fall 2005.

Kwong, Yoke Lye. "Spiritual/Pastoral Care in Worlds Beyond: Ministry to International and Immigrant Patients." In *Professional Spiritual and Pastoral Care—a Practical Clergy and Chaplaincy Handbook*. Edited by Stephen B. Roberts. Woodstock, VT: SkyLight Paths Publishing, 2001.

Lao Tzu, *Tao Te Ching*. New York: HarperCollins Publishers, 1988.

Lawrence-Lightfoot, Sara. *I've Known Rivers: Lives of Loss and Liberation*. Reading, MA: Addison-Wesley Pub., 1994.

Lerner, Gerda. *Teaching Women's History*. Washington, DC: American Historical Association, 1981.

———. *The Creation of Patriarchy*. New York: Oxford University Press, 1986.

———. *The Creation of Feminist Consciousness*. New York: Oxford University Press, 1997.

Lee, Charlene Jin. "Response #2." In *Society of Asian North American Christian Studies* 2 (2010): 63–67.

Lee Park, Sun Ai. "A Theological Reflection." In *We Dare to Dream: Doing Theology as Asian Women*. Edited by Virginia Fabella M. M and Sun Ai Lee Park. Maryknoll, NY: Orbis Books.

Lee, Sang Hyun. *From a Liminal Place: An Asian American Theology*. Minneapolis, MN: Fortress Press, 2010.

Lee, Yueh-ting, Heather Haught, Krystal Chen, and Sydney Chan. "Examining Daoist Big-Five Leadership in Cross-Cultural and Gender Perspectives." *Asian American Journal of Psychology* 4, no. 4 (12) (2013): 267–76.

Lipsky, Suzanne. "Internalized Oppression," *Black Re-Emergence*, no. 2, (Winter 1977).

Longkumer, Limatula, "Women in Theological Education from an Asian Perspective." In Dietrich Werner, David Esterline, and Namsoon Kang, eds. *Handbook of Theological Education in World Christianity: Theological Perspectives, Ecumenical Trends, Regional Surveys*. -75. Eugene, OR: Wipf and Stock, 2010.

Lutz, Jessie Gregory, ed. *Pioneer Chinese Christian Women: Gender, Christianity, and Social Mobility*. Studies in Missionaries and Christianity in China. Bethlehem, PA: Lehigh University Press, 2010.

Mananzan, Sr. Mary John, OSB. *Nun Stop: A Pilgrim's Tale*. Manila: Institute of Women's Studies, 2015.

McDade, Carolyn. *Sorrow and Healing*. Wellfleet, MA: Surtsey Publishing, 1993.

McRae, Mary B., and Lee L. Short. *Racial and Cultural Dynamics*. Thousand Oaks, CA: Sage Publication, 2009.

Melchert, Charles F. *Wise Teaching: Biblical Wisdom and Educational Ministry*. Harrisburg, PA: Trinity Press International, 1998.

Menegon, Eugenio. *Ancestors, Virgins, and Friars: Christianity as a Local Religion in Late Imperial China*, Harvard-Yenching Institute Monograph 69. Cambridge, MA: Harvard University Asia Center for the Harvard-Yenching Institute. Distributed by Harvard University Press, 2009.

Miller, Jean B. "Women and Power." In Thomas Wartenberg, ed., *Rethinking Power*. Albany, NY: SUNY Press, 1992.

Moore, Mary Elizabeth. *Teaching as a Sacramental Act*. Cleveland: Pilgrim Press, 2004.

Moraga, Cherrie, and Gloria Anzaldua, *This Bridge Called My Back: Writings by Radical Women of Color*. New York: Kitchen Table: Women of Color Press, 1983.

Nelavala, Surekha. "Liberation beyond Borders: Dalit Feminist Hermeneutics and Four Gospel Women." PhD diss. Drew University, 2008.

Nelavala, Surekha. "Smart Syrophoenician Woman: A Dalit Feminist Reading of Mark 7:24–31." *Expository Times*, v. 118, no. 2 (2006): 64–69.

Ng, David, ed. *People on the Way: Asian North Americans Discovering Christ, Culture, and Community*. Valley Forge, PA: Judson Press, 1996.

O'Connor, Kathleen M. *The Wisdom Literature*. Collegeville, MN: The Liturgical Press, 1988.

Pacheco, Diego. *Kyūshū Kirishitanshi kenkyū*. Tokyo: Kirishitan Bunka Kenkyūkai, 1977.

Pak, Su Yon. "Women Leaders in Asian American Protestant Churches." In *Religious Leadership: A Reference Handbook*. Edited by Sharon Henderson Callahan, 287–96. Thousand Oaks, CA: Sage, 2013.

Pak, Su Yon, Jung Ha Kim, Unzu Lee, and Myung Ji Cho. *Singing the Lord's Song in a New Land: Korean American Practices of Faith*. Louisville, KY: Westminster John Knox Press, 2005.

Pakaluk, Michael. *Aristotle's Nicomachean Ethics: An Introduction*. New York: Cambridge University Press, 2005.

Palmer, Parker J. *The Courage to Teach: Exploring the Inner Landscape of Teacher's Life*, San Francisco, CA: Jossey-Bass, 1997.

Park, Andrew Sung. *Racial Conflict and Healing: An Asian-American Theological Perspective*. Eugene, OR: Wipf and Stock, 2009.

Parks, Sheri. *Fierce Angels: Living with a Legacy from the Sacred Dark Feminine to the Strong Black Woman*. Chicago: Chicago Review Press, 2013.

Pasque, Penny A. "Women of Color in Higher Education: Feminist Theoretical Perspectives." In Gaëtane Jean-Marie and Brenda Lloyd-Jones, eds., *Women of Color in Higher Education: Turbulent Past, Promising Future, Diversity in Higher Education*, vol. 9. 2011.

Phan, Peter C. *Mission and Catechesis: Alexandre de Rhodes and Inculturation in Seventeenth-Century Vietnam*. Faith and Cultures. Maryknoll, NY: Orbis Books, 1998.

Pisano, Luca. "Taiwanese Composers and Piano Works in the XX Century: Traditional Chinese Cultures and the Taiwan Xin YinYue." *Kervan: Rivista Internazionale di Studii Afroasiatici* no. 1 (2005): 49–71.

Pyke, Karen D. "What Is Internalized Racial Oppression and Why Don't We Study Acknowledging Racism's Hidden Injuries?" *Sociological Perspectives*, vol. 53, no. 4 (Winter 2010).

Reventlow, Henning Graf. "Basic Issues in the Interpretation of Isaiah 53." In *Jesus and the Suffering Servant: Isaiah 53 and Christian Origin*. Edited by William H. Bellinger Jr. and William R. Farmer. Harrisburg, PA: Trinity Press International, 1998.

Rubin, Donald L., and Kim Smith. "Effects of Accent, Ethnicity, and Lecture Topic on Undergraduates' Perceptions on Nonnative English-Speaking Teaching Assistants." *International Journal of Intercultural Relations* 14.3, 1990.

Rumbaut, Rubén G. "Vietnamese, Laotian, and Cambodian Americans." In *Contemporary Asian America: A Multidisciplinary Reader*. Edited by Min Zhou and James V. Gatewood, 175–206. New York: New York University Press, 2000.

Russell, Letty. *Church in the Round: Feminist Interpretation of the Church*. Louisville, KY: Westminster/John Knox Press, 1993.

Salvatierra, Alexia, and Peter Heltzel. *Faith Rooted Organizing: Mobilizing the Church in Service to the World*. Downers Grove, IL: Intervarsity Press, 2014.

Sandberg, Sheryl. *Lean In: Women, Work, and Will to Lead*. New York: Knopf, 2013.

Schüssler Fiorenza, Elisabeth. "Introduction: Exploring the Intersections of Race, Gender, Status, and Ethnicity in Early Christian Studies." In Laura Nasrallah and Elisabeth Schüssler Fiorenza, *Prejudice and Christian Beginnings: Investigating Race, Gender, and Ethnicity in Early Christian Studies*. Minneapolis: Fortress Press, 2009.

Schüssler Fiorenza, Elisabeth. *Jesus: Miriam's Child, Sophia's Prophet: Critical Issues in Feminist Christology*. New York: Crossroad, 1985.

———. *Sharing Her Word: Feminist Biblical Interpretation in Context*. Boston: Beacon Press, 1998.

———. *Wisdom Ways: Introducing Feminist Biblical Interpretation*. New York: Orbis Books, 2001.

Skovholt, Thomas M. and Michelle Trotter-Mathison. *The Resilient Practitioner: Burnout Prevention and Self-Care Strategies for Therapists, Counselors, Teachers, and Health Professionals*, 2nd ed. New York: Routledge, 2011.

Smith, Andrea. *Conquest: Sexual Violence and American Indian Genocide*. Cambridge, MA: South End Press, 2005.

Smythe, Elizabeth, and Andrew Norton. "Leadership: Wisdom in Action." *Indo-Pacific Journal of Phenomenology* 11, no. 1 (2011).

Song, Choan-Seng. *Third-Eye Theology: Theology in Formation in Asian Settings*. Maryknoll, NY: Orbis Books, 1979.

Stjerna, Kirsi I. *Women and the Reformation*. Malden, MA: Blackwell Pub., 2009.

Strasser, Ulrike. "A Case of Empire Envy? German Jesuits and an Asia-born Saint from Colonial America." *Journal of Global History* (2007): 23–40.

Suyemoto, Karen L., Grace S. Kim, Miwa Tanabe, John Tawa, and Stephanie C. Day. "Challenging the Model Minority Myth: Engaging Asian American Students in Research on Asian American College Student Experiences." In Samuel D. Museus, ed. *Conducting Research on Asian Americans in Higher Education: New Directions in Institutional Research.* San Francisco, Jossey-Bass, 2009.

Swim, Janet K., Roybin Mallett, and Charles Stangor. "Understanding Subtle Sexism: Detection and Use of Sexist Language. *Sex Roles,* 51 (2004).

Tai, Pao-tsun. *The Concise History of Taiwan.* Translated by Ruby J. Lee. Nantou: Taiwan Historica, 2007.

Taussig, Hal. *A New New Testament: A Bible for the Twenty-first Century.* Boston, MA: Houghton Mifflin Harcourt, 2013.

————. *The Thunder: Perfect Mind: A New Translation and Introduction.* New York: Palgrave Macmillan, 2010.

Taylor, Barbara Brown. *Learning to Walk in the Dark.* 1st ed. New York: HarperOne, 2014.

————. *Leaving Church: A Memoir of Faith.* New York: HarperOne, 2016

Teng, Emma. "An Island of Beautiful Women: The Discourse on Gender in Ch'ing Travel Accounts of Taiwan." In *Women in the New Taiwan: Gender Roles and Gender Consciousness in a Changing Society.* Armonk, NY: M. E. Sharpe, 2004.

Thuong, Manh, and Quang Thuy. Tu Đien Viet-Anh: Vietnamese-English Dictionary. Ha Noi: Nha Xuat Ban Van Hoa Thong Tin, 2003.

Tseng, Timothy, et al. "Asian American Religious Leadership Today: A Preliminary Inquiry." Durham, NC: Pulpit and Pew Research on Pastoral Leadership (2005) 29–34.

Tuan, Mia. *Forever Foreigners or Honorary Whites?: The Asian Ethnic Experience Today,* New Brunswick, NJ: Rutgers University Press, 1998.

Tzu, Sun. *Sun Tzu and the Art of War: The Oldest Military Treatise in the World.* Translated by Lionel Giles. Champaign, IL: Project Gutenberg, n.d. eBook Collection (EBSCOhost).

Vergas, Lucila. "When the 'Other' is the Teacher: Implications of Teacher Diversity in Higher Education." *Urban Review* 31:4 (1998).

Wainwright, Elaine. "A Voice from the Margin." In *Reading from This Place.* Edited by Fernando F. Segovia and Mary A. Tolbert. Minneapolis: Fortress Press, 1995.

Ward, Haruko Nawata. "Good News to Women? The Jesuits, Their Pastoral Advice and Women's Reception of Christianity in the Portuguese East Indies; Goa and Japan." In *Jesuits in India: History and Culture.* Edited by Délio de Mendonça. Goa: Xavier Centre of Historical Research, 2007.

————. *Women Religious Leaders of Japan's Christian Century: 1549–1650.* Women and Gender in the Early Modern World. Aldershot, England and Burlington, VT: Ashgate Publishing, 2009.

————. "Naitō Julia and Women Catechists in the Jesuit Mission in Japan and the Philippines." In *Putting Names with Faces: Women's Impact in Mission History.* Edited by Christine Lienemann-Perrin, Atola Longkumer, and Afrie Songco Joye. Nashville: Abingdon, 2012.

Weiler, Kathleen. "Freire and a Feminist Pedagogy of Difference." *Harvard Educational Review.* November 1991.

Wheatley, Margaret J. *Leadership and the New Science: Discovering Order in a Chaotic World.* 3rd ed. San Francisco: Berrett-Koehler Publishers, 2006.

Wicki, Josef, ed. *Documenta Indica [DI].* Rome: Monumenta Historica Societatis Iesu, 1948–.

Wiesner, Merry E. *Women and Gender in Early Modern Europe.* 3rd ed. Cambridge, UK, and New York: Cambridge University Press, 2008.

Wiesner-Hanks, Merry E. "Gender and the Reformation." *Archive für Reformationsge-schichte / Archive for Reformation History*, vol.100 (2009): 363–64.

———. *Christianity and Sexuality in the Early Modern World: Regulating Desire, Reforming Practice* 2nd ed. London: Routledge, 2010.

Wimberly, Anne Streaty. "Daring to Lead with Hope." *Religious Education* 98, no. 3 (2003): 277–95.

Winter, Miriam Therese, Adair Lummis, and Allison Stokes. *Defecting in Place*. New York: Crossroad, 1994.

Ya, Wu Fu. *Women in the Christian Church: The Taiwanese Case*, DMin Thesis. Episcopal Divinity School, 1996.

Yamamoto, Hisaye. *Seven Syllables and Other Stories*. New York: Kitchen Table Press, 1988.

Yee, Gale A. *Poor Banished Children of Eve: Women as Evil in the Hebrew Bible*. Minneapolis: Augsburg Fortress Publishers, 2003.

Zander, Rosamund Stone, and Benjamin Zander. *The Art of Possibility*. New York: Penguin Books, 2002.

Contributors

Laura Mariko Cheifetz is an ordained minister in the Presbyterian Church (U.S.A.). She is the Deputy Director of Systems and Sustainability with the National Asian Pacific American Women's Forum. Of Japanese and white Jewish descent, she grew up a double-pastors' kid in the Pacific Northwest. She was an intern with the Presbyterian United Nations Office in New York, coordinating the denomination's participation in the UN World Conference against Racism, Racial Discrimination, Xenophobia, and Related Intolerance. She also directed a program at McCormick Theological Seminary for Asian American young adults and pastors and worked with the then Fund for Theological Education (now the Forum for Theological Exploration) in Decatur, Georgia, with new pastors and strategic partners in theological education and ministry. Prior to her current position, she served as Vice President of Church and Public Relations at the Presbyterian Publishing Corporation.

"I am a leader committed to a church embodying the struggle for justice who seeks to build relationships among and between people of diverse backgrounds and experiences."

Min-Ah Cho is a novice of the Society of the Sacred Heart of Jesus (RSCJ), a Roman Catholic Religious congregation for women. Before she joined RSCJ, she taught theology and spirituality at St. Catherine University in St. Paul, Minnesota. She received her doctoral degree from Emory University. Min-Ah's research interests focus on medieval women's spirituality, contemporary Christian spirituality, Asian and Asian American religion and spirituality, sacramental theology, feminist theology, and postcolonialism. Min-Ah finds her leadership voice bridging activism and the academy in light of the gospel. Through her experiences as a human and women's rights activist working with female industrial workers, survivors of sexual slavery, and homeless women, she has created communities within and around the academy concerned with social and political issues surrounding women and the marginalized.

"I am a leader who bridges activism and the academy."

Jin Young Choi is Assistant Professor of New Testament and Christian Origins at Colgate Rochester Crozer Divinity School. She earned her PhD from Vanderbilt University. She is also a Louisville Institute fellow. She is the author of *Postcolonial Discipleship of Embodiment: An Asian and Asian American Feminist Reading of the Gospel of Mark* (Palgrave Macmillan Press, 2015). She served as a cochair of the Asian and Asian American Hermeneutics group at the Society of Biblical Literature (SBL).

"I embrace differences as rich resources for theological imagination and integration. As a biblical scholar, I hope to bring positive change to church and society by incorporating voices from the margins into my scholarly work."

Helen Kim Ho is a civil rights attorney, community organizer, and immigrant rights advocate. In 2010, Helen founded Asian Americans Advancing Justice–Atlanta (formerly Asian American Legal Advocacy Center, or AALAC), the first nonprofit law center dedicated to promoting the civil, social, and economic rights of Asian immigrants and refugees in the South. Prior to founding and leading Advancing Justice–Atlanta, she worked as an attorney for the Mexican American Legal Defense and Educational Fund (MALDEF) among other nonprofits. Helen began her career as a corporate securities attorney at large law firms in New York and Houston, Texas, before committing herself to full-time public interest work. She is married to Rodney Ho, Entertainment Columnist for the Atlanta Journal Constitution, and is the mother of two adorable dogs.

"I am a faith-filled but also fear-filled leader. I believe the best people to create and lead change are those most intimately impacted. I am inspired by the courage, insights, and challenges of my fellow immigrants and refugees. I am fear-filled because I never want my ego or personal limitations to get in the way of movement building."

Hannah Ka is Associate Pastor of Discipleship at Korean United Methodist Church of San Diego, California. She graduated from Claremont Graduate University with specialties in theology, ethics, and culture. She is also a recipient of the Women of Color (WOC) Scholarship and Mentoring program in the United Methodist Church (UMC).

"I am an enthusiastic and easily accessible leader. I work well with others and complement the gifts they bring to our shared ministry. I feel indebted to everyone's presence and contributions to our faith community. Each day, I strive to embrace both theory and praxis not only in my teaching and ministry but also in my daily life."

Grace Y. Kao is Associate Professor of Ethics at Claremont School of Theology and codirector of its Center for Sexuality, Gender, and Religion (CSGR). She is the author of *Grounding Human Rights in a Pluralist World* (Georgetown University Press, 2011) and coeditor, with Ilsup Ahn, of *Asian American Christian Ethics: Voices, Methods, Issues* (Baylor University Press, 2015). She is a second-generation Taiwanese American and the first female of Asian heritage to have been awarded tenure at Claremont School of Theology. She is an emerging leader in the guild who has served in a variety of leadership roles in the American Academy of Religion (AAR), Society of Christian Ethics (SCE), and Pacific Asian North American Asian Women in Theology and Ministry (PANAAWTM) as well as on the editorial boards of several academic journals: namely, *Journal of the Society of Christian Ethics* (JSCE), *Journal of Religious Ethics* (JRE), and *Journal of Race, Ethnicity, and Religion* (JRER).

"I am an academic leader who cares deeply about training and mentoring the next generation of emerging scholars, particularly students of color."

Hee Kyung Kim came from Seoul, Korea, to Boston to study theology in 1999. She received her M.Div in 2003 and her PhD in 2012 from Boston University. Her doctoral dissertation is titled, "Dialectical Harmony of Self and Other: Implications of Philosophical and Religious Anthropology for Social Justice and Fundamental Ethics." She has served a local Korean immigrant church as a leader of children's ministry for twelve years. Currently she is a homemaker, with a husband and a three-year old daughter, and a part-time professor, teaching philosophy, ethics, and religion in colleges in the Boston area.

"I am not an authoritative nor self-sacrificial leader who is the sole originator of leadership. I believe leadership is a product of communal process, and I try to be an active participant who contributes to this process of leadership making."

Jung Ha Kim is a sociologist and Director of Undergraduate Studies at Georgia State University. She served as the first cochair of the Asian North American Religion and Culture Group at the American Academy of Religion and also served as the chair and cochair of the Women and Religion Section of the AAR. She is the founder of the Asian American Community Research Institute at CPACS (Center for Pan Asian Community Services), the oldest and largest nonprofit organization that provides comprehensive social and health programs for Asian Americans and other immigrant communities in the Southeast region. She is also a recipient of the Women's Legacy Award, 2012, of the United Way for her service and contributions in the community.

"Some of us are born to be leaders. Others of us are made to be leaders by social circumstances. I find myself wondering lately what type of leadership I've learned to embody. Such reflection is meaningful to me, especially when I'm faced with new challenges in the community; for it can guide me to different strategies and new opportunities to learn what it means to lead."

Boyung Lee is Senior Vice President for Academic Affairs and Dean of the Faculty, and Professor of Practical Theology at Iliff School of Religion in Denver, Colorado. She is the first Korean American woman academic dean at the Association of Theological Schools in the Unites States and Canada. Prior to this position, she taught at Pacific School of Religion and the Graduate Theological Union for fifteen years where she became the first woman of color to receive a tenure in 2007. She is also an ordained United Methodist minister who served churches in California, Connecticut, Massachusetts, and Korea. She received her MDiv from Claremont School of Theology and her PhD in theology and education from Boston College. She is the author of *Transforming Congregations through Community: Faith Formation from the Seminary to the Church* (Westminster John Knox Press, 2013) and three forthcoming books. Her research and teaching interests include intercultural/interreligious pedagogy, critical religious pedagogy, postcolonial biblical studies, Asian/feminist theology, and Protestant spiritual formation in the global South.

"I am a travel-guide-like leader who wants the fellow travelers to be guides for others, with their own itinerary after our common journey together."

Yoke Lye Kwong is a certified clinical pastoral educator with the Association for Clinical Pastoral Education. She is a leader of spiritual and pastoral care educator in a healthcare system. She supervises ministers and seminarians who are committed to learn from patients, families, and healthcare teams. Through experiential discovery of pastoral formation, reflection, and competence, she teaches people to become caregivers from the depth of their souls.

"I am a leader in the healthcare system. I see my role in a corporate world to advocate the sacredness of the human presence. Advocacy is work of compassion; it influences how care is delivered by a medical team when caring for the vulnerable as imago Dei."

Deborah Lee has worked at the intersection of faith and social justice as an educator and organizer on issues of race, gender, antimilitarism, LBGTQ, and economic and immigrant justice. She is an ordained minister of the United Church of Christ and in the past has worked to bridge theological education with pastoral ministry and spiritually rooted activism through an Asian American Pacific Islander lens for many years at the Graduate Theological Union and Pacific School of Religion in Berkeley, California. She is currently the Immigration Program Director for the Interfaith Movement for Human Integrity, inspiring faith communities to shape public policy and actively engage in solidarity and accompaniment of immigrant communities. Her work has consistently bridged different ethnic and socioeconomic communities, generations, and geographies in transformational leadership processes to bring about healing, solidarity, and social change.

"I am a prophetic leader. I inspire and lead people of faith and spirit to address the underlying root causes of injustice and to cross the borders that divide us as a human family so that all may live a dignified life."

Suk Jong Lee was born in Seoul, Korea, and came to the United States in 1971. After graduating from Queens College of CUNY, she worked as a chemist before attending Princeton Theological Seminary. She was ordained by the Presbytery of the City of New York, Presbyterian Church (U.S.A.), in 1989 and worked at the YWCA in Flushing, New York, before joining the Army as a chaplain. While in the Army, she completed an MS in counseling psychology and served as a Family Life Chaplain. As an officer and chaplain, her last assignment in the Army included overseeing the religious program of an Army installation with nine staff and numerous volunteers. She retired from the military service after twenty-three years in active duty in 2015. Currently she is studying Chinese medicine at AOMA Graduate School of Integrative Medicine.

"I consider myself a 'consensus building' leader."

Unzu Lee is an Asian American woman of Korean descent who grew up in a family deeply grounded in the life and teachings of Jesus of Nazareth. Theologically trained at Princeton Theological Seminary, Women's Theological Center, and Episcopal Divinity School, she has tried to live out her feminist commitment in her ministries, which has meant exercising antipatriarchal leadership moment by moment—leadership that is deliberate, strategic, focused and always in the service of a collective dance of liberation. She is ordained in the Presbyterian Church (U.S.A.).

"The key to my leadership has been about cultivating the wisdom to know when and how to enter various dance processes."

San Yi Lin is a minister of Word and Sacrament in the Reformed Church in America. She currently works as a chaplain at Huntington Hospital in Pasadena, California, and regularly meets with other pastors and lay leaders in the Presbyterian Church (U.S.A.) to support the future of the Taiwanese American church.

"I am a servant leader."

Keun-Joo Christine Pae is Associate Professor of Religion/Ethics at Denison University. She is also an Episcopal priest and has served congregations in New Jersey, Ohio, and California. As a social ethicist, she is interested in the intersection of gender, race, religion, and U.S. military imperialism from a transnational perspective. She considers PANAAWTM her spiritual and intellectual home.

> *"I see myself as an intellectual and spiritual leader in both academia and church. As a leader, I am trying to bring ethical reflection on social issues to the classroom and the congregational life where I intellectually, psychologically, and spiritually engage college students and the diverse body of the church."*

Su Yon Pak is the Senior Director and Associate Professor of Integrative and Field-Based Education at Union Theological Seminary in the City of New York. In this hybrid faculty-administrator position, she envisions, creates, and oversees the curricular and co-curricular work of the Office of Integrative Education including field education, clinical pastoral education, life-long learning, and ministerial formation. She is the chair of the Professional Conduct Task Force of the American Academy of Religion (AAR); is the past chair of the Status of Women in the Profession Committee; and has served as the cochair of the Asian North American Religion, Culture, and Society program unit and on a steering committee of the Women and Religion Section of the AAR. She is on the board of Pacific Asian North American Asian Women in Theology and Ministry (PANAAWTM). She currently serves on the board of United Board for Christian Higher Education in Asia. Deeply committed to interfaith theological education, she serves on the advisory board of the Center for Pastoral Education at the Jewish Theological Seminary. She volunteers at the Bedford Correctional Facility, the only maximum security New York State prison for women.

> *"I lead by setting the table for others to participate. Nurture and hospitality are two important modes of leadership for me. Recognizing the desires, gifts, and presence each person brings to the table, I celebrate and nudge them toward their own leadership."*

Elizabeth S. Tapia is teacher, pastor, wife, theologian, poet, and missionary. She is a committed leader born and raised in the Philippines and taught at Union Theological Seminary, Philippines, for ten years before taking a faculty position at Bossey Ecumenical Institute, World Council of Churches, Switzerland. She also worked at Drew University Theological School as Director of its Center for Christianities in Global Context. She served as Director of Mission Theology, Global Ministries of the United Methodist Church, New York City. Currently, she is back in the Philippines and serving as missionary teacher at John Wesley College in Cagayan.

> *"As a leader, I teach theology and Christian ministry courses with MDiv and Doctor of Ministry students in rural Cagayan Valley in Northern Philippines. I am interested in roles of lay and clergy in a postcolonial Christianity, mission studies, theological education, and social transformation."*

Mai-Anh Le Tran is Associate Professor of Religious Education and Practical Theology at Garrett-Evangelical Theological Seminary and Past-President of the Religious Education Association. A 1.5-generation Vietnamese American, her research and writing include contributions to the *Religious Education Journal*; *Ways of Being, Ways of Reading: Asian American Biblical Interpretation*; *Teaching for a Culturally Diverse and Racially Just World*; *Educating for Redemptive Community*. Her book *Reset the Heart:*

Unlearning Violence, Relearning Hope (Abingdon, 2017) is a practical theological exploration of religion and education in the making and unmaking of violence, particularly the violence of racism.

> *"I am a theological educator and ordained United Methodist who is accountable to both academic and ecclesiastical bodies. I see myself as a 'flexible leader' who simultaneously belong to multiple communities of study, service, and practice."*

Haruko Nawata Ward is Professor of Church History at Columbia Theological Seminary. She teaches women's histories in the larger streams of ecumenical and global Christian movements. Her courses are designed to awaken students' awareness of diverse women leaders, reformers, and theologians in the past and present and to guide her students to hear the wisdom of these women, born out of their struggles, often overcoming suppression by male hierarchy. She is also an ordained minister of the Presbyterian Church (U.S.A.) and writes and leads liturgies using the words of women leaders in hope of instilling a new sense of leadership from a historically informed, wholesome, inclusive, collaborative, caring, and wise perspective.

> *"I am a historian of women's history. I specialize in research and publication on women religious leaders from early modern Japan and Asia, interconnected with European Reformations, missions, commercial expansion, and colonialism, and grounded in their respective Asian religious cultures. In all I do in the academy and church, I lead to encourage women to see themselves as wise leaders."*

CPSIA information can be obtained
at www.ICGtesting.com
Printed in the USA
LVHW08s0415121018
593278LV00015BA/334/P